CLINICAL TREATMENT OF THE VIOLENT PERSON

CLINICAL TREATMENT OF THE VIOLENT PERSON

Edited by

LOREN H. ROTH, MD, MPH
Western Psychiatric Institute and Clinic
University of Pittsburgh

GUILFORD PRESS
New York   London

© 1987 The Guilford Press
A Division of Guilford Publications, Inc.
200 Park Avenue South, New York, N.Y. 10003

PRINTED IN THE UNITED STATES OF AMERICA

Library of Congress Cataloging-in-Publication Data

Clinical treatment of the violent person.

Reprint. Originally published: Rockville, Md.:
U.S. Dept. of Health and Human Services, Public Health
Service, Alcohol, Drug Abuse, and Mental Health
Administration, National Institute of Mental Health,
1985.
    Includes bibliographies and index.
    1. Violence—Psychological aspects. 2. Prison
violence. 3. Psychotherapy. I. Roth, Loren H.
RC569.5.V55C57   1987b   616.85′82   86-19543
ISBN 0-89862-277-8 (hard cover)
ISBN 0-89862-914-4 (paperback)

In Memoriam: Vivian Romoff (1946–1983)

This book is a memorial to Vivian Romoff, R.N., M.S.N, a courageous nurse, administrator, and contributor to this monograph.

Vivian was loved and respected by all who knew her, for her persona, and her ability to lead staff and effectuate the highest standards of patient care.

Providing treatment to violent persons was a subject of great interest to Vivian; she brought considerable expertise to this challenge.

Loren H. Roth, M.D., M.P.H.

Contents

Contributors

Gene G. Abel, M.D., Department of Psychiatry, Emory University School of Medicine, Atlanta, Georgia.

Judith V. Becker, Ph.D., College of Physicians and Surgeons, Columbia University, The Research Foundation for Mental Hygiene, New York, New York.

George E. Dix, J.D., University of Texas, School of Law, Austin, Texas.

Donna M. Hamparian, Federation for Community Planning, Cleveland, Ohio.

Dorothy Otnow Lewis, M.D., Department of Psychiatry, New York University, School of Medicine, New York, New York.

Robert Paul Liberman, M.D., Mental Health Clinical Research Center and Rehabilitation Research and Training Center, Camarillo State Hospital, UCLA Department of Psychiatry, Brentwood VA Medical Center, Camarillo, Brentwood, California.

John R. Lion, M.D., Department of Psychiatry, University of Maryland, School of Medicine, Baltimore, Maryland.

Denis J. Madden, Ph.D., Department of Psychiatry, University of Maryland, School of Medicine, Baltimore, Maryland.

Vivian Romoff, R.N., M.S.N., Western Psychiatric Institute and Clinic, Department of Psychiatry, School of Medicine, University of Pittsburgh, Pittsburgh, Pennsylvania.

Loren H. Roth, M.D., M.P.H., Western Psychiatric Institute and Clinic, Department of Psychiatry, School of Medicine, University of Pittsburgh, Pittsburgh, Pennsylvania.

Linda Skinner, Ph.D., Department of Psychology, University of Hartford, Hartford, Connecticut.

Katherine Slama, Ph.D., Department of Psychiatry, School of Medicine, University of South Dakota, Yankton, South Dakota.

Paul H. Soloff, M.D., Western Psychiatric Institute and Clinic, Department of Psychiatry, School of Medicine, University of Pittsburgh, Pittsburgh, Pennsylvania.

Joe P. Tupin, M.D., Department of Psychiatry, Davis Medical Center, University of California, Davis, California.

Stephen Wong, Ph.D., Acoma Research and Rehabilitation Unit, Las Vegas Medical Center, Las Vegas, New Mexico.

Foreword

You have in your hands a remarkable book. Remarkable not because it is the best book available on treating violent people—although it is clearly that—but because it is one of the few books on any mental health topic that so clearly succeeds at consolidating clinical, empirical, and administrative concerns.

Clinical Treatment of the Violent Person combines the most pertinent and up-to-date empirical research with the kinds of clinical insights that are forged not in the laboratory but on the ward and in the therapy rooms over years of practice. Added to this is a heavy and welcome dollop of a topic virtually never addressed outside the covers of mimeographed staff manuals: just how a program for treating violent persons is actually run. Yet without administrative procedures tailored to the clinical requirements suggested by research and experience, any program for treating violent persons is likely to have a Hobbesian life: nasty, brutish, and short.

In the not so distant past, a book titled Clinical Treatment of the Violent Person would have been expected to discount the notion that one could clinically treat the violent person and condescendingly chastise the reader for ever having been naive enough to think otherwise. The question, "What works?" in altering the behavior of violent persons could be answered, we all knew, not with an essay but in a word: "nothing."

The issues are less clear than they once seemed to be. The quality of the research that "proved" that nothing works has been reassessed. The National Academy of Sciences (1981, p. 9), for example, concluded that "existing studies cannot yield useful knowledge" (p. 00) about whether or not violent behavior can be treated successfully. Further, the policy alternatives to attempting to treat violent behavior—which in the main have consisted in meting out precisely calibrated amounts of "justly deserved" punishment—have not worn as well as many had so confidently foretold.

The message that Loren Roth and his colleagues bring is not that a new Age of Treatment is dawning. They are fully as skeptical as the critics of treatment about the state of scientific evidence in the field. But they part company with the nihilists in their belief that the effectiveness of treatment is a live issue rather than the dead one the nihilists perceive, and in their conviction that the benefits of successful treatment, if possible, are so great for the patient and for society that the grueling work necessary to attempt it is worth the effort.

Often, in edited books, the editor seeks artificially to generate "interest" or cleverly to manufacture "balance" by soliciting as contributors those who take extreme positions on the issues of concern. The hope is that exposing a reader to, say, a biological reductionist in tandem with an ideological environmentalist will somehow result in an integrated, or at least an evenhanded, portrait of a field. The organizing principle of <u>Clinical Treatment of the Violent Person</u>, however, was not to put rigidities in equipoise. Rather, Professor Roth has gathered here a nuanced group of reasonable people, each, to be sure, with his or her own relative expertise and points of emphasis, but all genuinely committed to the position that violent behavior admits of no single cause and responds to no single cure.

One of the clearest strengths of this book is the attention it concentrates on the treatment staff. In their attempt to divert the proclivities of violent patients and inmates, treating mental health professionals are buffeted by threats from three quarters. First and most unmistakeably, they are confronted with threats to their personal safety. Many a clinician working with violent patients has literally received his or her education at the school of hard knocks.

In addition to being placed in jeopardy of being victimized by their patients, therapists increasingly feel threatened by the lawyers of their patients' other victims. It takes only a few cases in which therapists are found liable to third parties for injuries at the hands of their patients for therapists to begin to think that not only their lives but their net worth is on the line.

Finally, working day in and day out with what is by all accounts one of the most difficult and resistant of clinical populations can threaten a clinician's professional self-concept and cause even a guarded hope for producing lasting changes in behavior first to flicker and then burn out.

Roth and his colleagues strike back at each of these risks. Specific procedures for securing the physical safety of treatment staff are offered. Pragmatic advice on how to minimize the chance of being sued is given. I can only hope to strengthen by repetition Denis Madden's observation that participating in clinical research on violent behavior can help sustain staff enthusiasm and retard the growth of cynicism.

If the clinical treatment of the violent person is a daunting problem now, it shows every sign of becoming even more so in the future. Consider the criminal justice system. Many states, confronted with growing public dissatisfaction about crime rates and a collapse in professional support for indeterminate sentencing and coerced prisoner rehabilitation, responded by enacting determinate sentences whereby every second offense robber, for example, spent the same time in prison as every other similarly situated offender. Such a rule-bound sentencing scheme, whatever its other virtues, will ineluctably result in some individuals receiving a shorter sentence than is believed appropriate "in this specific case." How will it be possible to put discretion back into a sentencing system that was explicitly created to reduce or eliminate discretion? The answer: by mandating the clinical treatment of violent offenders.

Take the example of California, a state that had moved strongly to a determinate, "just deserts" sentencing scheme. As of 1986, the Penal Code (Section 2960) was amended to read as follows:

> The Legislature finds that there are prisoners who have a treatable, severe mental disorder which caused, was one of the causes of, or was an aggravating factor in the commission of the crime for which they were incarcerated. Secondly, the Legislature finds that if the severe mental disorders of those prisoners are not in remission or cannot be kept in remission at the time of their parole or upon termination of parole, there is a danger to society, and the state has a compelling interest in protecting the public. Thirdly, the Legislature finds that in order to protect the public from those persons it is necessary to provide mental health treatment until the severe mental disorder which was one of the causes of or was an aggravating factor in the person's prior criminal behavior is in remission and can be kept in remission.

If the prisoner is found to have a severe mental disorder, he or she can be kept institutionalized, with one year renewals, for an indeterminate period. In this manner, providing clinical treatment to disordered inmates can be the escape hatch through which "just deserts" are jettisoned.

Not only in criminal justice is concern with the clinical treatment of violent persons accelerating. Recent court decisions finding therapists liable for injuries sustained by third parties at the hands of their patients are often viewed as challenging the <u>predictive</u> skills of mental health professionals. Yet often these cases might better be viewed as implicating the <u>treatment</u> abilities of the therapist: The therapist knew (or should have known) the patient presented a risk of violence and the therapist did nothing to reduce, that is, to treat, that risk. I would assert with some confidence the belief that in the foreseeable future a plaintiff's lawyer, seeking to establish that his or her client's injuries were the result of the offender's negligent treatment by a therapist, will cross-examine the therapist by asking, "Are you aware, Doctor, of recent advances in the clinical treatment of violent behavior?" It is the fortunate witness who will be able to answer, "Yes, I've read <u>Clinical Treatment of the Violent Person</u>.

As the criminal justice system struggles to choose between rules and discretion for handling criminal offenders, and as courts sort out the mixed messages they give the mental health system (i.e., preserve confidentiality and protect the public) the issues considered in <u>Clinical Treatment of the Violent Person</u> will become increasingly prominent, and the manner in which they are addressed here will become even more impressive.

John Monahan, Ph.D.
University of Virginia
School of Law

Preface

In recent decades, there has been growing public concern over the alarming degree of violence in American society and the adequacy and effectiveness of existing mental health and correctional programs for violent persons. While there exists a fairly extensive clinical literature on the treatment and management of such persons, much of it is scattered among professional journals that are not readily available to mental health and correctional administrators, State and county executives, mental health and correctional staffs, and other persons concerned with the management and treatment of violent persons. The goal of this monograph, The Clinical Treatment of the Violent Person, is to provide a comprehensive, authoritative overview of what is currently known and believed about appropriate ways of treating and managing violent persons in mental health and correctional settings.

Dr. Loren H. Roth, the editor of and a contributor to this monograph, has had extensive clinical experience in dealing with violent persons in both mental health and penal-correctional settings. After graduating from Harvard Medical School, he served for 2 years as a General Medical Officer in a Federal penitentiary. Since 1974, he has been Director of the Law and Psychiatry Program at the Western Psychiatric Institute of the University of Pittsburgh and became Chief of Adult Clinical Services at this facility in 1983. Dr. Roth was a major contributor to a 1974 American Psychiatric Association task force report entitled Clinical Aspects of the Violent Individual. He is the author of more than 30 publications pertaining to various topics covered in this monograph.

To assist him in preparing this overview volume, Dr. Roth enlisted the support of 14 contributors located in various parts of the Nation. Many of these are nationally known experts in their respective fields. Others, like the late Vivian Romoff, R.N., M.S.N., to whom this monograph is a memorial, bring to their exposition the wisdom born of many years of direct clinical experience in working with violent persons.

This publication is one of several monographs on topics pertaining to interactions between legal and mental health concerns that have been developed in recent years by the NIMH Center for Studies of Antisocial and Violent Behavior (formerly NIMH Center for Studies of Crime and Delinquency). Previous monographs were Competency to Stand Trial and Mental Illness (1973, reprinted 1977), Mental Health and Law: A System in Transition (1975, reprinted 1976), Criminal Commitments and Dangerous Mental Patients: Legal Issues of Confinement, Treatment, and Release (1976, reprinted 1977), Dangerous Behavior: A Problem in Law and Mental Health (1978), Legal Aspects of the Enforced Treatment of Offenders (1979), and The Clinical Prediction of Violent Behavior (1981).

It is our hope that, like its predecessors in this series, the monograph by Dr. Roth and his colleagues will be of interest and value to mental health and correctional personnel, program administrators, lawyers, judges, and other persons concerned with issues pertaining to treatment of violent persons and violent offenders.

Saleem A. Shah, Ph.D.
Chief, Center for Studies of
Antisocial and Violent Behavior

Introduction

Clinical Treatment of the Violent Person describes the treatment and management of violent persons in various outpatient and inpatient settings, including psychiatric emergency rooms, community mental health centers, mental hospitals, juvenile institutions, prisons, and jails. Correctional staffs, psychologists, psychiatrists, nurses, program administrators in mental health and corrections-related fields, social workers, probation workers, and counselors will find these chapters instructive in their day-to-day activities in the arena of treating and handling violent persons.

The following chapters do not attempt to summarize the voluminous clinical and experimental literature (much of it admittedly not very encouraging) relating to treating violent persons. The reader will, however, become acquainted with most of what is currently known and believed about treating and managing individual violent behavior.

This monograph is not limited to summarizing information about treating violence from the perspective of medicine, psychiatry, psychology, social work, nursing, or other professions whose members largely treat individual "psychopathology." The chapters not only relate to treating and managing "diseases" or "disorders" but also touch more generally on the psychology of "persons," "situations," and other determinants of individual violent behavior (see generally Shah 1981; Steadman 1982; Monahan and Klassen 1982).

Not all persons who manifest violent behavior are, nor should they be, labeled "patients" or even "clients." Violent behavior does not mean that a person is necessarily "crazy" or that his or her behavior must be treated and managed according to medical principles or even by medical personnel. Like all people, however, violent persons manifest both a "psychology" and a "social psychology" that must be understood and addressed if their behavioral change is to be facilitated. Violent behavior occurs within a social context that includes both antecedents and consequences. Some of the rules and recommendations provided in this monograph for treating and managing violent persons also apply to treating and managing violent persons who are not patients; for example, persons who act violently in criminal justice settings.

CHAPTER SUMMARIES

The following summaries highlight the chapters that follow.

In chapter 1, John R. Lion, M.D., presents practical information about how to assess violent persons so as to begin the process of treatment. Lion stresses the importance of a multicausal framework for evaluation, giving attention not just to the person's manifest psychopathology or affective (emotional) responses, but also to the environmental precipitants of the patient's behavior and to the impact of the setting where the evaluation is conducted. Lion also summarizes certain aspects of the "organic evaluation" that are relevant to determining the causes for the person's violence.

In chapter 2, Stephen Wong, Ph.D., Katherine Slama, Ph.D., and Robert Paul Liberman, M.D., summarize the behavioral approach to treating violence. This approach requires specifying aggressive behavior and modifying the environmental antecedents and consequences controlling that behavior. A variety of psychosocial techniques are described that may be used for treating aggressive and destructive behavior of psychiatric and developmentally disabled patients, e.g., activity programming, social skills training, differential reinforcement of other behavior, time out from reinforcement, use of mild aversives, overcorrection, and contingent restraint. The effectiveness of these treatments is illustrated primarily by the use of single-case experimental studies in which the patient serves as his or her own control.

In chapter 3, Denis Madden, Ph.D., presents an overview of outpatient psychotherapy with the violent person. He emphasizes the importance of gaining the patient's trust and setting limits, while also teaching the patient how to use group therapy and the availability of the therapist to gain control over the patient's violent impulses. Madden stresses the importance of helping violent persons become more sensitive to the needs of others while they learn to better monitor their own affective and cognitive (intellectual) responses to provocative situations.

Dr. Madden also reviews the outcomes of some of the best known institutional programs that have relied upon psychotherapeutic approaches for treating violent patients and inmates.

In chapter 4, Joe P. Tupin, M.D., reviews the value of medication for treating violent persons. Breaking down classes of drugs into those useful for the short-run "control" of violent behavior and those useful over the long run for treating psychiatric disorders accompanied by violence, Tupin also indicates that a risk/benefit assessment must be performed when medication is employed. Long-term drug treatment is usually indicated only when a patient's violent behavior is secondary to some identifiable psychiatric condition.

In chapter 5, Gene G. Abel, M.D., Judith V. Becker, Ph.D., and Linda Skinner, Ph.D., discuss outpatient treatment of violent sexual offenders. The authors summarize techniques for decreasing deviant arousal; increasing nondeviant arousal; correcting cognitive distortions; and providing skills training, sex education, and sex dysfunction therapy. The authors conclude that, at this time, decreasing the person's deviant sexual arousal through a technique of "masturbatory satiation" offers great promise. This chapter also provides useful guidelines for training staff to work with violent patients, and offers advice on how to secure institutional support for outpatient treatment programs.

In chapter 6, Paul H. Soloff, M.D., presents a concise overview of the use of physical controls with violent patients. Many arguments have taken place about whether such physical controls are truly required and also about how (when required) they may be used safely and effectively. Despite advances in modern psychiatry, including advances in the use of medication, physical controls still serve a needed and useful function for controlling violent patient behavior in institutional settings.

In chapter 7, Dorothy Otnow Lewis, M.D., summarizes special diagnostic and treatment issues concerning violent juveniles. She gives special attention to conducting an adequate neurodiagnostic interview for these youths, thus teaching the examiner how to take a medical, family, and social history; to evaluate mental status; and to check on the youth's educational and psychological achievements. The chapter also summarizes treatment implications for this type of "neuropsychological" approach to the violent delinquent.

In chapter 8, Donna M. Hamparian describes some special programs (most of an institutional type) that have been developed in various locations and settings for rehabilitating violent juvenile offenders. Programs such as continuous case management, the Unified Delinquency Intervention Services (UDIS) project, a juvenile corrections model, a joint mental health-juvenile corrections model, private profit-making models, and secure treatment units are described, and their common features are delineated in a set of guidelines. Hamparian indicates the importance of providing community followup and intervention for violent youths who have finished an institutional phase of treatment.

In chapter 9, George Dix, J.D., reviews important legal and ethical controversies relevant to treating and managing violent persons. These controversies include the need for the clinician to balance the patient's right to confidentiality with the clinician's obligation to protect other persons from harm by the patient, the legal and ethical limits of the institutionalized person's right to refuse treatment with medication, and his or her right to be free from aversive or other behavioral modification programs (see also Winick 1981). Practical advice is given to mental health clinicians to help them organize and direct their behavior so as to avoid liability when treating violent persons.

In chapter 10, Loren H. Roth, M.D., presents information about treating and managing violent behavior in prisons, jails, security hospitals, and other such units for mentally disordered offenders. Roth examines problems such as overcrowding in penal institutions, intrainstitutional assaults, and problems of inadequate medical and psychological services. Drawing from the work of others (and from his own experiences), Roth discusses a conceptualization of violent behavior that attempts to integrate social-psychological, behavioral-cognitive, and other approaches to thinking about and treating violent behavior over the long term.

In chapter 11, Vivian Romoff, R.N., M.S.N., addresses practical and extremely important administrative and staffing considerations relating to the treatment of violent persons. Units treating or managing violent persons need to develop and implement systematic and detailed policies for managing such behavior, e.g., policies relating to security procedures, admissions to the unit, prevention of violence, and seclusion. Specific policies used to address these matters at the Western Psychiatric Institute and Clinic in Pittsburgh are reproduced or cited.

SOME COMMON THEMES

Assessment

As noted in several of the chapters in this volume, adequate assessment (what psychiatrists call "differential diagnosis" and what other mental health clinicians usually refer to as "evaluation" or "assessment") is the first step in determining the nature and characteristics of the problem and in planning treatment approaches and interventions for violent persons. While assessment is especially indicated when "long-term" treatment interventions are contemplated (see, for example, chapters 1, 2, 3, 4, 5, 7, and 10), such an evaluative approach, fused with management, is also recommended when immediate response to a patient's violence is required (see, for example, chapters 1, 6, and 11).

Violence is multifactorial in origin. Rarely is there a single cause for a person's violent behavior. This same principle applies equally to treatment approaches. For example, in the medical arena, it has been noted that "there is currently no drug which is specifically antiaggressive" (Valzelli 1981, p. 161). Violent behavior, like all other human behaviors such as altruism or submission, must be understood and addressed through an interactive framework, giving attention to psychological, situational, medical, and/or other variables. As noted in chapter 1, some violent and aggressive behaviors may even be normal and adaptive.

Thus, prior to or early in the process of intervening with a violent person, the causes and patterns of the person's violence must be sought and understood. A very recent conceptualization of violence is provided by Monahan and Klassen (1982) modifying Novaco (1979). This conceptualization focuses on stressful events, the person's cognitive processes, affective reactions, and subsequent behavioral coping responses. This conceptualization is specifically amplified in chapter 10. Virtually all of the other chapters in this monograph also provide helpful information relevant to treating and managing behavior through such an interactive framework.

Treatment Effectiveness

This monograph does not review all that is known about the effectiveness of treatment for violent persons. Some of the longer term institutional studies (those relying upon individual or group psychotherapeutic techniques) are alluded to in chapters 3 and 10. Chapters 2, 5, and 8 cite some additional outcome data. Unfortunately, results from longterm treatment programs for violent persons in institutional settings have not been very encouraging. Problems posed by overreliance on the efficacy of institutional treatment are suggested by information presented in chapters 1, 3, 5, 7, 8, and 10. The information in these chapters clearly suggests that long-term community followup is required in the treatment of violent behavior. If, as proposed by Monahan and Klassen (1982), violent behavior often emerges because of an interaction between stressful life events, a person's cognitions and affects, and a person's behavioral coping responses, then effective treatment of violent persons requires their exposure to real-life situations.

In most institutions, violent persons are not confronted with the types of stresses with which they must learn to cope when returned to the community. Thus, as suggested by Gunn and Robertson's (1982) study of psychiatric treatment of prisoners at the Grendon Prison in England, treatment in an institution affects mainly what is going on in the prison. Institutional treatment has little to do with life in the community and perhaps little to do with the offender's subsequent adjustment (see also Gunn et al. 1978). The therapist's or program manager's "double bind" in planning and delivering institutional treatment for violent persons is thus obvious. On the one hand, security must be provided and the public must be protected; on the other, the violent person must be "under control" (either through internal or external controls) while also being exposed to provocations and situations in order to learn and relearn alternative behaviors to violence (see chapters 3 and 10). In this respect, very tightly controlled community-based programs become an essential part of the rehabilitation of such persons (see chapters 8 and 10).

Legal and Ethical Issues

Another major theme in this monograph is the importance of legal and ethical issues in treating violent persons. While chapter 9 provides a comprehensive overview of the multiple legal and ethical issues confronting the clinician, several other chapters (e.g., chapters 2, 5, 6, 10, and 11) touch on important ethical principles, such as the necessity of obtaining the patient's consent for treatment whenever possible, of considering or trying "lesser means" before more intrusive treatments are employed, and of distinguishing between the ethics of emergency and nonemergency interventions. Thinking through ethical issues in treating violent persons, while at times difficult, affords a kind of "creative tension" for the therapist that helps to guide the reasonableness of the therapy (chapter 9; see also Roth and Meisel 1977; Roth 1979; Roth 1980).

Learning From Experience

Here the "experience" alluded to is that of clinicians, therapists, correctional staff members, and program administrators—not patients. Treating violent persons should never be a theoretical exercise. Careful review and critique ("management autopsy") of past violent incidents and their management, including "near-miss analysis," is essential to improving the clinician's and the correctional staff member's future behavior. Thus, units treating violent persons must adequately train and prepare staff, formulate policies to guide program and administrative staff, and initiate review of past violent incidents to understand their genesis. The aim is to improve (through a "feedback process") the management of future violence (see especially chapters 2, 6, 10, and 11).

A conceptualization helpful for clinicians (and patients) is that of cognitive and behavioral review of past violent incidents and their management (see, for example, Meichenbaum 1977, p. 162; Frederiksen and Rainwater 1981). Here cognitive (intellectual) review means considering in great detail what happened, what the staff's expectations were, why staff believes the patient acted in a violent manner, what was done, and what could or should have been done instead. Such an "exercise" by staff is the essence of how best to "learn by experience" to treat and manage violent persons.

Therapist Burnout and Attitudes

A final theme running throughout the following chapters relates to the behavior and feeling of therapists. It is not easy to work with violent patients. Their behavior is frustrating and can stimulate fantasies on the part of clinicians who fear for their own and others safety (see, for example, chapters 1, 3, 5, 10, and 11). Therapists' attitudes and difficulties in treating such patients continually threaten the validity of the work as well as the enjoyment of the work. Problems of therapist burnout are frequent. Thus, chapter 3 suggests that therapists work with and share their experiences with colleagues. Chapter 5 provides a sensitive overview of the importance of a preventive-educational approach for staff members who work directly with violent patients, while chapter 11 indicates the importance of staff review of the management of violent behavior.

It has been the editor's experience that therapists should not take it upon themselves to treat violent persons exclusively nor, optimally, a very large number of them. Burnout is almost inevitable under these conditions, particularly in correctional settings where multiple roles and professional stresses bear down on the clinician (see chapter 10).

Treating violent persons, while frustrating, is nonetheless interesting and rewarding. No other activity makes such a strong demand upon the therapist to be a complete clinician. Psychological, medical, interpersonal, and administrative skills must all be brought to bear in treating violent persons. Above all, treating violent persons requires that the clinician exercise both logic and common sense. Hopefully, the chapters in this monograph point in these directions.[1]

Loren H. Roth, M.D., M.P.H.
Western Psychiatric Institute and Clinic
School of Medicine
University of Pittsburgh

REFERENCES

Bittner, E., and Messinger, S.L., eds. Criminology Review Yearbook, Vol. 2. Beverly Hills: Sage, 1980.

Frederiksen, L.W., and Rainwater, N. Explosive behavior: A skill development approach to treatment. In: Stuart, R.B., ed. Violent Behavior: Social Learning Approaches to Prediction, Management and Treatment. Brunner/Mazel, 1981.

Gunn, J.; Robertson, G.; Dell, S.; and Way, C. Psychiatric Aspects of Imprisonment. New York, Academic Press, 1978.

---

[1] To obtain a broader policy perspective on treating violent persons and/or to learn about other types of criminal justice programs or strategies that may be helpful in treating violent criminal offenders, readers may wish to consult Criminal Violence (Wolfgang and Weiner 1982), New Directions in the Rehabilitation Of Criminal Offenders (Martin et al. 1981), and Violent Juvenile Offenders: An Anthology (Mathias et al. 1984). Readers who wish to acquaint themselves more broadly with what is known about psychology and criminology may find useful Psychology of Crime and Criminal Justice (Toch 1979) and a chapter by Monahan and Splane on psychological approaches to criminal behavior found in volume 2 of the Criminology Review Yearbook (Bittner and Messinger 1980). Two recent valuable resources regarding seclusion, restraint, and assaults within psychiatric facilities are The Psychiatric Uses of Seclusion and Restraint (Tardiff 1984) and Assaults Within Psychiatric Facilities (Lion and Reid 1983).

Gunn, J., and Robertson, G. An evaluation of Grendon prison. In: Gunn, J., and Farrington, D.P., eds. Abnormal Offenders, Delinquency, and the Criminal Justice System. Vol. 1. New York: Wiley & Sons, 1982, pp. 285–305.

Lion, J.R., and Reid, W.H., eds. Assaults Within Psychiatric Facilities. New York: Grune & Stratton, 1983.

Martin, S.E.; Sechrest, L.B.; and Redner, R., eds. New Directions in the Rehabilitation of Criminal Offenders. Panel on Research on Rehabilitative Techniques. Washington, D.C.: National Academy Press, 1981.

Mathias, R.A.; DeMuro, P.; and Allinson, R.S. Violent Juvenile Offenders: An Anthology. Newark: National Council on Crime and Delinquency, 1984.

Meichenbaum, D. Cognitive-Behavior Modification: An Integrative Approach. New York: Plenum Press, 1977.

Monahan, J., and Klassen, D. Situational approaches to understanding and predicting individual violent behavior. In: Wolfgang, M.E., and Weiner, N.A., eds. Criminal Violence. Beverly Hills: Sage, 1982, pp. 292–319.

Monahan, J., and Splane, S. Psychological approaches to criminal behavior. In: Bittner, E., and Messinger, S.L., eds. Criminology Review Yearbook. Vol. 2. Beverly Hills: Sage, 1980, pp. 17–47.

Novaco, R. The cognitive regulation of anger and stress. In: Kendall, P., and Hollon, S., eds. Cognitive behavioral Interventions: Theory, Research, and Procedures. New York: Academic Press, 1979, pp. 241–285.

Roth, L.H., and Meisel, A. Dangerousness, confidentiality, and the duty to warn. American Journal of Psychiatry 134(5):508–511, 1977.

Roth, L.H. To respect persons, families, and communities: Some problems in the ethics of mental health care. Psychiatry Digest, pp. 17–26. October 1979.

Roth, L.H. Correctional psychiatry. In: Curran, W.; Peety, C.; McGarry, A.L.; eds. Modern Legal Medicine, Psychiatry and Forensic Science. Chapter 28. Philadelphia: F.A. Davis, 1980, pp. 677–719.

Shah, S.A. Dangerousness: Conceptual, prediction and public policy issues. In: Hays, J.; Ray, R.; Kevin, T.; and Solway, K.S.; eds. Violence and the Violent Individual. New York: SP Medical & Scientific Books, 1981, pp. 151–178.

Steadman, H.J. A situational approach to violence. International Journal of Law and Psychiatry 5(2):171–186, 1982.

Tardiff, K., ed. The Psychiatric Uses of Seclusion and Restraint. Washington, DC: American Psychiatric Association, 1984.

Toch, H., ed. Psychology of Crime and Criminal Justice. New York: Holt, Rinehart and Winston, 1979.

Valzelli, L. Psychobiology of Aggression and Violence. New York: Raven Press, 1981.

Winick, B.J. Legal limitations on correctional therapy and research. <u>Minnesota Law Review</u> 65(3):331–432, 1981.

Wolfgang, M.E., and Weiner, N.A., eds. <u>Criminal Violence</u>. Beverly Hills: Sage, 1982.

1

Clinical Assessment of Violent Patients

John R. Lion, M.D.

Like most conditions in medicine, assessment of violent behavior precedes treatment. Many difficult and pressing questions confront practitioners faced with the assessment of a violent individual. What should they do? How should they quiet down the patient? What risk to others does the patient pose? Why has the patient been violent? The aim of this chapter is to provide guidelines that can help to answer these questions and facilitate assessment.

GENERAL CONSIDERATIONS

In the 1974 *American Psychiatric Association Task Force Report on Clinical Aspects of the Violent Individual*, the violent patient is defined as "one who acts or has acted in such a way as to produce physical harm or destruction" (American Psychiatric Association 1974). This description emphasizes *physical behavior*. In this chapter, violent *ideation*, including *verbal aggression*, will be discussed as well.

A caution also is in order. Not all violent behavior is pathologic, and some aggressive behavior may represent health. For instance, a once passive adolescent may become rebellious at home in an effort to separate from a pathogenic family. In such a case, rebelliousness is an index of growth and change. A person who shouts back at an employer may be in need of self-assertion.

Physical violence is usually more ominous, though subcultures

1

exist in which violence is more the norm than elsewhere. Thus, a young man in a ghetto may get into frequent fights as an adaptation; his middle or upper socioeconomic class counterpart may be referred for psychiatric help if he gets into a single fist fight. Thresholds for mental health intervention vary. A patient who can channel aggression within acceptable social bounds is healthier than if he or she were either excessively labile or overinhibited with regard to displays of violence.

The clinician is apt to see not only patients who have been violent but also individuals who are fearful of becoming violent and verbalize fears of "going out of control" or injuring a specific person, such as a spouse or child (Lion et al. 1969). Premonitory sentiments play a role in violence just as does the "cry for help" of the suicidal patient (Lion et al. 1968).

The origins of violence are many. Violence often is precipitated by or accompanies a psychosocial event. Violence may stem from a situational reaction, as in the case of a Saturday-night barroom brawl. Violence may be a symptom of underlying psychopathology or the manifestation of a functional illness, such as schizophrenia or toxic psychosis from amphetamine abuse (Ellinwood 1971). Violence often is associated with characterologic disturbances and is a prominent part of the Antisocial Personality or Passive–Aggressive Personality (Lion 1981). Violence is an integral part of disorders of impulse control such as Intermittent Explosive Disorder (American Psychiatric Association 1980). Violence may be a component of an affective disease, such as agitated depression or manic excitement. Violence may result from organic disease processes in individuals with overt brain damage or more subtle cases of "minimal brain damage," as described in the Diagnostic and Statistical Manual III (DSM III) classification of Attention Deficit Disorder (Ibid. 1980). Violence may accompany sexual dysfunction and be the dominant drive in rape (Cohen et al. 1971). The point to be emphasized is that the clinician must look for underlying etiologies and not view violent patients as uniform generic entities (Lion and Penna 1974). A careful assessment must be made and psychosocial factors elucidated.

Recently, there has been talk of "violence syndromes," such as childbattering and wifebattering in the lay press and professional literature. While useful for purposes of social and legislative reform, such clusters of behavior are conceptually imprecise; etiologic clarification is required. A man who abuses his children may have a disordered personality or suffer from a depression or psychosis. Spouse abuse is embedded in a complex dyadic relationship requiring detailed psychological and social understanding. For example, an abused wife may be clinically depressed; her abusing husband may have a disorder of impulse control; both may come from family backgrounds in which they were abused; both may live in a subculture that perpetuates family violence as a norm. These examples are purposely complex to illustrate assessment challenges facing the clinician.

EMERGENCY ROOM ASSESSMENT

In emergency room settings, management and assessment of the violent patient are invariably intertwined. It is impossible to assess the violent patient until the patient is calmed down. Certain principles of management are requisite (Lion 1972a).

Typically, a belligerent and combative patient is brought into the emergency room by police officers and taken to a seclusion room where the patient is restrained or held until the psychiatrist becomes available. The evaluating clinician should be aware that the patient's propensity for violence may be heightened when surrounded by a number of people. Hence, if the patient is brought to the evaluator by others, it may be beneficial to ask these individuals to wait down the hall, still in view of the patient, but far enough removed so that the latter does not feel overwhelmed and react to helplessness with intensified hostility. This is not a hard and fast rule. The clinician may reasonably feel that the patient is dangerous and prefer to have someone else in the examining room during the initial phase of the interview.

During early talks, the anger of the patient should be acknowledged. At the same time, the clinician must indicate the possibility of exerting control over the patient's violent propensities. Offering patients oral medication is often a suitable way of beginning to establish control even if the patient refuses to accept the medication. Since violent patients tend to fear loss of control over their own aggression, helpful comments can be "You seem to be very angry. I'm going to help you calm your anger. Let's talk so that you can tell me what made you upset." The evaluator's goal, whenever possible, is to convert physical agitation and belligerence into verbal catharsis. This principle holds true irrespective of the etiology of the patient's violence.

Some patients are so out of control that physical restraints are necessary (Rosen and DiGiacomo 1978; Gutheil 1978). Simple principles hold here as well. Restraints should not be haphazard but carefully rehearsed and carried out by a skilled medical team in a special room.

All members of the medical team should be familiar with parenteral neuroleptilization (Donlon et al. 1979) so that they can tranquilize the patient promptly and humanely (see chapter 4). However, medication is not a substitute for the tasks of evaluation that must also be performed.

Matters pertaining to hospitalization and risk tend to be the initial focuses for evaluation. Some patients are a greater risk than others. Patients with well-formed delusional symptoms and command hallucinations urging homicide are quite clearly dangerous to society regardless of whether they are "noisy" or "quiet." Persons with paranoid schizophrenia and individuals with acute paranoid toxic psychoses may be quite tractable but still harbor dangerous ruminative fantasies. Psychotically depressed patients may harbor both suicidal and homicidal ideation. The clinician should not assume that suicide is the only act that a despondent patient is capable of carrying out but should ask appropriate questions.

Patients such as those described above are obvious candidates for hospitalization. Less obvious are patients who do not seem to have homicidal or suicidal thoughts, but who come or are brought to the emergency room after having been combative or belligerent. Often, these patients have been drinking and have been involved in a family argument. The temptation is to dismiss them as drunks who will get over it, but family violence that results in admission to the emergency room is serious. In many cases, the violence has been repetitive. Other members of the family may need to be seen (Harbin 1977), since violence does not occur in a vacuum but rather in response to psychological, social, and environmental stress. The evaluator must ask what that stress is and whether it can recur.

In addition to inquiring about stress, the clinician may need to ask questions about availability and ownership of weapons, use of such weapons, past violence, and past criminality. Queries such as "What is the most violent thing that you have ever done?" may be revealing. Unfortunately, many clinicians are uncomfortable in this role and do not sufficiently inform themselves about a patient's violent propensities.

Risk is determined by a conglomerate of findings. For example, an evaluator needs to know whether the patient has been incarcerated for violence. Does the patient drink alcohol? Is the patient's marriage deteriorating? Does the patient's history reveal an impulse control disorder? If the answers to inquiries such as these are positive, the conclusion is likely to be that the patient poses a risk of violence. The severity of risk can be determined through additional interviews with family, by assessment of the patient's support system, and by formation of a clinical alliance in which the patient does or does not show a willingness to cooperate with treatment.

Another important parameter is the patients' own affect toward their violence and their thoughts of harm. Patients who seem unconcerned may seriously be at risk.

Generally, it may be desirable to keep a patient overnight for reassessment the next day, unless the clinician has a good understanding of the causes of the patient's violence. Appearances of tranquility in a previously violent person can be deceptive. Discharging the patient can be an error when the problem has not really been resolved. The clinician must consider whether anything has really changed and whether the patient is likely to become aggressive again if discharged from the hospital.

Violent patients sometimes come to emergency rooms after having engaged in self-mutilation (Bach-y-Rita et al. 1971a). Clinicians seeing such individuals are often asked to determine whether these patients will be aggressive toward others. This is a difficult question to answer, since inward direction of violence is often a manifestation of impaired ego function (Cain 1961). In individuals with impaired ego function, either on a functional or organic basis, aggression can be turned inwardly and outwardly almost randomly.

Patients may exhibit varied behaviors in the emergency room (Lion et al. 1969). Some patients complain about specifically directed violent urges and express fear that they are going to harm a certain person, such as a spouse or child. Other patients voice more diffusely directed violent urges and say that they are afraid of "hurting someone," even though no target or vector is named. In the former group, there may be a pathologic relationship in which some violence has already occurred. In the latter instance, the diffuseness of the patient's urges represents a defense that protects the patient from awareness of the true object of rage. Risk exists in both instances.

Other patients voice or exhibit anger primarily in association with alcohol. Alcohol is ubiquitously implicated in all kinds of violence, but its specific association with paroxysmal rage outbursts, particularly when alcohol use is minimal, should draw attention to the phenomenon of pathological intoxication (Bach-y-Rita et al. 1971b; Marinacci 1963). A patient's repeated rage outbursts or temper problems in the absence of alcohol should make the clinician consider the diagnosis of Intermittent Explosive Disorder.

CLINIC AND OFFICE PRACTICE SETTINGS

In the clinic or office the task is not to restore order and accomplish disposition but to assess the patient's longterm outlook and treatability. The atmosphere in this setting is usually more relaxed. Many patients are sent for consultation by other practitioners or by the criminal justice system. Some patients come on their own (Lion et al. 1976).

Violent patients evaluated in clinic and office settings are less dramatic and belligerent than patients seen in emergency rooms. Even so, the clinician is apt to see patients with histories of violent outbursts and temper who usually have (1) personality disorders of the Antisocial, Passive-aggressive, or Paranoid types or (2) Intermittent Explosive Disorders and a history of problems with aggression. Other patients may have adjustment disorders and affective disorders. The clinician may also see some patients with obsessional character structures and others with schizoid traits. These individuals often are referred to as "over-controlled" (Megargee 1966). They typically have good work adjustment histories, are devoid of impulsivity and mood lability, have a history of only one circumscribed temper outburst or a history of a series of outbursts that are very alien to their personalities. Unlike impulsive patients, these individuals are overly inhibited with respect to aggression. Some are clinically depressed, while others experience marital or financial difficulties that lead to their irritability.

Forensic evaluation typically requires that the clinician determine whether a patient's violence is associated with mental disease that might exculpate the patient from responsibility. The clinician may find that the violence was associated with a personality disorder, psychosis, depression, or situational factors.

Evaluation of sexually aggressive patients needs to focus on the heightened drive states that accompany such behavior as rape or pedophilia. In many instances, patients will complain of the need to engage repetitively in a behavior over time. The compulsiveness of this drive state, together with its component of violence, signals risk of violence and the need for appropriate psychological or pharmacologic therapy.

VIOLENCE WITHIN SPECIAL SETTINGS

Assessment of violence within special settings, such as schools and prisons, requires interfacing with knowledgeable individuals, such as teachers or guards. If a child is violent at school, teachers who have observed the child must be consulted. Such consultation is common when evaluating attention deficit disorders in children but is less likely to be considered when dealing with violent children and adolescents.

The same principle holds within the prison system. It is not unusual for a psychiatrist to be referred a patient who is prone to violence and temper outbursts that are unusual even in this milieu. Patients of this type are often shunned by other prisoners and usually are individuals with severe psychopathology that may be of psychotic proportions or stem from characterologic immaturity. Guards can provide the clinicians with information on such persons and this information can greatly aid assessment.

Beyond this subgroup of violent patients within the prison is the prison population itself, a group that typically contains many individuals incarcerated for serious crimes of violence. Here the clinician is often requested by the authorities to identify "treatable" individuals and develop treatment programs. The clinician may be asked to consult on individuals already in therapy or about to be released. Often queries arise about a prisoner's seeming lack of conscience and how such a person might be "reformed." Questions may be asked about a prisoner's remorse for the crime and capacity for recidivism.

While clinicians may be tempted to play the prophet in response to such inquiries, they should remember that officials usually have far more experience in such matters and far better intuition. Clinicians should remain in their proper role and avoid manipulation by prisoners and staff. The clinician's task is to identify disorders, psychodynamic vulnerabilities, therapeutic needs, and conditions responsive to treatment and medication (see chapter 10).

VIOLENCE WITHIN HOSPITALS

Perhaps the most common form of hospital violence involves the adolescent patient in a State hospital who previously has been violent in a private hospital. Another familiar type of violent patient is the agitated psychotic patient who requires restraint and seclusion.

The milieu shapes much violence, and tolerance for violent behavior differs markedly in various institutions. Private facilities have a variety of means for dealing with violent behavior, including treatment of the patient, discharge, and transfer to a State hospital. The State hospital must accept and try to treat any violent patients sent there. A "downward drift" of violence thus occurs so that the State facilities end up with the most violent and difficult to manage patients.

Violence problems within mental hospitals tend to escape public scrutiny. Some data suggest that violence among patients and between patients and staff in mental hospitals is generally underreported for a variety of reasons (Lion et al. 1981). First, filling out injury forms is time consuming. Second, there are fears that nurses or other staff who sustain injury will be perceived as ineffective or "bad" and that authorities may launch an investigation into whether retaliatory violence by a staff member took place. Third, staff members in mental hospitals are often inured to the violence that occurs.

Most literature concerning the identification of patients likely to be assaultive in hospitals indicates that such individuals are youthful and psychotic (Tardiff and Sweillam 1980; Shader et al. 1977; Depp 1976). Some more recent work (Tardiff 1981) indicates that patients with mental retardation and personality disorders are more likely to be violent.

Serious attention to violence within a mental hospital is important. Only by documenting and discussing what occurs can intelligent policies be developed for dealing with violence. For example, staff may decide that a patient is too assaultive to remain in a particular ward and should be transferred elsewhere. Hospital policy could dictate that patients must pay for destroyed articles and broken furnishings. Criminal charges of assault may be pressed against a nonpsychotic patient who has been violent (Schwarz and Greenfield 1978). Small epidemics of hospital violence indicate changes in morale and leadership that require prompt attention.

Issues of group transference and countertransference are significant in ward management. Many violent patients use belligerence and verbal hostility to distance themselves from staff members. If the latter are not aware of this dynamic, they may choose to handle the issue by over-sedating the patient or placing the patient in seclusion (Lion and Pasternack 1973). Alienation then can deepen, as the patient, feeling more helpless, intensifies belligerence. This vicious cycle can be broken by bringing the patient out of seclusion and lessening medication. Isolation is usually a devastating affair for a patient (Wadeson and Carpenter 1976) and can have a destructive impact upon the ward, as in cases in which patients hear an isolated patient screaming throughout the night. A modified restraint camisole or other device that enables the patient to interact with other patients on the ward can be a humane alternative to isolation.

Another common dynamic on the ward is for staff to perceive the patient as more dangerous than the patient really is. This misperception can easily occur when the staff does not like a particular patient and handles its anger by projection.

Some patients, often including individuals in State hospital systems who have some degree of organic impairment together with a chronic psychosis, are notorious for their chronic violence. They are virtually imprisoned within the system and retained on large amounts of antipsychotic medication or placed on experimental paradigms and mixtures of antipsychotic, anticonvulsant, or lithium medication. The rationale for these regimens is often unclear. Attempts to take these patients off medication to clarify the underlying picture can be difficult because of strong affective responses by staff members who insist that the patient must remain medicated. Often, these patients are best transferred for evaluation to another unit of the hospital where the staff is more tolerant.

In evaluating the dosage needs of these types of patients, the clinician should construct a chart showing the name of each drug given to the patient, the length of time it was used, the maximum dosage, and the effects noted. Control should also be established over PRN medications of the patient while the evaluation is in progress. In this manner, the clinician can rule on the adequacy of the drug regimen (Lion 1978). More often than not, the fact that a patient has been "tried on everything" means that the patient has been exposed to small amounts of numerous medications for inadequate lengths of time rather than placed on any systematic regimen. One drug at a time is the rule, and that drug should be titrated to show inefficacy or toxicity before it is deemed ineffective (see chapter 3).

ANAMNESTIC ISSUES

Common sense dictates which variables in the patient's history are most ominous with regard to violence. Some clinicians believe that lack of capacity for interpersonal warmth and for positive object relations places a patient at risk for future violence (Kozol et al. 1972). For example, a patient who was treated cruelly as a child can grow up to be aloof to the suffering of others, indifferent to hurting others, and prone to excessive discipline of children or pets. It is important to assess the nature of childhood upbringing as well as the clinician's own attitude and feelings after having assessed the patient. Is the patient one with whom a therapeutic alliance could be formed? Does the patient have some reverence for the lives and value systems of others, or is the patient cold, cynical, and nonremorseful? Such queries shape an intuitive assessment of the patient's potential for aggressiveness.

Past violence, of course, is the best predictor of future violence. It is thus essential that the clinician assiduously inquire into the patient's history of violence. Much has been made of a childhood history of enuresis, pyromania, and cruelty to animals (Hellman and Blackman 1966). These neuropathic factors cannot predict violence, but they have been retrospectively associated with it. The evaluator should also note that violence in childhood can shape the patient's response to future behavior. Violence tends to breed violence, so persons abused during childhood learn a style of coping that they may use in later life with their own offspring and with others.

Violence is a behavior traditionally associated with parental deprivation, alcoholism, and traits seen in delinquent and antisocial individuals. More subtle aspects of psychological assessment have to do with defense structure and a patient's tendency to blame problems on the externals while avoiding introspection. Paranoid traits may become evident during an interview. The level of the patient's hostility and belligerence may surface during repeated interviews.

Assessment of the patient's self-esteem is important. Low self-esteem, coupled with projection, often forms the substrate for the brittle defensiveness seen in aggressive patients. Some individuals who cannot tolerate insults to their tenuous sexual identity or who have a pervasive fragility try to protect themselves by lashing out at others. Patients' vulnerability to object loss can often be ascertained from their case histories. Patients' ability to tolerate ambivalence and to see both good and bad is an effective index of whether they can respond adaptively to insults to their value system, or whether they are so rigid in their beliefs that they are apt to respond hostilely. Patients' degree of passivity or hostility, which can be gleaned from projective psychological tests, may give the evaluator important information about patients' level of rage and the targets of their anger (see chapter 5).

The capacity for aggression needs to be judged (Lion 1972b). Some violent patients, unable to tolerate introspection, convert any criticism into external rage and a physical outburst. Other patients are more able to dwell on the consequences of their acts, have a more established sense of fantasy, and are able to premeditate the consequences of their actions. Some patients can recognize their affective states as well. Others perceive anger as a vaguely alien condition that requires suppression:

they may feel the need for deviant behavior (e.g., go out and get drunk) when they feel "bad." The ability to fantasize, to premeditate outcome, and to identify anger are important parameters in assessing a patient's aggressiveness.

ORGANIC PARAMETERS

Organic factors play a role in many behavior disorders that are characterized by lability of moods and affect, impulsivity, and aggressiveness. Such disorders include the so-called "minimal brain dysfunction" syndromes now described for adults as well as for children (Bellak 1979). Organic factors also play a role in Intermittent Explosive Disorder as well as in Idiosyncratic Alcohol Intoxication; for example, brain tumors in the limbic system have been implicated in violence (Malamud 1967).

The literature on the role of epilepsy in violence is extensive (Mark and Ervin 1970; Sweet et al. 1969). Unlike the entity of depression or schizophrenia, which exists for weeks or months, a patient's violence comes and goes in a matter of moments; hence, it is episodic and often viewed as "epileptoid." The evidence to support this view is very controversial. Opinions differ about the occurrence of violence during ictal, interictal, or postictal states of such entities as psychomotor epilepsy (Rodin 1973; Goldstein 1974; Benson and Blumer 1975; Delgato-Escueta et al. 1981). These controversies seem somewhat academic for the clinician whose job is to determine the existence of an underlying or organic pathology that might be treated successfully with an anticonvulsant (Monroe 1970).

Organic impairment needs to be evaluated through neurologic assessment, psychological testing, and electroencephalographic examination. Basically, clinicians should proceed as though they had a mentally retarded child in whom they are trying to establish an etiology. Thus, historical questions need to be asked about head trauma, periods of unconsciousness, episodes of convulsions, and other similar phenomena. Psychological tests for organicity, such as the Reitan-Halstead test battery (Reitan and Davidson 1974), deserve consideration. These are basically tests of psychomotor function and visual–motor coordination, but they may also give valuable indications of a patient's lability and impulsivity associated with subtle brain dysfunction in the frontal, temporal, or parietal lobes. Neurologists interested in cortical function may be used as consultants to detect signs of organic impairment. Such findings as reflex asymmetries or difficulty in motor coordination point to neurologic dysfunction that may be associated with temporal or parietal lobe impairment.

An electroencephalogram (EEG) examination can yield evidence of brain dysfunction; on occasion, direct evidence of focal and specific changes, such as a temporal lobe spike, may be elicited. Nonspecific changes, such as the 14- and 6-per-second spike and wave form or slow waves, often associated with behavior disorders (Kiloh 1963), may give the clinician a rationale for anticonvulsant treatment. If the clinician suspects organic impairment, EEG's are best carried out during sleep, since the incidence of interictal abnormalities for those epilepsies associated with violence such as psychomotor seizures is small (Ervin 1967). Repeated sleep tracings may be required if the first recording yields nothing. Sleep also promotes hypersynchrony, which is conducive to the discovery of limbic system abnormalities; an awake tracing is far less valuable. The clinician must therefore spend some time with both the patient and the laboratory technician to procure a good sleep tracing.

Two forms of violence associated with brain dysfunction have been mentioned above and will be discussed in some detail here. Intermittent Explosive Disorder, a new DSM III entity, is characterized by episodes of loss of control over aggressive impulses. The term replaces the Explosive Personality seen in DSM II. The associated feature portion of DSM III concerning Intermittent Explosive Disorder notes that "features suggesting an organic disturbance may be present such as nonspecific EEG abnormalities or minor neurologic signs and symptoms thought to reflect subcortical or limbic system dysfunction." It is evident from further discussion of this entity that an organic evaluation is an important way to assess this disorder.

Alcohol Idiosyncratic Intoxication has been mentioned above. This is also a DSM III term; the DSM II term was "Pathologic Intoxication." The essential feature is a "marked behavioral change—usually to aggressiveness—that is due to recent ingestion of an amount of alcohol insufficient to produce intoxication in most people" (American Psychiatric Association 1980). The predisposing factors section of DSM III mention that "a small percentage of individuals with this disorder have been reported to have temporal lobe spikes on an electroencephalogram after receiving small amounts of alcohol." This phenomenon is rare, but the clinician should attempt to establish organic pathology through good sleep EEG studies and a careful history.

The general diagnostic issues confronting the clinician do not neatly separate into psychosocial or organic categories. As mentioned above, violence can be the manifestation of brain dysfunction but often is the result of psychological variables that are reflected in character pathology or more serious illness such as psychosis. Both organic dysfunction and psychosocial factors can coexist, and they are not mutually exclusive. For example, a patient with minimal brain dysfunction may have a personality disturbance that leads to overreaction to stress and violence when provoked. Aggression can occur particularly when alcohol lowers the threshold to impulsivity. Alcohol, the availability of a victim, the availability of a weapon, characterologic defects that lead to aggressive propensities, and threshold alterations on impulsivity resulting from subtle organic impairment can thus all contribute to the patient's violence. In such a case, each parameter should be individually assessed. The clinician needs to perform an organic evaluation, assess character strength and weakness, establish drinking patterns, note the availability of the weapon, and perhaps interview the victim.

TOXIC FACTORS

A host of toxic factors have been implicated in violence. Most hallucinogens, such as LSD or PCP (National Institute on Drug Abuse 1978), or inhalants, such as glue fumes (Cohen 1975), have been associated with aggression and homicidal behavior. Abuse of amphetamines (Ellinwood 1971) can lead to homicidal aggressiveness, and abuse of barbiturates (Tinklenberg and Woodrow 1973) can have a disinhibitory effect leading to aggression. If the clinician determines that the patient is likely to abuse these drugs, the patient is less predictable and hence riskier.

Some literature suggests that use of benzodiazepines may liberate aggression (Lion et al. 1975), but this literature is based upon violence simulated in a laboratory under very controlled conditions (Gardos et al. 1968). The existence of "paradoxical rage reactions" caused by benzodiazepines is rather rare (Lion 1979). Basically, the effect seems to be a disinhibitory one similar to the use of barbiturates or alcohol.

Contrary to popular belief, narcotics do not liberate violence but rather suppress it (Lion 1975). In fact, a drug such as marijuana has a distinct pacifying effect on the patient who uses it. Since persons become violent in order to procure narcotics, there is some association between these drugs and aggressiveness. In addition, alcohol remains the most frequent toxic substance linked to violence (National Commission on the Causes and Prevention of Violence 1969).

VICTIMS AND POTENTIAL VICTIMS

The evaluator's job is to determine first whether a victim or potential victim exists, then what danger the victim is in, and finally whether any ongoing pathology between victim and assailant can be resolved. Sometimes these tasks are urgent, as in the case of the homicidal patient. More often these tasks can be performed through traditional types of diagnostic conferences and treatment, when the treatment needs and treatability of the victim can be ascertained.

Confronting an identified or prospective victim is often considered to be beyond the purview of the clinician's role, yet the intervention rarely does harm and can be a means of identifying and resolving potentially violent dyadic relationships. A simple interview may uncover a vast range of psychopathology. Victims may prove to be passive, provocative, culpable, or innocent (Symonds 1978). It can often be a serious mistake to treat only the patient.

The <u>Tarasoff</u> decision (see chapter 9) about the therapist's responsibility to warn victims has aroused a defensive stance on the part of the mental health profession (Roth and Meisel 1977). In actual clinical practice, the patient usually welcomes intervention and rarely resists contact between the therapist and the potential victim.

RISK AND THE POTENTIAL FOR VIOLENCE

As used here, "risk" describes the patient's propensity to inflict future harm. The clinician is faced with assessing immediate and long-term risk. Three case vignettes illustrate the varieties of risk assessment, often referred to in the literature as "prediction of dangerousness."

Case 1. A paranoid patient is admitted to an emergency room with command hallucinations urging him to kill his wife. The wife is immediately contacted, corroborates the patient's deviant behavior, and acknowledges her fear of him.

Case 2. A patient phones the clinician for an appointment regarding his severe temper. He struck his wife and vaguely threatened to harm her. He sounds composed on the phone. Although offered an immediate appointment, he opts for a week's delay because of out-of-town business. When he appears on time for his evaluation, he relates a 6-month history of explosive temper outbursts and spouse abuse. He admits perplexity regarding these events and asks for treatment. The clinician ascertains that the wife has sustained bruises in the past. The patient admits to owning a weapon and to mild alcoholism.

Case 3. man charged with murder was found not guilty by reason of insanity and committed to a hospital for the criminally insane. He has served 6 years in this forensic facility. His behavior has been exemplary. The staff meets to discuss his release to a halfway house.

These examples confront the evaluator with differing types of risk assessment. Short-term risk assessment is the most urgent, yet not difficult when the problem is as blatant as in the first case. The second case is more problematic in that mental status gives few clues about risk. The clinician needs to probe more deeply into the patient's past, assess the variables already mentioned (ownership and use of weapons, alcoholism), and interview the spouse. Only then can the relative explosiveness of the situation be determined. For example, the evaluator may discover that the patient does not know that his wife is planning to leave him. This impending loss may evoke the patient's rage in the future and significantly increase risk unless therapy intervenes.

The third case is even more difficult since the violence occurred so long ago and has not recurred. Although the man has been a model patient for a long time, his ability to adjust to life outside the institution is essentially unknown. Through a graduated release procedure, control can be maintained over the patient while he comes in contact with real-life stresses that can be used to assess risk for violence—e.g., an argument with an employer, economic hardship, adverse family circumstances.

Clinical prediction is far more liable to error than many clinicians realize. It is important to be familiar with literature in this area to understand the limitations and hazards of prediction thoroughly (National Institute of Mental Health 1981).

As with a depressed patient, the clinical state and the environment change with time and growth. No violent patient is always at risk or always safe. Good followup is the key to good assessment in all aspects of medicine, particularly with patients who are prone to impulsiveness and aggressiveness. The clinician needs to ascertain whether a particular patient seeks help in times of stress and has someone to whom to turn. Without these safeguards, any violent patient is at risk.

The evaluator also needs to consider whether the violent patient has an ongoing clinical relationship with a therapist or an institution and whether this relationship is sufficiently strong to help in moments of stress. Violent patients are frightened by their urges, but they can be taught to call for help rather than translate affect into behavior. As with a suicidal patient, initial evaluation and disposition are not the end of the matter but the beginning of what may need to be a long treatment process.

A point should be made about the benefit of collegial help in evaluating violent patients. Since strong transference sentiments are aroused by these individuals, the clinician may wish to seek a second opinion. When significant differences emerge between evaluators in their perception of the patient's dangerousness, transference or countertransference issues may well be involved.

Denial of violence can occur in the context of ongoing psychotherapy. Some patients try to make fun of their own violent fantasies and may even talk to therapists about violent thoughts directed toward them. Jests, fantasies, and veiled threats must be taken seriously, for they reflect transference material that can escalate to psychotic proportions in borderline and paranoid individuals. The existence of violence in the thoughts and lives of patients must be monitored as closely as depression. For example, violent behavior within the home by an adolescent patient in treatment should be evaluated as possibly representing an acting out of conflicts from the therapy setting.

A final plea is made for clinicians to become actively involved in the evaluation of violent patients. Without direct exposure to such individuals, assessments are sterile textbook exercises that increase rather than bridge the gap between theory and practice.

REFERENCES

American Psychiatric Association. Diagnostic and Statistical Manual of Mental Disorders. Washington, D.C.: the American Psychiatric Association, 1980.

American Psychiatric Association. Task Force Report 8. Clinical Aspects of the Violent Individual. Washington, D.C.: the American Psychiatric Association, 1974.

Bach-y-Rita, G.; Lion, J.R.; Climent, C.E.; and Ervin, F. Episodic dyscontrol: A study of 130 patients. American Journal of Psychiatry 127(11):1473–1478, 1971a.

Bach-y-Rita, G.; Lion, J.R.; and Ervin, F.R. Pathological intoxication: Clinical and electroencephalographic studies. American Journal of Psychiatry 127(5): 698–703, 1971b.

Bellak, L. Psychiatric Aspects of Minimal Brain Dysfunction in Adults. New York: Grune and Stratton, 1979.

Benson, F.D., and Blumer, D. Psychiatric Aspects of Neurologic Diseases. New York: Grune and Stratton, 1975.

Cain, A.C. The presuperego "turning-inward" of aggression. Psychoanalytic Quarterly 30:171–243, 1961.

Cohen, M.L.; Garofalo, R.; Boucher, R.; and Seghorn, T. The psychology of rapists. Seminars in Psychiatry 3(3):307–327, 1971.

Cohen, S. Inhalant abuse. Drug Abuse and Alcoholism Newsletter 4(9):1975.

Delgado-Escueta, A.V.; Mattson, R.H.; King, L.; Goldensohn, E.S.; Spugel, H.; Madsen, J.; Crandall, P.; Dreifuss, F. The nature of aggression during epileptic seizures. New England Journal of Medicine 305(12):711–716, 1981.

Depp, F.C. Violent behavior patterns on psychiatric wards. Aggressive Behavior 2(4):295–306, 1976.

Donlon, P.T.; Hopkin, J.; and Tupin, J.P. Overview: Efficacy and safety of the rapid neuroleptization method with injectable haloperidol. American Journal of Psychiatry 136(3):273–278, 1979.

Ellinwood, E.H. Assault and homicide associated with amphetamine abuse. American Journal of Psychiatry 127(10):1170–1175, 1971.

Ervin, F.R. Brain disorders. IV: Associated with convulsions (epilepsy). In: Freedman, A.M., and Kaplan, H.I., eds. Comprehensive Textbook of Psychiatry. Baltimore: Williams and Wilkins, 1967, pp. 795–816.

Gardos, G.; DiMascio, A.; Salzman, C.; and Shader, R.I. Differential actions of chlordiazepoxide and oxazepam on hostility. Archives of General Psychiatry 18:757–760, June 1968.

Goldstein, M. Brain research and violent behavior. Archivesof Neurology 30(1):1–35, 1974.

Gutheil, T.C. Observations on the theoretical bases for seclusion of the psychiatric inpatient. American Journal of Psychiatry 135(3):325–328, 1978.

Harbin, H.T. Episodic dyscontrol and family dynamics. American Journal of Psychiatry 134(10):1113–1116, 1977.

Hellman, D.S., and Blackman, N. Enuresis, firesetting and cruelty to animals: A triad predictive of adult crime. American Journal of Psychiatry 122:1431–1435, June 1966.

Kiloh, L.G. The electroencephalogram in psychiatry. Postgraduate Medical Journal 39:34–47, January 1963.

Kozol, H.L.; Boucher, R.J.; and Garofalo, R.F. The diagnosis and treatment of dangerousness. Crime and Delinquency 18(4):371–392, 1972.

Lion, J.R.; Bach-y-Rita, G.; and Ervin, F.R. The selfreferred violent patient. Journal of the American Medical Association 205(7):503–505, 1968.

Lion, J.R.; Bach-y-Rita, G.; and Ervin, F.R. Violent patients in the emergency room. Americen Journal of Psychiatry 125(12):1706–1711, 1969.

Lion, J.R. Evaluation and Management of the Violent Patient. Springfield: Charles C. Thomas, 1972a.

Lion, J.R. The role of depression in the treatment of aggressive personality disorders. American Journal of Psychiatry 129(3):347–349, 1972b.

Lion, J.R., and Pasternack, S.A. Countertransference reactions to violent patients. American Journal of Psychiatry 130(2):207–210, 1973.

Lion, J.R., and Penna, M. The study of human aggression. In: Whalen, R., ed. The Neuropsychology of Aggression. New York: Plenum, 1974.

Lion, J.R. Conceptual issues in the use of drugs for the treatment of aggression in man. Journal of Nervous and Mental Diseases 160(2):76–82, 1975.

Lion, J.R.; Azcarate, C.L.; and Koepke, H. Paradoxical rage reaction during psychotropic medication. Diseases of the Nervous System 36(10):557–558, 1975.

Lion, J.R.; Madden, D.J.; and Christopher, R.L. A violence clinic: Three years' experience. American Journal of Psychiatry 133(4):432–435, 1976.

Lion, J.R. The Art of Medicating Psychiatric Patients. Baltimore: Williams and Wilkins, 1978.

Lion, J.R. Benzodiazepines in the treatment of aggressive patients. Journal of Clinical Psychiatry 40(2):70–71, 1979.

Lion, J.R. Personality Disorders: Diagnosis and Management. Baltimore: Williams and Wilkins, 1981.

Lion, J.R.; Synder, W.; and Merrill, G. Underreporting of assaults in a mental hospital. Hospital and Community Psychiatry 32(7):497–498, 1981.

Malamud, N. Psychiatric disorder with intracranial tumors of the limbic system. Archives of Neurology 17:113123, August 1967.

Marinacci, A.A. Special type of temporal lobe (psychomotor) seizures following ingestion of alcohol. Bulletin of Los Angeles Neurological Society 28(4):241–250, 1963.

Mark, V.H., and Ervin, F.R. Violence and the Brain. New York: Harper & Row, 1970.

Megargee, E.I. Undercontrolled and overcontrolled personality types in extreme antisocial aggression. Psychological Monographs 80(3):1–29, Whole No. 611, 1966.

Monroe, R.R. Episodic Behavior Disorders: A Psychodynamic and Neurophysiologic Analysis. Cambridge: Harvard University Press, 1970.

National Commission on the Causes and Prevention of Violence. The role of alcohol, narcotics, dangerous drugs in individual violence, Chapter 15. In: Crimes of Violence: A Staff Report. Vol. 12, by Mulvihill, D.J.; Tumin, M.M.; and Curtis, L.A., pp. 641–651. Washington, D.C.: Supt. of Docs., U.S. Govt. Print. Off., 1969.

National Institute on Drug Abuse. Phencyclidine (PCP Abuse): An Appraisal, by Peterson, R.C., and Stillman, R.C. Research Monograph 21 DHEW. Washington, D.C.: U.S. Govt. Print. Off. 1978.

National Institute of Mental Health. The Clinical Prediction of Violent Behavior, by Monahan, J. Crime and Delinquency Issues Monograph. DHHS Pub. No. (ADM) 81-921. Washington, D.C.: U.S. Govt. Print. Off., 1981.

Reitan, R.M., and Davidson, L.A. Clinical Neuropsychology:Current Status and Applications. Washington: V.H. Winston, 1974.

Rodin, E.A. Psychomotor epilepsy and aggressive behavior. Archives of General Psychiatry 28:210–213, February 1973.

Rosen, H., and DiGiacomo, J.N. The role of physical restraint in the treatment of psychiatric illness. Journal of Clinical Psychiatry 39(12):228–232, 1978.

Roth, L.H., and Meisel, A. Dangerousness, confidentiality and the duty to warn. American Journal of Psychiatry 134(5):508–511, 1977.

Schwarz, C.J., and Greenfield, G.P. Charging a patient with assault of a nurse on a psychiatric unit. Canadian Psychiatric Association Journal 23(4):197–200, 1978.

Shader, R.I.; Jackson, A.H.; Harmatz, J.S.; and Appelbaum, P.S. Patterns of violent behavior among schizophrenic inpatients. Diseases of the Nervous System 38(1):13–16, 1977.

Sweet, W.H.; Ervin, F.R.; and Mark, V.H. The relationship of violent behavior to focal cerebral disease. In: Garattini, S., and Siggs, E.G., eds. Aggressive Behavior. New York: John Wiley & Sons, 1969.

Symonds, M. The psychodynamics of violence-prone marriages. American Journal of Psychoanalysis 38(3):213–222, 1978.

Tardiff, K., and Sweillam, A. Assault, suicide, and mental illness. Archives of General Psychiatry 37:164–169, February 1980.

Tardiff, K. Emergency control measures for psychiatric inpatients. Journal of Nervous and Mental Disease 169(10):614–618, 1981.

Tinklenberg, J.R., and Woodrow, K.M. Drug use among assaultive and sexual offenders. In: Frazier, S.H., ed. Human Aggression: Proceedings of the 1972 Annual Meeting of the Association for Research in Nervous and Mental Disease. Baltimore: Williams and Wilkins, 1973.

Wadeson, H., and Carpenter, W.T. Impact of the seclusion room experience. Journal of Nervous and Mental Diseases 163(5):318–328, 1976.

2

Behavioral Analysis and Therapy for Aggressive Psychiatric and Developmentally Disabled Patients[1]

Stephen E. Wong, Ph.D.
Katherine M. Slama, Ph.D.
Robert Paul Liberman, M.D.

Aggression by patients within mental hospitals is a major clinical and administrative problem. At Camarillo State Hospital, with 1,400 psychiatric and developmentally disabled patients, a study revealed 400 violent incidents reported each month. Since official reports account for only one-fifth of the violent incidents that actually occur (Lion et al. 1981), a more accurate estimate of aggressive incidents might be 2,000 incidents per month. This estimated hospital-wide rate of 70 aggressive acts per day compares with a rate of 1 aggressive act per half hour of waking time recorded on two richly staffed and actively programmed units at a regional psychiatric hospital in Illinois (Paul and Lentz 1977).

With the documented significance and prevalence of aggression among psychiatric patients, methods are needed for examining and understanding the factors controlling aggressive responses. Like other behavior, aggression is the result of both biological and environmental processes. Behavioral analysis and therapy provide a framework for studying environmental influences by analyzing stimuli that precede and follow aggressive behavior. Antecedent stimuli can elicit aggression

[1] The authors express appreciation to B.D. Marshall, Jr., M.D.; Lorelle Banzett, M.S.W.; Mark Terranova, M.A.; and the nursing staff of the Clinical Research Unit as well as Martha Johnson, Unit Supervisor; Diane Bannerman, B.S., Jan Lapointe, R.T.; and the nursing staff of the female Behavior Adjustment Unit for their technical expertise and tireless efforts, some of which are described in this chapter.

as a reflexive reaction or prompt aggression by signaling occasions in which aggressive behaviors will be rewarded. Consequent stimuli, on the other hand, can function as reinforcement (positive events that increase the probability of a behavior) or punishment (negative events that decrease its probability). Reinforcing and punishing stimuli are both determined empirically by their actual effect on aggressive responding. In using behavior analysis and therapy, one identifies controlling environmental stimuli and modifies them to produce desired changes in behavior. This chapter will elucidate environmental causes of aggression in psychiatric patients and behavioral treatments for this disorder.

The material for this chapter is drawn from published behavioral research and the authors' work at Camarillo State Hospital (CSH) and its Clinical Research Unit (CRU) in Camarillo, California. Located 50 miles north of the metropolitan area of Los Angeles, CSH houses approximately 800 psychiatric and 600 developmentally disabled patients. Separate programs within the facility treat patients classified as mentally retarded, autistic, child, adolescent, acute and chronic adult psychiatric, or geriatric. The CRU is a 12-bed unit in the CSH that receives male and female referrals from all sectors of the hospital and the State system. The CRU is affiliated with the Neuropsychiatric Institute, Department of Psychiatry, University of California at Los Angeles, and is specially staffed and funded for innovative behavioral treatment, research, and training. Aggressive psychiatric and developmentally disabled patients are treated on the CRU and on many units within the CSH.

BEHAVIORAL ANALYSIS OF AGGRESSION

The usual question facing clinical staff members treating aggression is: "What is causing this behavior and how can it be changed?" A careful examination of the aggressive response and environmental stimuli associated with it can be the first step in answering this question. An operant, "ABC" analysis proceeds by (1) identifying antecedents of aggression or stimuli correlated with the behavior's onset; (2) specifying the behavior fully; and (3) noting consequences that may be maintaining the behavior. This information, considered along with the patient's treatment history, reinforcers, intellectual functioning, and concomitant treatments, can be used to develop an effective behavioral program.

Antecedents of Aggressive Behavior

Aspects of the physical and social environment often provoke aggression. It is important to note these potential antecedents and to consider them when devising a treatment program. Laboratory studies have shown that unpleasant stimulation such as pain (Azrin et al. 1965) and the withdrawal of food (Azrin et al. 1966) can directly elicit aggressive behavior. Inpatient settings are fraught with undesirable elements that might lead to aggression. Crowding is one (Boe 1977; Rago et al. 1978); irritating noise and boredom are probably others. The frustrations that accompany institutional living add to the aversive quality of an environment (Cataldo and Risley 1974). Peers are also a continuing source of annoyance. Since patients in these facilities tend to be socially unskilled, interactions between them often include teasing, insults, and roughhousing. A frequent reaction is to return the abuse, creating a cycle that can rapidly escalate into violent conflict.

Other situations prompt antagonistic behavior by offering clear incentives for aggressive acts. These are generally recurring circumstances in which aggression secures some reward and is likely to go unpunished. Aggressive patients quickly discriminate occasions when other patients can be assaulted with impunity, such as when staff are few in number, untrained, or easily intimidated. The patients learn which of their peers are unable to defend themselves and areas of the unit which are poorly supervised. A weak, isolated patient possessing a desired cigarette or another favored item may be an irresistible target.

Also serving to encourage aggression is seeing how this behavior secures reinforcement and social dominance for the aggressor. It is well established that aggression can be prompted by modeling (Bandura 1973).

Institutions can both reduce aversive features that elicit aggression and remove or alter discriminative stimuli that prompt it. Conditions predisposing patients to antagonistic behavior may be changed by alleviating inactivity, crowding, and excessive noise. Patients' free time can be filled with activities fashioned around their interests. Recreational gatherings can be scheduled outside the unit or with small groups. Prosocial group activities may effectively replace assaultive behavior.

Other measures can be taken to modify situations that facilitate and invite aggression. Patients can be kept out of areas of the unit that are impossible to supervise properly. Staff can coordinate their actions so that small, physically weak workers can apply negative consequences as effectively and safely as large, muscular workers can. On units with a high rate of assaults, staff might wear whistles to bring immediate aid from others when needed. Physically or verbally abusive patients can be segregated from persons for whom they model aggression. These are but a few of the possible ways to restructure an environment to avoid triggering aggression.

Specification of Aggressive Behaviors

When designing a behavioral intervention, the topography, intensity, frequency, and duration of the target behavior must be specified. This information can help staff decide on the need for treatment and exactly what behaviors they will modify. Specification can emerge from a series of questions: How does the patient assault others—with hands and feet or with an object? What force is used? How often does the patient attack someone? How long does the assault last? If the patient punches at people's faces or throws chairs, even one instance of aggression may be so serious that staff will gladly undertake a complex and arduous treatment that will minimize this response. On the other hand, if the patient slaps people lightly on their seats, it may suffice to have staff agree to ignore this behavior. Observing and recording the occurrence of aggression may at times reveal the "mountainous problem" to be a "molehill." Objective measurement of a patient's aggressiveness can often yield surprising information that conflicts with casual impressions of that individual.

Empirical information helps to determine not only the appropriate treatment procedure but also what aspect of the behavior to change. For example, suppose there are four patients on a ward who grab at people. With Bob, who reaches for other people's private parts, staff might decide to change the topography of his behavior by teaching him to shake hands, pat shoulders, and touch people in more appropriate ways. For Carol, who grabs those around her so hard that she bruises or scratches, staff members might want to decrease the intensity of grabbing. The intervention in this case might be to tell her not to hold so hard, praise her is she complies, and apply timeout if she does not. With Don, who pulls on staff members' arms to make a request several times each hour, the program might reduce the frequency of this behavior by praising him at the end of each half hour that he has not grabbed anyone. Finally, for Evelyn, who clings to staff for long periods, treatment might entail rewarding her at the end of each hour with points toward a backrub if she touches others for periods of 2 seconds or less.

Consequences of Aggressive Behavior

The environmental events that occur after aggressive acts are perhaps the strongest determinants of the probability of future aggression. Consequences that increase aggressive behavior, known as "reinforcers," can be either positive or negative. Positive reinforcement involves presenting pleasurable stimuli following the performance of a behavior; negative reinforcement involves removing unpleasant stimuli following the performance of a behavior.

Staff members can inadvertently provide abundant positive reinforcement for aggressive behavior in psychiatric settings. If, for example, a female patient has just struck someone, what happens? Staff run to the patient, ask her why she hit another person (giving a mixture of positive attention and admonishment), touch her as they move her from the victim, and give her a PRN medication (more attention and physical stimulation) if she continues to act in a hostile way. Other positive reinforcement may be more subtle, such as being shunned by staff and being allowed to engage in one's preferred activities (e.g., self-stimulation, isolation, ritual performing, sleep). The reaction of other patients can also strengthen the patient's behavior. They may accord her a higher status out of fear or admiration for her manipulation of staff members. Other patients may try to purchase protection by giving her cigarettes and small change.

Various types of negative reinforcement may also maintain the same patient's aggressive behavior. The behavior may enable her to avoid or escape a boring workshop or therapy session. Aggression may drive away annoying or abusive fellow patients who do not respond to verbal pleas.

The general treatment strategies involving reinforcement are to separate it from aggressive behavior, to reinforce other appropriate or incompatible responses, and to program response cost, timeout, or aversive consequences for aggressive acts. One set of interventions might include (1) requiring the aggressor to pay the victim a certain number of tokens for "damages"; (2) sending the aggressor to a timeout room; (3) avoiding use of PRN medication for the aggressor; and (4) making the aggressor attend regularly scheduled activities.

Knowledge of response chains, i.e., behaviors that reliably follow each other, can be a helpful way to prevent aggressive behavior. For example, intense acts of aggression, such as biting other patients' noses, may be preceded by less noxious behavior, such as placing one's face within 6 inches of the victim's face. Staff can devise an intervention for the earlier behavior in the chain and prevent the more damaging behavior from occurring. Response chains become troublesome, however, when they lead to unintentional reinforcement of inappropriate behavior. As a simple example, Fred begins tapping on George's shoulder and causes George to yell out. Fred continues until a staff member hears George yelling and tells Fred to stop. Fred stops and the staff member praises him for leaving George alone. Eventually, someone realizes that Fred is obtaining praise at the end of the chain for an undesirable behavior earlier in the chain. Once this is known, staff can provide more appropriate consequences, such as requiring Fred to stop touching George, and then avoid attending to Fred until he engages in appropriate behavior for several minutes.

Other Considerations In Choosing Interventions

Besides the components of the initial behavioral analysis, several additional factors should be reviewed when developing a treatment program for an aggressive patient. These include the individual patient's strengths and deficits, the stimuli he or she characteristically finds reinforcing and aversive, and an overall risk-benefit analysis of the alternative treatment procedures.

DESIGNING A BEHAVIORAL PROGRAM

Patient Strengths and Deficits

When designing a behavioral program, knowledge of a patient's individual skills and shortcomings can have several applications. For example, level of intellectual functioning can determine the best types of activities and environmental stimulation to offer a patient. A severely retarded person might be entertained by giant cartoons and simple games, toys, and puzzles. Such a patient may not be adequately stimulated by an environment featuring impressionist art, word games, and a television. Level of intelligence often indicates the strategy that should be used to teach behaviors that are incompatible with aggressive responses. While modeling and verbal coaching may suffice to show a patient of normal intelligence how to touch other people in a socially acceptable manner, manual guidance may be required to teach the same behavior to a developmentally disabled patient.

Assessment of an individual's social skills can also guide the se-

lection of treatment procedures. A patient who responds to social disapproval may not need more aversive punishment to decrease aggression. Someone who already has basic conversational skills may simply require assertion training in how to express complaints before becoming frustrated. On the other hand, a patient lacking in language skills may respond faster to timeout and other less verbally oriented procedures.

Mental status is another area that should be evaluated when fashioning treatment programs. More subtle cognitive behavior modification procedures will often be ineffective with a hallucinating acute schizophrenic until an antipsychotic drug regimen helps to organize the cognitive processes. For severely depressed people, ignoring mildly aggressive behavior and reinforcing its absence is unlikely to be as therapeutic as prompting and reinforcing positive self-statements.

Age and other physical characteristics also help to determine which treatments are indicated. Overcorrection (Foxx and Azrin 1972) for a resistive client may be much more feasible for a 5-year-old child than for a strong adult. The patient's physical health must be considered if an intervention requires strenuous activity. In general, appropriate treatment interventions build upon a patient's abilities and skills and remediate a patient's weaknesses.

Individual Reinforcers and Aversives

Perhaps even more than most people, institutionalized patients have idiosyncratic tendencies. Without empirical testing, it is difficult to judge whether a given stimulus will be reinforcing, aversive, or neutral for any particular patient. Social disapproval is probably the most familiar example; some patients find it unpleasant, but a great many find it reinforcing because it directs attention to themselves and stirs up activity in a typically low-interaction environment. A similar example is the isolation involved in timeout procedures; although most patients seek to avoid it, autistic and schizophrenic patients may find it reinforcing.

One factor that can shape a patient's response to aversive consequences is treatment history. A patient who has been exposed to very aversive procedures is less sensitive to subsequent punishment, perhaps because of habituation (Hobbs and Forehand 1977). For this reason and for ethical ones, it is wise to begin with the least restrictive procedure that seems likely to decrease the aggressive behavior within the time required by its severity. If the procedure fails and is properly evaluated, the knowledge thus gained will contribute to the selection of a more effective treatment.

Risk-Benefit Analysis

Treatments vary along a number of important dimensions, and a risk-benefit analysis can assist in determining the most suitable therapeutic procedure for a given patient. Possible benefits of a treatment can include (1) anticipated reduction in the frequency and intensity of the target behavior and (2) positive side effects and benefits that may accompany the primary behavior change (such as increased adaptive behaviors, improved social adjustment, or movement to a more normal environment). Risks connected with treatment can include (1) physical danger and amount of discomfort to the patient; (2) degree of interference with the patient's life; and (3) known or possible negative side effects of the procedure (e.g., social withdrawal). The treatment emerging from this analysis with the most favorable risk-benefit ratio is probably the therapy of choice.

The remainder of this chapter describes some novel and some well-recognized behavioral treatments for aggression and presents data that have been obtained on the effectiveness of treatment. The procedures to be discussed are activity programming, social skills training, differential reinforcement of other behavior, timeout from reinforcement, mild aversives (in particular, water mist), overcorrection, and contingent restraint. The treatments are presented in order of their judged aversiveness and restrictiveness, from least to most.

ACTIVITY PROGRAMMING

As outlined earlier, aggressive behavior may occur in institutional environments that do not encourage alternative responses and allow long periods of patient inactivity. Although the relationship between boredom and aggression has not been thoroughly investigated, preliminary data suggest that reinforcing client participation in recreational activities can lessen inappropriate behavior, including aggressive and self-injurious responses. The following paragraphs summarize a study conducted in a CSH unit for the severely retarded. The study evaluated the effects of structured leisure activities on several aspects of patient functioning. A complete report of this research has been presented elsewhere (Slama et al. 1981).

Researchers observed all residents on a ward for aggressive, developmentally disabled patients using a 15second time sampling procedure for 1 hour each day. On-task behavior, toy play, and a number of other desirable responses were recorded under an "appropriate behavior" category, while aggression, self-stimulation, selfabuse, and other undesirable responses were placed under an "inappropriate behavior" category. During baseline sessions, the patients had access to a variety of toys and games (puzzles, picture books, peg boards, art supplies), but staff did not prompt or reinforce patient involvement with these materials. During sessions with programmed activities, staff verbally and manually directed patients to use the present recreational equipment and delivered social and consumable reinforcement (cookies and

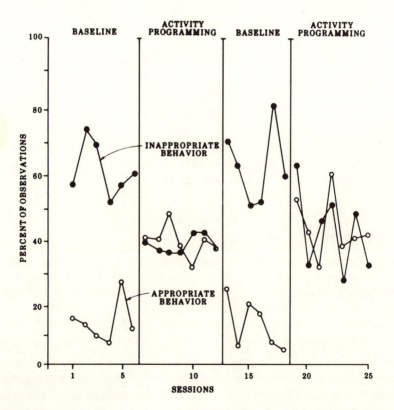

Figure 1. Percent of Observations Scored Appropriate and Inappropriate Behavior During Baseline and Activity Programming

candy) when patients used these materials in an acceptable manner. At first, staff administered prompts and reinforcement very frequently, but gradually instructions were faded and the intervals between reinforcements were lengthened. The intervention was evaluated within an ABAB design (Hersen and Barlow 1976) in which, following a baseline phase, activity programming was introduced, withdrawn, and then reintroduced.

Averaged data for the entire ward of aggressive retarded patients shown in figure 1 indicate that activity programming was highly effective in reducing inappropriate behavior while simultaneously promoting appropriate behavior. Inappropriate responses decreased by approximately 30 percent from baseline levels and appropriate behavior increased slightly over 100 percent from the baseline. The impact on aggressive and self-injurious behavior was also noteworthy, as these responses were reduced by nearly 60 percent when structured activities were offered. This encouraging outcome seemed to suggest that activity programming can be a positive strategy for indirectly suppressing aggressive and other socially undesirable behaviors.

SOCIAL SKILLS TRAINING

Aggression can be considered not only as an excess in the intensity and frequency of certain responses but also as a deficit of more acceptable forms of behavior. People may use force to satisfy their needs if they lack skills for effective solicitation, persuasion, and negotiation. Behavioral clinicians have used social skills training to establish interactive behavior that is both instrumentally and contextually appropriate. Training usually involves several component procedures: (1) instructions describing and providing a rationale for the behavior being taught; (2) demonstration or modeling of the desired response; (3) behavior rehearsal arranging for repeated enactment of the behavior; and (4) feedback or social reinforcement for correct performance of the response (Center for Studies of Schizophrenia 1980). This treatment package can be applied alone or combined with other techniques to control aggression (Wallace et al. 1973).

Social skills training generally proceeds through successive instruction in numerous minute behaviors that make up a competent social performance. Desirable interactive responses that have been taught as alternatives to aggressive behavior in recent studies are appropriate affect, facial expressiveness, assertive posture (Matson and Stephens

1978), direct eye contact (Bornstein et al. 1980; Frederiksen et al. 1976; Matson and Stephens 1978), appropriate requests (Frederiksen et al. 1976), and requests for the listener to change his or her behavior (Bornstein et al. 1980; Elder et al. 1979). All of the previous investigations also applied training procedures to weaken a host of antagonistic or disruptive behaviors. Although the above studies primarily assessed and trained patients' responses within role-played situations, a few also demonstrated generalization of treatment gains to naturalistic encounters occurring on the ward (Bornstein et al. 1980; Frederiksen et al. 1976).

The following case study describes how social skills training was employed at CSH to teach elementary, positive interactive behaviors to a retarded woman who violently attacked others. In this clinical intervention, training of prosocial responses was combined with timeout from reinforcement to modify a dangerous antisocial pattern.

Case Study of Barbara. Barbara was a 28-year-old moderately retarded woman hospitalized since the age of 6 with an initial diagnosis of childhood schizophrenia. Her bouts of aggression were frequent (more than 3 times per week) and very intense; on several occasions, she severely injured staff members she attacked. Aggression appeared to be provoked by minimal social stimulation, such as close physical proximity or attempts to engage her in conversation. When confronted with these situations, Barbara would respond by tensing her hands by her face and making loud sounds. If the situation continued, Barbara's screaming increased, and she often attacked the other person in a frenzied manner. Because of her aggressiveness, staff were afraid to involve Barbara in recreational and training activities in the unit. As a result, she spent most of the day rocking by herself.

Barbara received social skills training, as did four other patients who exhibited some verbal skills but lacked the ability to initiate positive interactions. Training sessions lasting 30 minutes were conducted 3 times per week over a period of 4 months. Patients were taught four basic greeting responses: making eye contact, presenting a pleasant facial expression, saying "Hi" and addressing the conversant by name, and speaking at an appropriate volume. Due to these patients' limited verbal repertoires, staff used oral instructions and physical prompts to introduce desired responses and delivered edibles (sugared cereal, bits of candy) with praise as reinforcement for correct responses.

Results indicated that training was effective in teaching Barbara elementary social skills. During a baseline assessment, she spoke loudly enough 50 percent of the time but totally lacked the remaining three greeting responses. After 4 months of training, the three greetings improved substantially, and later appeared in 80 percent of the assessments conducted. Measures taken on the unit indicated that these skills also generalized to Barbara's daily environment.

Nursing staff recorded the number of screaming tantrums and incidents of physical attack during the 4 months of Barbara's social skills training and for 9 months thereafter. In the fourth month of training, a locked timeout procedure was instituted on her unit to control physical aggression. Barbara's tantrums gradually declined in frequency, from 55 in the first month of training to 14 in the fourth month. During the subsequent 9-month period in which timeout was employed, the mean number of tantrums was 6.7 per month. The number of attacks per month also declined over the same period, although this second behavior was initially less frequent and the changes were less pronounced. The mean number of attacks during the 4 months of social skills training was 3.25; the corresponding value for the subsequent 9 months while timeout was in effect was 1.22.

Data suggested that social skills training contributed to a reduction in screaming tantrums, and contingent timeout was associated with a diminution of violent attacks. Improvements in Barbara's social responsiveness were noted by unit staff members, who were now able to involve her in much of the standard routine. She was more compliant and tolerated an industrial therapy assignment, adult education classes, and off-unit activities. Barbara began to make requests for things she wanted and to engage in conversations of three to five sentences or longer. Close proximity of another person no longer evoked aggression, and Barbara even was observed requesting the physical contact of others (e.g., backrubs).

DIFFERENTIAL REINFORCEMENT OF OTHER BEHAVIOR

Differential reinforcement of other behavior (DRO), or omission training, reduces behavior by reinforcing all responses other than the target aggressive behavior. In practice, reinforcement is delivered after a specific interval has passed with no aggression. For various reasons, DRO has often been combined with timeout to control aggressive behavior (Bostow and Bailey 1969; Vukelich and Hake 1971; Repp and Deitz 1974). These two techniques can complement one another; the

DRO schedule adding to the reinforcing value of the "timein" situation and, by contrast, amplifying the punishing properties of the timeout condition (Vukelich and Hake 1971; Solnick et al. 1977). Furthermore, the decelerative impact of DRO schedules when applied alone is somewhat unreliable; it is effective with certain subjects and responses but not with others (Harris and Ersner-Hershfield 1978).

An example of a program developed for a highly aggressive patient referred to the CRU will clarify how a DRO procedure might be applied. In this clinical study, a DRO schedule and response cost (token fines) modified threatening verbalizations and gestures. Physical assault by this patient was treated separately with locked timeout.

Case Study of Robert. Robert was a 52-year-old male with a 30-year history of psychiatric hospitalization and aggressive behavior. Although originally diagnosed as schizophrenic, Robert continued to be institutionalized primarily because of his frequent and unprovoked attacks on others. Robert had been the subject of many determined attempts to reduce his violence, including 3 lobotomies and over 100 electroconvulsive treatments, but none engendered any clear improvement.

When aggressive, Robert both intimidated and injured those around him. He often confronted other patients and staff members with menacing facial expressions and gestures. Robert was almost nonverbal, but occasionally he would emit loud sounds and profanities. Physical violence usually entailed threatening and then punching patients or staff members in the face. During his first week on the CRU, Robert injured three patients and one staff member by blows to the head or face.

The treatment for aggressive behavior was composed of contingent timeout to reduce acts of assault and response cost plus a DRO schedule of reinforcement to control gestural threats. All hitting was punished with a 1-hour timeout through confinement in a "quiet room" (described in detail in the following section on timeout). Staff members punished threats, usually exhibited in the form of finger pointing or fist shaking accompanied with a scowl, by fining Robert one token per incident. Conversely, Robert received token reinforcement when no threats were observed for certain intervals of time, which were gradually increased from 15 to 45 minutes. Tokens initially could be traded for coffee or cigarettes every 30 minutes, but this interval was also progressively increased until exchange times were 90 minutes apart.

Both the frequency of assaults and threats improved significantly during treatment. The number of assaults, recorded on a daily basis, declined from an average of 1.6 per day during the first 20 days on the CRU to an average of 0.15 during the last 20 days of therapy. Threats were quantified by a fixed-interval recording system, with the occurrence or nonoccurrence of the behavior being scored for each DRO reinforcement interval. The threats fell from an average of 17.7 percent of all observed intervals per day to an average of 4.9 percent.

After 6 months of treatment, Robert's aggressiveness had decreased sufficiently to justify his release from the CRU. He was transferred with the recommendation that the DRO procedure be continued to suppress aggressive behavior and enrich Robert's density of reinforcement. Follow-up contacts with this patient, however, revealed a recurrence of violent behavior after he left the CRU and his aftercare program was neglected. He was returned to the CRU, where reinstitution of the previously successful set of interventions again brought his aggression under control. A second effort at designing a maintenance program was carried out with greater attention to staff training at the aftercare site. Subsequent follow-up revealed sustained reduction in Robert's aggression.

TIMEOUT FROM REINFORCEMENT

Timeout, the temporary removal of reinforcement contingent on the performance of an undesired response, is probably the most widely used behavioral procedure for reducing aggression and property destruction. During timeout, all normally accessible social and tangible reinforcers are made unavailable. In some of its better known forms, timeout is accomplished through placement in a barren, locked room (Tyler and Brown 1967), a small booth (Bostow and Bailey 1969; Clark et al. 1973), or an open but restricted area (Porterfield et al. 1976; Wong et al. 1982). Behavioral researchers investigating optimal timeout durations have found that longer intervals are generally more punishing, but that periods as brief as a minute can have decelerative effects on aggression (White et al. 1972).

Contingent timeout is often the preferred procedure for controlling aggression because it is relatively easy to apply and does not require direct administration of aversive stimuli. Because of proven efficacy, practicality, and social acceptability, timeout is also the primary method for treating aggressive behavior on the CRU. Three case studies will describe the standard CRU program for controlling assault and property destruction: a two-stage timeout procedure plus response cost are involved. These decelerative procedures operate concurrently with the unit's positive programming to foster overall adaptive functioning.

Case Studies of Carl, George, and Brian. The following three patients were referred to the CRU during the same 1-year period specifically for problems of assaultive and/or destructive behavior. Carl was a 29-year-old schizophrenic of normal intelligence who frequently displayed bizarre and infantile behavior as well as delusional speech. His violent outbursts, seemingly without provocation, involved punching, kicking, pulling hair, and throwing objects. George was a 24-year-old man with borderline retardation, diagnosed as a chronic undifferentiated schizophrenic. He had problems of noncompliance, inappropriate interpersonal behavior, and severe tantrums. When disturbed or frustrated, George would abuse himself (bite his knuckles), flail his arms wildly, scream insults, strike others, and destroy property. Brian, the highest functioning patient in the trio, was a 31-year-old schizophrenic with an average I.Q. and good verbal and social skills. Brian's major difficulty comprised the destructive behavior of kicking over ashtrays and trash cans. No reliable antecedents preceded this possibly attention-seeking behavior, which led to his current hospital commitment. All three patients had a history of multiple psychiatric admissions.

The CRU token economy (Liberman et al. 1974; Elder et al. 1982) structured environmental contingencies to improve social, self-care, and rehabilitative work performance. Patients earned credits for daily tasks, such as participating in unit activities, grooming, and cleaning their rooms. The credits entitled them to consumable reinforcers and privileges on the ward and hospital grounds. Each week, staff reviewed the ratings given to patients for completing these assignments. Patients who performed satisfactorily would be promoted to a higher level in the economy, where additional reinforcers could be purchased, where they received less supervision, and where they could develop better self-management skills.

Assaultive and destructive behaviors were treated with timeout from reinforcement and response cost procedures. These two classes of behavior were carefully specified so that staff members would be consistent in administering consequences for patient actions. "Assault" was defined as any jab, push, hit, kick, bite, scratch, spit, or public contact with another's genital area. "Property destruction" was defined as striking any furniture, wall, window, etc.; slamming doors; tearing paper or clothes; or throwing objects. When an example of either behavior was observed, staff members directed the patient to one of several quiet areas (QA's) on the unit. Lines painted on the floor in corners of certain rooms served as boundaries for QA's. The program required that the patient go to an assigned QA within 30 seconds after being instructed and remain there for 15 minutes. At the end of 15 minutes, if the patient was still loud or agitated, the time in the QA was extended until the patient had been quiet for at least 2 full minutes. If the patient refused to voluntarily enter the QA or left the QA before the 15 minutes were up, a stronger consequence would be assigned—30 minutes in the quiet room (QR), a lighted, well-ventilated, locked room devoid of any furniture. The patient would be escorted to the QR by staff, and observed through a window in the QR door. Both QA and QR served as a timeout when rewarding activities were inaccessible. In addition to the absence of rewards, time in the QA or QR was associated with fines of one and two credits per minute, respectively.

Results of the timeout program on individual patient behavior are shown in figure 2. The frequency of assaultive and destructive acts during the first week following admission ranged from 10 to 12. These incidents varied in intensity from serious attacks that injured staff members and other patients (Carl) to merely disruptive events (Brian). Both Carl and George showed very gradual declines in aggression over 20 to 30 weeks until aggression was at a low level. In contrast, Brian's destructive pattern was virtually eliminated in 2 weeks. During their last month on the CRU, none of the three patients exhibited more than one occurrence of assault or property destruction per week.

Objective behavioral data demonstrated the efficacy of timeout and response cost for decreasing assaultive and destructive responses in these three patients. Aggressive acts declined during treatment by approximately 90 percent for George and Brian and 80 percent for Carl. All three patients also exhibited concomitant gains in their interpersonal behavior, self-care skills, and work performance while participating in the unit token economy. The ongoing positive programming on the CRU probably contributed to lessened aggression by providing reinforcement for alternative behavior patterns. The presence of a reinforcement system also enabled the use of response cost (credit fines) as a supplementary consequence.

The CRU timeout procedure deserves some elaboration. Punishment for aggression on the CRU is a two-stage operation in which patient cooperation with a timeout assignment results in a less severe penalty (being restricted in the QA rather than being locked in the QR). Although there has been no attempt to compare empirically the effec-

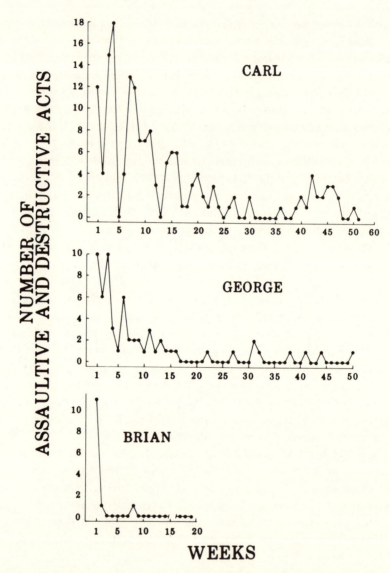

WEEKS

Figure 2. Number of Assaultive and Destructive Acts During Treatment with Timeout From Reinforcement

tiveness of this procedure to that of a simpler, one-stage time-out, the CRU technique appears to offer several practical advantages. First, because the QA consequence is relatively mild, there is greater inclination to use it each time an infraction has occurred. This regularity, in turn, probably enhances the decelerative impact of the contingency (Clark et al. 1973). Second, when needed, additional QA's can readily be made by painting more lines on the floor, which is much less costly than constructing extra QR's. Third, because QA assignments are verbal, physical contests between staff members and patients are avoided. Patients are given an incentive for complying with staff instructions to go to the QA and accepting this negative consequence of their inappropriate behavior.

MILD AVERSIVES

An aversive procedure is the presentation of a noxious stimulus immediately after a maladaptive behavior occurs. For a decade between the mid-1960's and mid-1970's, painful but harmless electric shock applied to the forearm was the most frequently employed aversive stimulus. Behavior therapists utilized it principally for self-injurious behavior, but occasionally for aggressive behavior as well. As problems with generalization and maintenance came to light and as social controversy regarding its use developed, electric shock became less popular (Harris and Ersner-Hershfield 1978). Milder aversives such as bad-tasting or bad-smelling substances (lemon juice, ammonia, Tabasco sauce) were devised in the mid-1970's, but medical and procedural problems associated with these treatments later surfaced.

Another mild aversive, water mist administered to the face, has recently proved to be effective in reducing selfinjurious behavior, especially self-biting (Dorsey et al. 1980), in developmentally disabled patients. Like other aversives, water mist has some risks, but drying of skin appears to be the most serious. Advantages of the water mist lie in its ease of preparation and presentation as well as in its potentially rapid effect. Water mist was employed in the following case as the punishing stimulus to suppress severe aggression in a mentally retarded woman.

Case Study of Juanita. Juanita, a 44-year-old woman with mild to moderate mental retardation and idiopathic epilepsy, was first admitted to a CSH ward for aggressive developmentally disabled women 5 months prior to the present treatment. She had lived most of her life with her parents, who appeared to have taken care of all her needs and made very few demands on her. When her parents died, she lived for a short time with her sister who tried to encourage Juanita to take some responsibility for her own care. This effort precipitated a rash of aggressive acts that the sister could not handle.

During her first week on the CSH ward, Juanita bit staff and other residents 15 times, each time hard enough to require a physician's treatment. She also hit, kicked, and scratched others 16 times. These aggressive incidents generally occurred whenever she was instructed to perform some useful behavior. The frequency did not decrease toward the end of the week, despite close observation, reinforcement of appropriate behaviors, and administration of social disapproval and timeout for aggression.

The interdisciplinary team met at the end of the week when it had become clear that a different treatment was needed to control Juanita's aggression. Although the frequency of aggressive behavior had not lessened with the use of timeout, the team thought that Juanita might respond to the novel consequence of water mist. As prescribed by Dorsey et al. (1980), a hand-pump spray bottle was used to spray a mist of room-temperature water into the patient's face. The nozzle was adjusted to spray the finest mist possible. Staff applied the mist after each observed incidence of aggressive behavior while frowning and firmly shouting "No" or "Stop."

Figure 3 shows the effect of the water mist consequence on Juanita's aggressive behaviors. During her third week on the ward, the frequency of her aggression decreased to approximately 30 percent from her first week. Unfortunately, when Juanita accidentally smashed her thumb between two chairs, her aggressive behavior increased, although not to its previous level. At the end of 2 weeks, when her thumb had healed, Juanita's aggression fell to zero and remained there for 5 weeks.

During the tenth week, Juanita again attempted to bite, but stopped shortly after the water mist was applied. Her other two attempts at aggression occurred the week she was placed in an adult education class and the day of a grand mal seizure. Thereafter, she did not attempt to bite and made only one attempt to hit. The water mist intervention maintained Juanita's aggression at a low level, and staff reported that she was learning more acceptable means of fulfilling her needs. Since the water mist was paired with verbal commands ("No" and "Stop"), the treatment team could fade the mist consequence and control the patient's aggressive behavior with social disapproval alone. Juanita subsequently left the hospital to live in a community group home.

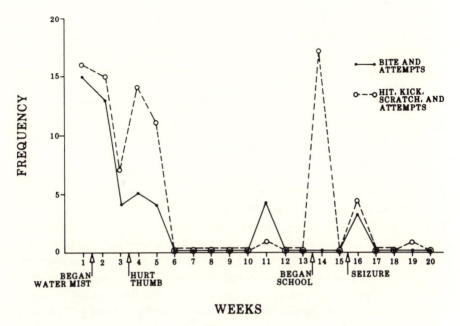

WEEKS

Figure 3. Frequency of Aggressive Behavior During Treatment With Contingent Water Mist.

OVERCORRECTION

Originally proposed as a treatment alternative to punishment, overcorrection has two forms: restitution and positive practice (Foxx and Azrin 1973). Restitutional overcorrection requires patients to restore and improve any aspect of the environment that they disturb. Positive practice overcorrection compels patients to perform acceptable behaviors repeatedly contingent on the occurrence of negative acts. Both forms of overcorrection are theoretically educative and have the following characteristics (Foxx and Azrin 1972): (1) involvement in an activity related to the undesired response (preferable to or remediating effects of that action); (2) initiation of the activity immediately following an inappropriate response (enhancing the potency of the activity as a decelerative consequence and interfering with whatever might ordinarily reinforce the undesired behavior); (3) engagement in the activity for an extended duration (serving as a timeout from reinforcement); and (4) performance of an effortful and continuous activity (making this an annoying task which serves as an inhibitory event). When first applying the procedure, the patient may be instructed and physically guided through the overcorrecting movements. Later, patients undertake the movements themselves to avoid manual guidance.

A relatively small number of specific overcorrection procedures have been applied in the treatment of aggressive and disruptive behavior. Foxx and Azrin (1972) in their research with retarded and brain-damaged patients successfully required household orderliness training (cleaning and rearranging floors and furniture) for disturbing residential furnishings; social reassurance (apologizing verbally or gesturally) for irritating and frightening others; and medical assistance (cleansing and medicating wounds) for assaulting others. Sumner et al. (1974) used a mandatory 30-minute verbal apology to achieve significant reductions in physical assault, verbal abuse, and property destruction in four psychiatric patients. Matson and Stephens (1977) required an apology and 5 minutes of picking up trash to treat potentially injurious object throwing in a chronic schizophrenic patient. More recently, Luce et al. (1980) applied an overcorrection-like procedure to modify verbal and physical aggression in two severely emotionally disturbed boys. Antisocial behaviors were almost completely eliminated by making brief exercise (standing up and sitting down on the floor 10 times) contingent on aggressive acts. It should be noted that this last treatment was effective even though it contained only two of the characteristic elements of overcorrection (items 2 and 4).

Despite the documented efficacy of overcorrection in reducing aggressive and disruptive behaviors, this procedure has not been widely adopted at CSH nor frequently applied within the CRU. The staff required to maintain the procedure makes the technique impractical for many hospital units. A large staff is required to respond to situations in which a patient refuses to engage in the overcorrecting activity and manual guidance is necessary. Under these circumstances, one staff member who is physically stronger than the patient or several staff members are needed to implement the procedure. In addition, to maintain a consistent treatment program, these personnel minimums must be maintained across three nursing shifts on a 24-hour basis. Such demanding prerequisites may explain why the four previously described studies using overcorrection to control aggression were conducted either with females (Foxx and Azrin 1972; Matson and Stephens 1977; Sumner et al. 1974) or with young children (Luce et al. 1980). Furthermore, in contrast to Foxx and Azrin (1972), the authors have found that nursing staff prefer simpler techniques (such as timeout) that do not entail the lengthy and exerting struggles with patients that are associated with overcorrection. This discussion is not meant to be a blanket criticism of overcorrection, but rather is intended to point out practical factors that can limit its utility.

CONTINGENT RESTRAINT

Restricting a patient's movements, first manually and then with devices such as ties and belts, is a traditional reaction to destructive and aggressive behavior in psychiatric institutions. Physical restraint generally has not been considered to be a treatment but rather an emergency action to terminate or prevent injury and property damage. This low status of restraint is probably warranted, given the frequent abuse of this procedure in the past. Recent findings also indicate that being restrained can be positively reinforcing for certain patients (Favell et al. 1978; Favell et al. 1981). When used systematically as the consequence for a class of responses, however, physical restraint can be a punishing stimulus in valid behavioral programs (Hamilton et al. 1967; Reid et al. 1981). The following characteristics distinguish restraint as a behavioral treatment from restraint as an emergency procedure: (1) a treatment plan specifying the behaviors that will result in restraint and consistent application of the procedure according to the plan; (2) a predetermined length of time during which the patient will remain in restraint (usually the shortest period thought to have a suppressive effect); and (3) a data collection system that evaluates the therapeutic value of the procedure.

Contingent restraint was used in the following case to treat destructive and assaultive behavior in a mentally retarded woman. The procedure involved brief manual restraint similar to that employed by Reid et al. (1981) to control stereotypic body rocking in profoundly retarded patients. The restraint consisted of briefly holding the patient's hands in her lap whenever she acted destructively or aggressively.

Case Study of Kate. Kate was a 19-year-old nonverbal, profoundly retarded woman with the diagnosis of cretinism. For several years, she had exhibited destructive and assaultive behavior complicated by episodes of anorexia. In the year preceding this study, Kate had refused food for long periods. When instructed to eat or perform other tasks, she tore up clothing, mattresses, and chairs while screaming loudly. In her worst week, Kate destroyed approximately $2,000 worth of property. She also hit, kicked, and bit people when they attempted to intervene.

The patient received behavioral treatment on a CSH ward for aggressive, developmentally disabled women. In this setting, Kate again screamed and tore her clothes when instructed to initiate a constructive task or to participate in an educational activity. Positive programming, in the form of a DRO schedule, was combined with contingent restraint to reduce destructive and assaultive acts. Within the DRO schedule, if Kate left her clothes intact for at least a half hour she was reinforced with music or walks outside the unit. She was no longer allowed to avoid going to school or other training activities by having a tantrum. When she tried to tear her clothing, a staff member immediately guided her hands to her lap and used the minimal force necessary to keep them there. Unfortunately, when Kate was prevented from being destructive, she hit, bit, kicked, and tore the clothing of the staff member who held her. Two staff members often had to work together to restrain Kate and protect each other. As soon as Kate ceased struggling and trying to tear her clothes, she was released and taken to her regular activity.

Results of the combined behavioral treatments were gratifying. The frequency of clothes tearing decreased from an average of 2.3 times per week during the first month of treatment with contingent restraint to 0.5 times per week in the eleventh month. During the same period, hitting frequency fell from an average of 3.5 to 2.0 times per week. This reduction was obtained despite the somewhat intrusive nature of the intervention, which might have been expected to provoke additional aggression.

As Kate's problem behaviors lessened, her adaptive skills advanced. She learned some sign language and improved her self-care. Kate also became more cooperative and sought affectionate touches and hugs from her group leaders. As her behavior improved she was able to return to a community placement.

TREATMENT EVALUATION

Because of individual differences in learning history, physiological makeup, or situational variables, one or more of the techniques described above may be ineffective with a given patient. The behavioral approach recognizes that idiosyncratic variables can determine the outcome of an intervention, therefore, ongoing evaluation of treatment programs is the sine qua non of behavior therapy.

Treatment evaluation ensures that clinical procedures have their intended impact. One straightforward, clinically relevant, and objective method of evaluation involves taking repeated frequency counts of reliably observed behaviors and graphing the data to produce a visual display. In most of the case studies given in this chapter, one or more treatment procedures were instituted and patients monitored for a specific time period. If a more refined investigation is desired, authors have discussed a variety of intra- or single-subject designs that permit experimentation with strong internal validity and allow definite inferences regarding the causality of obtained behavioral changes (Hersen and Barlow 1976; Wong and Liberman 1981). One of these designs, in which an intervention is sequentially introduced, withdrawn, and reintroduced, is depicted in figure 1. Utilizing either case study formats or single-subject designs, clinicians are provided with an ongoing record of patients' performance that can guide them in making intelligent decisions as to whether to retain or modify interventions.

The characteristic that distinguishes behavior therapy from other therapeutic approaches is its fundamental commitment to measuring and monitoring clinical change. Assessment is a continuing process that begins when the patient is initially evaluated. The behavioral model, depicted in figure 4, highlights the importance of ongoing assessment of progress in the clinical process. With repeated and regular assessments, the behavior therapist can collaborate with the patient and other staff in making decisions about terminating, continuing, or changing the goals and methods of treatment.

A final case study will illustrate the value of treatment evaluation in clinical practice. The patient in this difficult case was an assaultive, brain-damaged man with multiple behavior problems who received a series of treatments over a 32-month period. Staff repeatedly modified procedures in an effort to find a treatment that was effective yet minimally restrictive. In addition, staff attempted to fade special consequences designed for the patient and to control his aggression with the standard programs of his unit.

Case Study of Fred. Fred was a 31-year-old man who had been in an automobile accident in which he received a severe trauma to the left fronto-parietal section of his brain. Before the accident, Fred had led a normal life, working as a bartender for a catering firm while attending college at night. During his postoperative recovery, the patient

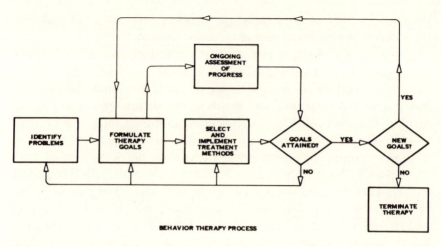

Figure 4. Flowchart of the Behavior Therapy Process

developed a multitude of antisocial and aggressive behaviors that resulted in 6 years of continuous institutionalization in a succession of private and public psychiatric hospitals. He exhibited a range of obnoxious and threatening behaviors at the time of his transfer to the CRU.

Fred's repertoire included lewd and obscene speech, high-frequency spitting (observed at a rate of over 1,000 times per day), physical abusiveness (furtive pinching, pushing, poking, and kicking of fellow patients), lying, stealing, and various destructive behaviors (e.g., setting fires and stuffing toilets). Probably as a result of his brain injury, Fred was also frequently incontinent and somnolent, often falling asleep in the middle of an activity. Despite his bewildering array of antisocial responses, Fred was a gregarious patient who regularly initiated conversations with others and invited them to join him in games of cards, checkers, and chess.

The first treatment used with Fred (Phase A) was a modified version of the standard CRU program for controlling aggression. If Fred spat on or assaulted another person, stole anything, destroyed property, or started a fire, he was placed in locked timeout for 15 minutes. Over 2–1/2 months, this procedure proved ineffective in reducing Fred's aggressive and destructive behavior.

A = Locked timeout for 15 minutes contingent on each aggressive or destructive act

Figure 5. Behavioral Interventions Employed With Fred Over a 32–Month Period

B = Same as A plus 24–hour period of deprivation in which Fred was denied access to all CRU reinforcers and staff totally ignored him. This deprivation period was gradually shortened to 4 hours by the end of the phase

C = Same as B plus the removal of personal clothing for the same 4–hour deprivation period

C^1 = Same as C except that the deprivation period lasted 6 hours

D = Required relaxation for 10 minutes contingent on each aggressive or destructive act.

In the second intervention (Phase B), after being released from the timeout room Fred was prohibited from exchanging his credits for cigarettes, coffee, or other items for 24 hours. He continued to receive his meals and kept his usual sleeping accommodations but lost access to the small luxuries available on the unit. During this period, staff also ignored him except for essential interactions. Since Fred was very sociable and enjoyed talking to staff, the withdrawal of staff attention was considered a potent negative consequence. To reenter the regular CRU program, Fred had to refrain from performing any of the above prohibited acts for 24 hours. As shown in figure 5, the second intervention seems to have had a beneficial effect on his aggressiveness. However, staff sought to refine Fred's program because, even though his behavior was much improved, he was still averaging over one aggressive or destructive incident per day.

In the third intervention (Phase C), the 24-hour period was gradually shortened to 4 hours, and Fred was given State-supplied clothing to wear during the interval. Since Fred preferred wearing his own clothes, staff felt that this additional penalty might further diminish his aggression. Indeed, as seen in figure 5, this new program lasted over a year and resulted in another decrease in the frequency of Fred's problem behaviors. By the end of the third intervention, Fred's aggressive and destructive behaviors occurred approximately once every 2 days.

In the fourth intervention (Phase C^1), lasting a month, the period of deprivation was increased to 6 hours, but no further reduction in problem behaviors was noted. At this point, several staff expressed their frustration at being unable to eliminate Fred's oppressive and destructive behaviors.

In the fifth intervention (Phase D), required relaxation (Webster and Azrin 1973) was employed as a treatment procedure. Any time Fred engaged in spitting, aggression, or property destruction, he had to lie down on the floor motionless without talking for 10 full minutes. If he spoke or moved, his 10-minute relaxation period would start over again. The almost total suppression of aggressive behavior for the 2 weeks following the introduction of the required relaxation, as shown in figure 5, was a result of Fred's spending most of his time lying on the floor. Required relaxation was discontinued when aggressive and destructive behavior began to recur after 2 weeks.

During the sixth intervention (Phase C), the staff members reinstituted the 4-hour deprivation procedure that previously seemed to have been beneficial. Fred spent 15 minutes in locked timeout for each aggressive incident and lost access to all CRU reinforcers and his clothes for 4 hours. The frequency of aggressive behavior fell to an acceptably low level during the 4 months of this program.

In the seventh and final phase (Phase A), Fred was placed back on the standard CRU program for aggression, which enabled him to live on the unit as any other patient. Engaging in an assaultive or destructive act merely led to 15 minutes of locked timeout. The standard CRU program maintained a low frequency of aggression in Fred for over 6 months.

In addition to the timeout, positive programs were devised to strengthen Fred's adaptive behavioral repertoire. Focusing on his lewd speech, staff provided differential attention: they responded with avid interest when Fred spoke politely and respectfully, but totally ignored him and walked away when he cursed or spoke lasciviously. Natural reinforcers, such as spontaneous conversation or playing cards or chess, were programmed as consequences for his appropriate speech content. Staff also taught Fred to speak more slowly, since his speech was so rapid that it was often unintelligible. He received training sessions in which he learned to pace his speech by using his fingers and talking in cadence.

The improvements in Fred's behavior over the past 3 years led to important changes in the quality of his life. He no longer needs psychotropic medication—having been taken off all drugs shortly after his arrival on the CRU—and he is free from the annoying and debilitating side effects that accompany these drugs. He is able to leave the hospital for brief trips to a local town and for extended visits and holidays with his parents, sometimes for as long as 2 weeks. He has even gone to Las Vegas with his parents for a vacation, a real treat for him as his favorite pastime is playing cards.

Fred's daily life on the CRU and in the hospital has also improved. Staff and other patients no longer avoid him but rather engage him in a high rate of social interaction. He has a job assisting the custodian and takes pride in his work and in the credits he earns. He has also been promoted to advanced standing in the token economy. Overall, Fred is considered one of the more successful patients treated on the CRU.

ETHICAL CONSIDERATIONS

Ethical problems and issues that confront behavior therapists are identical to those faced by other mental health and human service professionals. These issues center on selection of appropriate treatment objectives and intervention strategies, respect for the well-being and rights of patients, and sensitivity to the sometimes conflicting interests of individual patients, their families and close associates, and society and society's agents. Behavioral clinicians have been sensitized to ethical issues by abusive practices in the name of behavior therapy, misinterpretation of behavioral treatment in the popular literature, and the potential for misuse inherent in an effective technology for behavior change.

Behavior therapists practice in a wide range of settings with diverse patient groups. In providing services to involuntary and severely disabled people, ethical dilemmas are significant. Therapists working in institutions can resolve some of these dilemmas in several ways:

1. Maximizing patient involvement in goal setting and treatment planning to the extent possible, given the patient's disability and legal status.

2. Enriching institutional environments and using positive pro-

gramming whenever possible, while avoiding procedures that rely on deprivation and aversive control.

3. Using the least intrusive methods available to promote the patient's optimal level of interpersonal and independent functioning.

4. Extending patients' "freedom" by employing the natural contingencies of reinforcement in the patients' home and community environments (i.e., teaching behaviors that are valued and will be encouraged by parents, family members and group home staff).

5. Promoting practices in the hospital or care facility that will shape adaptive rather than institutionally convenient but nonadaptive behavior.

6. Arranging for reinforcement contingencies in patients' natural environments that will maintain patients' behavior when they leave the hospital or institution.

7. Having the courage to pursue controversial treatments when they are in the patients' interests and balancing the right to effective treatment with the patients' rights to liberty and personal integrity.

8. Resisting use of "behavior therapy" to legitimate retributive punishment, inhumane treatment, and sham token economies that reinforce behaviors beneficial only to institutions and caregivers.

9. Submitting proposed restrictive or aversive procedures to the institution's Human Rights Review Committee to ensure that patients' rights to treatment are impartially weighed against their other individual rights and freedoms.

10. Obtaining consent for treatment from the patient or the patient's legal representatives. Many institutionalized patients, even after being involved in the treatment decision, are unable to give valid informed consent because of underdeveloped or deteriorated mental capabilities. In such cases, guardians or court-appointed conservators should be involved in treatment selection and give written informed consent before treatment begins.

11. Continually assessing the effects of treatment, not only on a patient's aggressive behavior but also on other important areas of functioning that might be affected. Through this procedure, staff can determine whether the use of a controversial plan is justified by overall patient gains.

Ethical guidelines and review procedures for mental health services should not convey the impression that only behavioral interventions need scrutiny. No matter what the therapeutic modality, sensible guidelines will balance risks with benefits, avoid restricting innovation, and require evaluation of the treatment's worth. Guidelines are particularly needed to monitor clinical services to involuntary and severely disabled clients, especially when aversive or restrictive interventions are used. Behavior therapists participating in the development of guidelines can work toward developing standards that are technically accurate, flexible, easy to administer, and subject to revision in the light of new developments in the field.

SUMMARY

Behavior analysis leads to an understanding of how violent behavior in patients is influenced by the behavior's environmental antecedents and consequences. Behavior therapy provides intervention strategies for modifying those environmental influences that have been identified as promoting aggression.

Antecedents of aggressive behavior include physical pain, crowding, noise, boredom, teasing, insults, roughhousing, and poorly supervised ward settings. Through the process of modeling, the mere viewing of aggressive behavior can promote aggression in other patients.

The environmental consequences of violent behavior are the strongest determinants of future aggression. Abundant, albeit inadvertent, reinforcement for aggressive behavior may be furnished by the psychiatric staff and by other patients. In a setting where patients receive little attention from staff, violent acts can derive powerful reinforcement from the attention they attract. Even ministrations that accompany a PRN (parenteral medication) can provide reinforcement for aggressive behavior through the tactile, neuromuscular, and social contact involved. Aggression can also produce tangible reinforcers such as cigarettes and favors from intimidated patients and staff. Negative reinforcement can also promote violence, as when a patient gets "grounded" and thereby escapes a boring therapy session or a fatiguing workshop assignment. Reinforcers are idiosyncratic; for example, spending time in a quiet or secluded room may actually strengthen some patients' aggressive behavior.

Specifically pinpointing and operationally describing aggressive acts is a necessary first step in behavioral assessment, which helps to determine both the nature of the treatment procedure and the aspect of the behavior that is in need of change. For example, minor and relatively infrequent acts of aggression might be best managed by systematically ignoring them. The individual's strengths, deficits, and responsiveness to reinforcers are also important parts of the initial assessment prior to determining a treatment intervention. Treatments vary according to level of effort, complexity, cost, time, and intrusiveness. A risk-benefit analysis enables clinicians to weigh the potential advantages and disadvantages of treatment options.

A number of behavioral methods have been documented as effective in preventing, displacing, or suppressing aggressive behavior in psychiatric and retarded patients. These include, from least intrusive to most intrusive, activity programming, social skills training, differential reinforcement of other behavior, timeout from reinforcement, mild aversive stimuli (e.g., water mist), overcorrection, and contingent restraint. An adequate behavioral program frequently requires combining several of these interventions. An important rule of thumb in designing a treatment program, which also guards against abusive treatment, is to set goals of strengthening and increasing some desirable, prosocial behavior of the patient as well as reducing the unwanted aggressive behavior.

Behavior therapy is distinguished from other therapeutic approaches by its fundamental commitment to measuring behavioral change. Measurement requires a continuous system of monitoring changes in the frequency or quality of both desirable and aggressive behavior as a treatment program unfolds. The information obtained from ongoing assessment of the clinical process provides an empirical basis for deciding on timely and necessary alterations in goals and intervention methods. Ethical and effective use of behavior therapy in managing aggressive behavior can be enhanced by maximizing patient involvement in goal setting and treatment planning, enriching and humanizing institutions and their rules, using the least intrusive treatment consistent with enhanced functioning, and involving patient advocates and human rights committees.

REFERENCES

Azrin, N.H.; Hake, D.F.; and Hutchinson, R.R. Elicitation of aggression by a physical blow. Journal of Experimental Analysis of Behavior 8(1):55–57, 1965.

Azrin, N.H.; Hutchinson, R.R.; and Hake, D.F. Extinction induced aggression. Journal of the Experimental Analysis of Behavior 9(3):191–204, 1966.

Bandura, A. Aggression: A Social Learning Analysis. Englewood Cliffs, N.J.: Prentice-Hall, 1973.

Boe, R.B. Economical procedures for the reduction of aggression in a residential setting. Mental Retardation 15(5):25–28, 1977.

Bornstein, M.; Bellack, A.S.; and Hersen, M. Social skills training for highly aggressive children. Behavior Modification 4(2):173–186, 1980.

Bostow, D.E., and Bailey, J. Modification of severe disruptive and aggressive behavior using brief timeout and reinforcement procedures. Journal of Applied Behavior Analysis 2(1):31–37, 1969.

Cataldo, M.F., and Risley, T.R. Evaluation of living environments: The MANIFEST description of ward activities. In: Davison, P.O.; Clark, F.W.; and Hamerlynck, L.A., eds. Evaluation of Behavioral Programs in Community, Residential and School Settings. Champaign, Ill.: Research Press, 1974.

Center for Studies of Schizophrenia, National Institute of Mental Health, Alcohol, Drug Abuse, and Mental Health Administration. A review and critique of social skills training with schizophrenic patients, by Wallace, C.J.; Nelson, C.J.; Liberman, R.P.; Aitchison, R.A.; Lukoff, D.; Elder, J.P.; and Ferris, C. In: Schizophrenia Bulletin 6(1):42–54. Washington, D.C.: U.S. Government Printing Office, 1980.

Clark, H.B.; Rowbury, T.; Baer, A.M.; and Baer, D.M. Timeout as a punishing stimulus in continuous and intermittent schedules. Journal of Applied Behavior Analysis 6(3):443–455, 1973.

Dorsey, M.F.; Iwata, B.A.; Ong, P.; and McSween, T.E. Treatment of self-injurious behavior using a water mist: Initial response suppression and generalization. Journal of Applied Behavior Analysis 13(2):343–353, 1980.

Elder, J.P.; Edelstein, B.A.; and Narick, M.M. Adolescent psychiatric patients: Modifying aggressive behavior with social skills training. Behavior Modification 3(2):161–178, 1979.

Elder, J.P.; Liberman, R.P.; Rapport, S.; and Rust, C. Staff and patient reaction to the modernization of a token economy. The Behavior Therapist 5(1):19–20, 1982.

Favell, J.E.; McGimsey, J.F.; and Jones, M.L. The use of physical restraint in the treatment of self-injury and as positive reinforcement. Journal of Applied Behavior Analysis 11(2):225–241, 1978.

Favell, J.E.; McGimsey, J.F.; Jones, M.L.; and Cannon, P.R. Physical restraint as positive reinforcement. American Journal of Mental Deficiency 85(4):425–432, 1981.

Foxx, R.M., and Azrin, N.H. Restitution: A method of eliminating aggressive-disruptive behavior of retarded and brain damaged patients. Behavior Research and Therapy 10(1):15–27, 1972.

Foxx, R.M., and Azrin, N.H. The elimination of autistic self-stimulatory behavior by overcorrection. Journal of Applied Behavior Analysis 6(1):1–14, 1973.

Frederiksen, L.W.; Jenkins, J.O.; Foy, D.W.; and Eisler, R.M. Social-skills training to modify abusive verbal outbursts in adults. Journal of Applied Behavior Analysis 9(2):117–125, 1976.

Hamilton, J.; Stephens, L.; and Allen, P. Controlling aggressive and destructive behavior in severely retarded institutionalized residents. American Journal of Mental Deficiency 71:852–856, 1967.

Harris, S.L., and Ersner-Hershfield, R. Behavioral suppression of seriously disruptive behavior in psychotic and retarded patients: A review of punishment and its alternatives. Psychological Bulletin 85(6):1352–1375, 1978.

Hersen, M., and Barlow, D.H. Single Case Experimental Designs: Strategies for Studying Behavior Change. New York: Pergamon Press, 1976.

Hobbs, S.A., and Forehand, R. Important parameters in the use of timeout with children: A re-examination. Journal of Behavior Therapy and Experimental Psychiatry 8(14):365–370, 1977.

Liberman, R.P.; Wallace, C.; Teigen, J.; and Davis, J. Interventions with psychotic behaviors. In: Calhoun, K.S.; Adams, H.E.; and Mitchell, K.M., eds. Innovative Treatment Methods in Psychopathology. New York: John Wiley & Sons, 1974.

Lion, J.R.; Snyder, W.; and Merrill, G.L. Under-reporting of assaults on staff in a hospital. Hospital & Community Psychiatry 32(7):497–498, 1981.

Luce, S.C.; Delquadri, J.; and Hall, R.V. Contingent exercise: A mild but powerful procedure for suppressing inappropriate verbal and aggressive behaviors. Journal of Applied Behavior Analysis 13(4):583–594, 1980.

Matson, J.L., and Stephens, R.M. Overcorrection of aggressive behavior in a chronic psychiatric patient. Behavior Modification 1(4):559–564, 1977.

Matson, J.L., and Stephens, R.M. Increasing appropriate behavior of explosive chronic psychiatric patients with a social-skills training package. Behavior Modification 2(1):61–76, 1978.

Paul, G.L., and Lentz, R.J. Psychosocial Treatment for Chronic Mental Patients: Milieu versus Social-learning Programs. Cambridge: Harvard University Press, 1977.

Porterfield, J.K.; Herbert-Jackson, E.; and Risley, T.R. Contingent observation: An effective and acceptable procedure for reducing disruptive behavior of young children in a group setting. Journal of Applied Behavior Analysis 9(1):55–64, 1976.

Rago, W.V.; Parker, R.M.; and Cleland, C.C. Effect of increased space on the social behavior of institutionalized profoundly retarded male adults. American Journal of Mental Deficiency 82(6):554–558, 1978.

Reid, J.G.; Tombaugh, T.N.; and Heuvel, K.V. Application of contingent physical restraint to suppress stereotypic body rocking of profoundly mentally retarded persons. American Journal of Mental Deficiency 86(1):78–85, 1981.

Repp, A.C., and Deitz, S.M. Reducing aggressive and selfinjurious behavior of institutionalized retarded children through reinforcement of other behaviors. Journal of Applied Behavior Analysis 7(2):313–325, 1974.

Slama, K.M.; Bannerman, D.J.; Lapointe, J.; and Johnson, M.E. Reducing problem behaviors in developmentally disabled adults by activity programming. Unpublished manuscript, Camarillo State Hospital, 1981.

Solnick, J.V.; Rincover, A.; and Peterson, C.R. Some determinants of the reinforcing and punishing effects of timeout. Journal of Applied Behavior Analysis 10(3):415–424, 1977.

Sumner, J.H.; Mueser, S.T.; Hsu, L.; and Morales, R.G. Overcorrection treatment for radical reduction of aggressive-disruptive behavior in institutionalized mental patients. Psychological Reports 35:655–662, 1974.

Tyler, V.O., and Brown, G.D. The use of swift, brief isolation as a group control device for institutionalized delinquents. Behavior Research and Therapy 5(1):1–9, 1967.

Vukelich, R., and Hake, D.F. Reduction of dangerously aggressive behavior in a severely retarded resident through a combination of positive reinforcement procedures. Journal of Applied Behavior Analysis 4(3):215–225, 1971.

Wallace, C.J.; Teigen, J.R.; Liberman, R.P.; and Baker, V. Destructive behavior treated by contingency contracts and assertive training: A case study. Journal of Behavior Therapy and Experimental Psychiatry 4(3):273–274, 1973.

Webster, D.R., and Azrin, N.H. Required relaxation: A method of inhibiting agitative-disruptive behavior of retardates. Behavior Research and Therapy 11(1):67–78, 1973.

White, G.D.; Nielsen, G.; and Johnson, S.M. Timeout duration and the suppression of deviant behavior in children. Journal of Applied Behavior Analysis 5(2):111–120, 1972.

Wong, S.E.; Gaydos, G.R.; and Fuqua, R.W. Operant control of pedophilia: Reducing approaches to children. Behavior Modification 6(1):73–84, 1982.

Wong, S.E., and Liberman, R.P. Mixed single-subject designs in clinical research: Variations of the multiplebaseline. Behavioral Assessment 3(3–4):297–306, 1981.

3

Psychotherapeutic Approaches in the Treatment of Violent Persons

Denis J. Madden, Ph.D.

The treatment of the violent person is one of the most challenging of therapeutic endeavors because of incomplete understanding of the reasons violent persons act as they do. Violent persons are not always motivated to accept treatment, and clinicians feel at a disadvantage when attempting to treat them. Nevertheless, clinicians are called on to offer guidance and to help address the phenomena of violence and aggression (Shah 1977). Despite their inability to offer final solutions, clinicians can help address these problems.

The author's experience in this area stems from his work in a specialized clinic that treats violent persons, primarily through group psychotherapy in an outpatient setting. The work of this clinic is described elsewhere in the literature (Lion et al. 1974; Lion 1975; Lion et al. 1976; Madden 1977). While the clinic treats patients who manifest a range of psychopathology (including severe characterological disturbances, adjustment reactions, toxic and functional psychoses, and organic brain syndromes), in all instances the patient's past violent behavior or present impulses toward violence are a major focus of patient management and treatment.

A wide spectrum of persons may manifest violent behavior and request treatment. Persons who manifest violence or who complain of related symptomatology vary with regard to age, physical stature, socioeconomic background, ability to maintain relationships and jobs, and even degree of actual violence that they exhibit (Madden and Lion 1981). The youngest person seen in the clinic mentioned above was a

4-year-old child who poured glue into the eyes of his infant brother. The oldest was an elderly man in his 80's who had only one leg and was at the final stage of a terminal illness. Many clinic patients have committed seriously violent acts, including murder. Still others, although never having actually assaulted anyone, are tormented with the fear that they might someday commit such an act. Most clinic patients have been coerced into therapy; a small number enter willingly. Violent patients are not homogeneous with respect to the acts they commit or their motivation for treatment.

As defined by the <u>American Psychiatric Association Task Force Report on Clinical Aspects of the Violent Individual</u>, the violent person is "one who acts or has acted in such a way as to produce physical harm or destruction" (American Psychiatric Association 1974). Of course, not all criminals who commit violent acts should be deemed patients. Neither should all psychiatric patients necessarily be viewed as being at great risk for future violence or dangerousness (Rappeport 1974; National Institute of Mental Health 1981). However, the persons whose treatment is discussed in this chapter have either acted in accord with the above definition or have voiced a fear that they might (Lion et al. 1969).

WHY VIOLENT PATIENTS COME OR ARE REFERRED FOR HELP

The Patient's Complaint

Persons who come to clinicians with concerns about impending loss of control over violent urges, i.e., those who fear running amok or doing harm to others, are the most easily identifiable as potentially violent patients. Other persons have experienced spontaneously outbursts of rage or temper tantrums associated with the use of alcohol. Still others relate histories of labile moods associated with past assaultive or destructive acts. Some violent persons are sent to clinicians because they are perceived by others in their environment as dangerous or violent (Lion et al. 1969). Murderers, rapists, and perpetrators of other violent crimes may be sent for psychiatric evaluation to determine the existence of treatable psychopathology.

Some patients, while generally acknowledging a problem with violence, cannot give specific information about it. They may see themselves as "being mad" much of the time; they may feel like a "powder keg that is ready to go off." They do not appreciate the true precipitants of their behavior. When asked what is troubling them, these individuals respond that everything is wrong. When asked with whom they are angry, they include everyone.

Other persons target a specific victim for future violent behavior, yet this person may not appear to the clinician to be the true source of the patient's conflict or pain. Thus, the patient may speak about an employer rather than a spouse who may soon leave, or about a parent rather than a spouse. This denial is understandable. The loss of a relationship with a spouse or lover may be more threatening for the patient than the loss of a job (as threatening as that might be). The clinician should, therefore, make efforts to identify the true objects of the patient's concern or resentment and try to identify and understand the patient's feelings about other named or potential victims. Finding out about potential victims provides important information. Potential victims, as well as others in the patient's environment, may be acting in a provocative manner. These people may eventually need to be brought into therapy either alone or with the patient (Roth and Meisel 1977).

Referral Issues

Generally, neither violence nor its treatment takes place in a vacuum. While some patients may seek treatment themselves, violent persons come for help more commonly after they have been caught or threatened in some way. Thus, a man may finally seek help for his problem only after his wife has threatened to leave him. Other persons are told by the police, courts, probation officers, or other authorities to get help with their problem or to face an unpleasant alternative such as going to jail. While these incentives are less than optimal, they do get the patients into treatment, thereby affording them a period of time during which a clinician can determine whether help is indeed possible. A specific time period for treatment may have to be mandated.

The referral source can aid or hinder the process of treatment. Some spouses, for example, threaten to leave the patient if treatment is not sought. This can contribute to therapy if the spouse is making a good-faith request. It is not helpful, however, when the spouse has already decided to leave the patient regardless of how therapy progresses or if the spouse is already engaged in a more satisfying personal relationship with someone else.

Some probation officers or other referral sources may sabotage therapy, as shown in the following case example.

Case example. A young man with a history of many convictions for assaultive behavior was referred by a court for treatment following another conviction for assault with a deadly weapon. As was customary, the patient's probation officer was requested to provide the clinic with background information. Because many violent persons do not voluntarily provide accurate histories about their past violent behavior, obtaining such background information is critical to the treatment process. However, the requested information was not received from the probation officer until more than a year later, despite the clinic's repeated efforts to obtain it. By this time, the patient had once again been arrested and convicted for another violent act.

Attempts thus were made to involve the patient's probation officer in treatment. The probation officer, however, communicated the impression that he and his agency had no interest in assisting in the patient's treatment. To the contrary, the probation officer seemed to be waiting for the patient to fail or not comply with treatment so that punitive action might be taken against him.

It is unusual to encounter a violent individual who manifests an inner willingness to enter the therapeutic process. Some clinicians believe that without coercion, treatment of these individuals often is not possible (Rappeport 1974).

Assessing Motivation

As in all forms of therapy, the patient's motivation plays a crucial role in treatment (Schmideberg 1968; Madden 1977). Clinicians should remember, however, that violent patients may seek treatment impulsively, demanding that the therapist see them immediately. Clinicians may thus find themselves changing schedules to fit the patient in, only to have the patient not come or arrive a half-hour late for the first session. While such behavior can be viewed as showing a lack of motivation, it may also demonstrate a characteristic behavior of the patient that requires attention in subsequent therapy. Even after beginning therapy, the patient's attendance may be erratic. While voicing a keen desire to obtain some control over behavior, the patient may nevertheless frequently miss appointments or group therapy sessions. Just as violent patients are impulsive in their violent acts, many are impulsive in their work settings, living situations, personal relationships, and therapy.

Working with violent patients is a long process of unraveling in which understanding of the patient often is gained only after prolonged contact with the person. This characteristic is directly related to the issue of trust, an issue to be discussed later in this chapter.

CHOOSING THE MODALITY OF TREATMENT

Even in a teaching setting, in which psychiatric residents are usually willing to work with difficult patients, it has been the author's experience that many therapists are reluctant to undertake individual treatment with patients identified as violent (Madden et al. 1976). The group modality for treatment tends to be more practicable and offers a more efficient way to place these persons into treatment. More important, what little experience exists to date suggests that the group modality may provide the most efficacious treatment for these individuals (Carney 1976).

Group Treatment

Group therapy allows distance for the violent individual, which may be especially necessary at the beginning stages of treatment. Involvement with the group is less threatening for violent persons than involvement with an individual, even if that individual is a therapist. Group treatment allows the patient to come into contact with other persons who manifest the same kinds of difficulties as the patient, and has a socializing impact on the patient. The patient is able to identify with others and to recognize that they have similar problems. The group provides the patient with a forum and with a place to return when under stress. Many violent patients come to use the group on an "as needed" basis (in medical terms, a PRN). While the violent patient's irregular attendance at the group session should be of concern to the therapist, even intermittent attendance is often helpful for the patient and for others. Violent patients need to be encouraged to seek therapy when they are under stress, rather than to act on their impulses.

Family and Couples Treatment

Sometimes, providing family or couples therapy for violent patients is a worthwhile approach (Harbin 1977). Of course, not all violent patients have a spouse or family willing to enter therapy. Therapists should be wary of family or couples therapy when it only seems to provide a forum for a spouse or other family members to retaliate against the violent patient who has injured them. Importantly, however, family and couples therapy provides the therapist with an opportunity to observe family interactions that might not otherwise be apparent. These family interactions may help to explain the patient's pathology and concern.

Case example. A 17-year-old young man had a history of substance abuse and violent behavior toward others. The patient's family wished to enter therapy with him, even though their motivation for doing so was difficult to clarify. The family verbally abused this adolescent during much of the time in the family sessions.

After about 6 months of therapy, the adolescent verbally exploded during a family sesson. Screaming and crying, he revealed in the presence of all the other family members that he was privy to his family's secret, namely, that his mother was suffering from a life-threatening disease. Like his mother and father, he had kept this secret from the other members of the family.

In retrospect, the family's attack on the patient and his retaliatory and acting-out behavior seemed to relate to the hidden pressures that the family had not realized or acknowledged they were placing on this youth. The family therapy approach helped to identify the family's secret and clarify family dynamics that were contributing to the youth's behavior.

Clinical judgments must, of course, be made to determine the best treatment modality for a particular patient, including whether it is best to include others in the patient's treatment. Regardless of whether the patient is seen primarily as an individual or is treated through the group modality, it is still helpful for the therapist to have contact with the patient's spouse and/or other family members, on at least an intermittent basis. Such family consultation can and should take place early in the therapy, especially when the patient's violent behavior takes place in the home. Even when the patient's violent behavior is expressed outside the home, such behavior often brings added pressure to the home situation and the therapist should be knowledgeable about this pressure.

Role of Victims

The determination of the appropriate treatment modality may also depend on the therapist's assessment of the role of a victim or victims (Symonds 1975). While it has been argued that consideration of the possible provocative role of victims (especially when dealing with spouse abuse) is tantamount to "victim blame," the therapist must consider interactions between assailants and victims. Most violent crimes are committed against a person with whom the assailant has had some kind of personal relationship or acquaintance (Wolfgang 1978).

Even when the patient's victim is not a spouse or other family member, it is useful to understand the psychological role played by victims. Toch's work concerning the interactional quality of much angry and violent behavior is important here. As Toch notes:

> Violence is at least a two-man game. Even where the victim does no more than appear at the wrong time and place, his contribution is essential for the consummation of his destruction . . . . To understand violence, it is necessary to focus on the chain of interactions between aggressor and victims, on the sequence that begins when two people encounter each other—and which ends when one harms, or even destroys, the other (Toch 1969, pp. 5–6).

At times, violent behavior enacted against strangers may even be precipitated by the actions of a family member.

Case example. A young man viciously assaulted a young woman he did not know. In therapy, it was learned that the patient's spouse had repeatedly been sexually unfaithful to him and had also cheated him financially. The patient's wife had exhibited similar behavior in her previous marriage. The therapist initially believed that the patient's violent attack on the stranger might have been precipitated or encouraged by his troubled relationship with his wife. It later became apparent in therapy that immediately prior to the violent assault, the patient's mother had verbally attacked him. She had denigrated him for marrying his wife, but also, and more important, upbraided him for his lack of concern about his own mother. Prior to recounting in therapy his interactions with his mother, the patient did not recognize the importance of this interaction as prelude and stimulus to his violent behavior. Nor had he been able to acknowledge his complicated feelings and resentment about his mother's attack on him. This was a turning point in the therapy. Until the therapist learned about the events that had taken place between mother and son, the therapy had been going in the wrong direction.

This example indicates the need for the therapist treating violent persons to be aware of the patient's psychological relationships with others, including family, friends, and potential victims.

THE THERAPEUTIC PROCESS

Teaching the Patient

In many ways, treating violent patients takes on the guise of teaching. Such patients are often surprised to learn that they frighten those around them. Therapists may also inform patients of their alarm over patients' behavior. Telling patients that they are frightening alerts them to their behavior and how it affects others. Patients are thereby given the opportunity to learn why others reject them and do not want to be associated with them.

Violent patients must also learn to identify specific physiologic and psychological warning signs of loss of control, such as sweating, rapid heart beat, flushing, fear, or a rising tide of anger (Frederiksen and Rainwater 1981). They must learn to respond to these signs appropriately, not by losing control; for example, they might leave an explosive situation, take time to reflect on their thinking or mood, talk it out, or seek counsel with others such as a therapist with whom they can share their feelings.

Contact with a therapist who cares and is truly interested can also be a gratifying and worthwhile learning experience for patients. In individual and group therapy, patients have the opportunity to meet with and learn from other persons who are subject to pressures and to the hurt of insult and rejection, but who have learned to modulate their behavior and feelings effectively. The therapist's behavior can give patients a sense of hope that they also can learn to manage their behavior and feelings. Patients can learn that acting out impulsively is not the only way to respond.

When working with violent patients, it also becomes apparent that violent behavior is a screen that often serves to protect a fragile individual who is very afraid. Fear can lead anyone to perform at a lower level than usual. Thus, while the patient's violent behavior needs attention, the patient will not obtain a sense of "wellness" when the therapist attends only to the violent aspect of the patient's personality. The therapist must appeal to the healthier, more caring part of the patient. That appeal must, of course, also come from the healthier part of the therapist, that is, the part that does not reject or wish to punish the patient, but rather wants to assist and encourage constructive change.

Establishing Trust

Therapy with violent patients begins with establishing trust (Lion 1978; Carney 1978), a process that involves both patient and therapist.

Therapists must expect and trust that the patient will come to therapy sessions and will try to talk about problems rather than behave violently. Patients must expect and trust that the therapist will be available to them and will try to understand and help. This kind of rapport requires that the therapist consider and attend to the "whole person" while not being negatively influenced by patients' past deeds. Such attitudes and behavior on the part of the therapist signal to the patients that they need not be hypervigilant (suspicious and mistrustful) with the therapist.

The need for hypervigilance is a defense that protects violent patients from possible danger. Patients do not trust themselves or their own resources, so they cannot trust others. As Carney (1976) notes, violent patients accept nothing at face value. Meetings with them can become confrontations. Their "game" is to ferret out the therapist's "con" while at the same time "conning" the therapist. This interpersonal dynamic must be interrupted. Furthermore, the therapist should recognize that this type of behavior is, at least in part, a defense that can be addressed through the therapeutic process.

How do violent persons come to such a state? The author believes that violent patients have been taught what to expect. At crucial points in their lives, violent patients have learned, or have been taught, that it is inadvisable to trust. More basically, they have also been taught that they themselves are not trustworthy. Their self-image and self-esteem are damaged. Violent patients see themselves as needing to play roles: at one time to be tough, at another time dependent, at another overly trusting and caring, and at another cold and indifferent. Violent patients do not act in a consistent manner because they have not learned what it means to be responsible, to have internal and external controls, and to modulate life experiences (Quen 1978). Violent patients nevertheless complain repeatedly that "their trust" has been betrayed by spouses, lovers, or friends.

Limit Setting

In addition to the therapist's availability to patients and attempts to understand their behavior and feelings, setting limits helps the therapist establish trust and is crucial to good therapy (Chawst 1965). Once behavioral limits for the patient have been set and agreed upon by patient and therapist, they must be followed. Therapists can expect that patients will test the limits. While violent patients, especially at the initial stages of therapy, do not possess inner controls (and appear to reject imposed control), it is important for the therapist to remember that the search for control is what brought the patient to treatment. Furthermore, it is the patient's experience and reinforcement of control that holds the person in treatment.

To aid in the process of setting limits, the therapist should not make demands or set up situations that are conducive to patient failure. Thus, it is clinical good sense not to extend trust to patients beyond their demonstrated capacity to utilize such trust. Many violent patients, knowing that they are untrustworthy in some respects, will perceive that a therapist who is not aware of this does not really understand them.

The therapist's communications to the violent patient should always be straightforward. Certain kinds of patient behavior are unacceptable and must be dealt with honestly and consistently. Many violent patients have had "second chances" given to them by spouses, friends, and the courts. Conflict can arise in therapy between giving the patient "another chance" versus the necessity to deal straightforwardly with an unacceptable behavior. It is important for the therapist to respond to the patient's present conduct in a manner that is consistent with the behavioral limits that have been established. At the psychological level, the patient will perceive inconsistent behavior or lack of appropriate response by the therapist as equivalent to rejection.

Some patients test limits by missing sessions. In an inpatient setting or in a correctional institution, this may mean that the patient has violated the contract; the same is true in certain outpatient settings (Carney 1978). Patients may miss therapy or attempt to miss it when they feel anxious or when they have not yet begun to experience a sense of release or help through treatment. Flexibility can be beneficial in such cases, especially early in the therapeutic process when even intermittent participation by a patient may be helpful (Lion et al. 1977). On the other hand, repeated unexcused absences may mean that, at least at this time and in this particular setting, the patient may not be suitable for treatment.

Threats to report absentee patients to authorities who expect them to attend therapy can make patients angry. Such anger should not be viewed simply as another display of inappropriate behavior; it should also be seen as the patient's effort to cope with the honest response of another. Learning to live with and cope with anger is part of the patients' therapy.

The Patient's Experience of Therapy

Therapists treating violent patients have difficulty viewing them as experiencing either helplessness or hopelessness (Halleck 1967) because violent patients often act as if they were not afraid of anything, even of losing their lives. It is an error, however, to view all such outward patient behavior as being comfortable (syntonic) for the patient and none of it as uncomfortable (dystonic). Many violent patients act super-tough in order to maintain a sense of equilibrium. It is not that these individuals do not feel; instead, they feel so intensely that they seek relief by acting violently, for example, so that they can let others know that they are "somebody." The patients' quick acting out prevents them from having to experience something that is disturbing to them.

Violent patients must learn that "just talking" helps. For this reason, setting limits is critical to the therapeutic process. Patients must not be allowed to strike out but should understand that they may talk about anything and even shout. In treating violent patients, therapists must therefore be able to tolerate discussions that they may find personally upsetting. Having two therapists rather than one participate in therapy with patients assists in proper limit setting and helps the therapists tolerate uncomfortable discussions. Therapists must be able to tolerate not only the patients' verbal expressions but also uncomfortable feelings and affects that emerge when limits are placed upon behavior.

Sometimes patients do not express anger in therapy sessions because they sense that the therapist will not tolerate it. The patients instead express angry affects in other settings where such behavior cannot be addressed or evaluated therapeutically. Display of anger by violent patients should be viewed as a positive factor in patient therapy (Rothenburg 1975). The therapist should be suspicious when, in dealing over time with a violent patient, anger is not forthcoming, for it is a warning that not much is going on in therapy.

Lack of expression of anger by a violent patient can also be understood as the patient's attempt "to give the therapists what they are looking for"—i.e., to present a picture of a calm person who is in the process of developing insight. This picture can be highly deceptive. The author's experience is that patients who indicate how angry they are, even when they do so in a bellicose manner, are actually safer to be with than are patients who continue to experience anger but tell the therapist that nothing is bothering them.

Use of Fantasy

A helpful way to teach patients to deal with difficult emotions is through the use of fantasy. It is often asserted or believed that violent patients cannot fantasize. In the author's opinion, a more correct view is that violent patients have not learned what to do with their fantasies or how to express them in words rather than in actions. In the therapy of violent patients, it is thus useful to help them "push" the fantasy to the final point.

Patients may state initially that they don't care what happens to them. For example, they may allude to gun battles with police and indicate to the therapist they will "never be taken alive." Rather than accept this scenario, the therapist can help the patients by having them relate in a step-by-step manner all the actions that will take place in this particular drama. For example, patients can be asked to describe the setting, who is present, what actions the patients will take, what will happen to the patients in the end, and how others will feel. This approach (encouraging verbalization of fantasies) gives patients the opportunity to experience fantasies more fully, including potentially distasteful aspects and outcomes, while also providing the therapist with more information about the patients' inner worlds.

The use of fantasy is also a technique for initiating cognitive restructuring of the violent patient's expectations and/or characteristic ways of viewing or distorting the behavior of others. Drawing upon the work of Novaco (1976) and others, Meichenbaum has described how "stress-inoculation training" can teach patients to cope with angry feelings or misleading expectations. Self-exploration is "facilitated by having clients vicariously relive recent anger experiences by closing their eyes and 'running a movie' of the provocations, reporting their feelings and thoughts" (Meichenbaum 1977, p. 163). This technique, coupled with skills development, has been found useful in treating patients with a history of angry and explosive behaviors (Frederiksen and Rainwater 1981).

Empathy and the Violent Patient

Clark (1980) defines empathy as the "unique capacity of the human being to feel the experiences, needs, aspirations, frustrations, sorrows, joys, anxieties, hurt, or anger of others, as if they were his or her own." A personality feature of some violent patients is their seeming inability to empathize with the feelings of others. Kozol (1975) has described the importance of this phenomenon when attempting to assess the violent patient's future dangerousness.

The author's experience is that all persons can learn empathy, at least to some degree. Patients who display violent behavior are often able to develop and express some rudimentary form of empathy which must be reinforced and strengthened through the therapeutic process. For many patients, the initial challenge is to help them develop and display empathy through therapeutic appeals to the "whole person" and to higher principles. Attention to the development of empathy is important at the very start of therapy and is directly related to the development of trust. The violent patients who learn to display empathy must also have learned to trust that they will not be harmed by such a display.

The therapist should be cautious, however, of facile displays of empathy by patients with a history of violent behavior. In such cases, the patient may be acceding to the perceived wishes of the therapist, which may be more indicative of a "con" of the therapist than an internal shift. Typically, development of empathy requires sustained therapeutic work and rehearsal with violent patients for them to relate to the experiences and feelings of others. Relating interferes with their customary way of behaving.

Medication Issues

The literature reveals that there is a fairly large group of persons who commit violent acts who can be described as dependent (Saul 1972; Child 1954; Kalogerakis 1972; Madden1976). Such dependency leads some violent patients to make demands of the therapist for immediate relief by requesting medication.

Lion (1975) has writtten extensively on the use of medication in treating violent patients (see also chapters 1, 4, and 7 in this volume). There is no one medication for treating violence. The central principle in giving medication to violent patients is to treat the underlying psychiatric disorder if one is present. Thus, for example, major tranquilizers (antipsychotic drugs) can aid in reducing psychoses and hence the aggression that may at times accompany these conditions (Itil and Wadud 1975) (see chapter 4).

When giving medication, the therapist should recognize that impulsive, erratic individuals may also take their medication impulsively; they may take too much or not enough. Both of these possibilities need to be kept in mind, especially when prescribing medication that the patient can abuse.

For some patients, use of medication causes problems other than physical abuse. Some patients believe that taking a pill can solve their problems. This magical thinking can be a manifestation of the difficulty violent patients have in tolerating delay and controlling their behavior.

Just as there is no one drug for the treatment of violent behavior, no one principle can be offered regarding the giving or withholding of medication. The therapist must be aware of all the factors involved. Does the patient have a psychiatric disorder or other condition that is likely to respond to medication? If so, medication may be clearly indicated. Other concerns, however, must also be addressed: Will use of medication lead to more or less patient involvement in therapy? Will use of medication lead to more or less willingness by patients to accept responsibility for changing and helping to control their behavior?

It is critical to the therapeutic process with violent patients that they begin to accept responsibility for changing their behavior. If using medication dampens this aspect of the therapy, it may be best to support the patient in another way. For other patients, accepting medication and complying with a helpful medical regimen may signal the beginning of patients' willingness to accept responsibility for their behavior.

Giving medication to violent patients requires self-awareness and honesty on the part of the therapist. Over time, there is a tendency to grow tired of treating these difficult patients, either individually or as a group. The therapist is tempted to slip into managing patient behavior merely by supplying medication. At no time should medication be given, even when requested by the patient, without first considering its possible implications for the therapy as a whole.

Caution is particularly advised when a patient whose past violence has not been associated with depression begins to complain of depression. Some clinicians believe that it is important for some violent patients to move through a period of depression to achieve more lasting control over their impulsive behavior. According to Lion, "this melancholy heralds the beginning of a guilt-like process which can eventually lead to appropriate affects, attachments, and a normal life-style" (Lion 1978, p. 299). The patient's temporary experience of depression can be a helpful step toward the development and expression of needed empathy.

TERMINATION OF TREATMENT

Outpatient Settings

When a patient begins to stop acting violently and impulsively, demonstrates an ability to be more reflective, and manifests increased empathy for others, the treatment may have run its course. At this point most violent patients themselves consider terminating therapy. When treatment of violent patients is winding down, however, it is essential that patients know that the therapist will continue to be available to them after therapy has been formally terminated. Further contacts through periodic meetings and phone calls may be needed.

Situational variables have been shown to be very important in predicting and eliciting violent behavior (National Institute of Mental Health 1981). Even though a patient may have shown a personality change while in treatment, alterations in life circumstances may continue to elicit former behaviors and affects. The experience of many therapists indicates that therapy never ends for some violent patients. Instead, the frequency of therapeutic contacts may decrease over time as the patient matures and life circumstances improve.

Institutional Settings

When treatment takes place in prison settings, the termination of psychological therapy usually is determined more by the law than by clinical practice. Nevertheless, many of the same psychological issues and themes already discussed arise when working with patients in prison, hospitals, or other institutional settings (Carney 1978). It is critical to the violent patient's release from inpatient settings that provision be made for continued psychological treatment, medical treatment, and social support in the community (see chapters 4, 5, 7, 8, and 10).

SPECIAL ISSUES

Countertransference

Treating violent patients requires that therapists be sensitive to issues of countertransference, feelings and attitudes that arise in the therapist consequent to the patient's behavior. Some such feelings are justified whereas others are not (Lion and Pasternack 1973). While a number of pertinent issues have already been mentioned, some additional points require emphasis.

The ambience created by discussions about violence (by the patient's recounting past acts, present intentions, or fears) may be uncomfortable for both patient and therapist. The patient is aroused, but is not encouraged to act. Lack of action can be something new and uncomfortable, even frustrating, for the patient who may communicate the discomfort in turn to the therapist. When treating patients who have been violent (or who struggle with violent intentions), therapists may fear for their own safety or be concerned that others may be assaulted or murdered by the patient (Madden et al. 1976). Sometimes, when patients manifest an inability to control their own behavior, a fear is engendered in the therapists that they also may lose control. Therapists of violent patients sometimes must cope with their own retaliatory fantasies. They may also experience "professional worries" concerning the impact of possible violent behavior by one of their patients on their own professional standing and reputation.

The most helpful techniques for dealing with such feelings and thoughts are for the therapist to discuss these issues with other experienced colleagues, to seek case consultation, to participate in case teaching conferences, and conduct a self-examination. It is not always easy, however, to find helpful colleagues with whom one can discuss personal feelings about treating violent patients, especially when the therapist works alone in a private office. One of the advantages in treating violent patients in a clinical setting is that several colleagues can work together and share experiences.

When the therapist is made persistently uncomfortable by working with violent patients, it may be time for a career change, or it may be that some of the therapist's most difficult patients should be referred elsewhere. Usually, however, such drastic steps are not necessary. Consulting with colleagues and sharing experiences with others typically suffices. This is fortunate, since successful therapy with violent patients may require that therapeutic relationships with such persons be sustained over many years. Once therapy has begun, it is important that the patient not be rejected by the therapist. Therapists who work with violent patients should monitor and assess their own reactions and continuing ability to work with such patients to avoid becoming overburdened.

Hospitalization

Sometimes it is advisable to hospitalize the violent patient (see chapter 1). While discussion of this treatment modality is beyond the scope of this chapter, it is important to note that even recommending hospitalization to a violent patient may, at times, make the therapist feel uneasy. The therapist fears that such a recommendation will provoke the patient or reinforce the patient's fear of lack of control. This matter may be particularly delicate in a group therapy setting when and if it appears that a group member is at risk for imminent violent behavior. Some therapists worry that use of hospitalization for one patient can cause other group members to be more cautious about voicing their own conflicts or fears in the future.

In the author's experience, violent patients (whether being treated individually or in a group) are usually relieved to learn that a therapist is genuinely devoted to helping patients control their behavior, even if this means hospitalization. It should also be remembered that, in the modern era, psychiatric hospitalizations typically are quite brief. Violent patients can and should be assured that hospitalization does not mean prolonged or indefinite segregation.

Patient Requests

Violent patients frequently make requests that make the therapist uncomfortable and/or uncertain about how to respond. At such times it is important for the therapist to manifest a flexible approach, while at the same time adhering to some general rules.

As a general rule, many therapists believe that it is important for the violent patient to have the therapist's home telephone number. Admittedly, this practice sometimes results in the patient's calling the therapist at odd hours and even with odd requests. Nevertheless, having the therapist's home number affords much relief for the impulsive patient, for it is the therapist's way of communicating that "help is available" when urgently needed. Another way to make emergency assistance available is to give the patient the telephone numbers of psychiatric facilities for assessment, evaluation, and hospitalization at a time of crisis. Sometimes it is very helpful for the patient and the therapist to visit these locations together before there is any need for using them.

Violent patients make many other demands upon therapists. Some patients request that the therapist write letters on their behalf to obtain social services or (if they are unable to work) disability payments. In responding to such requests, the most important principle is to be honest and straightforward. While some violent patients will threaten to stop coming to therapy if the therapist does not comply with every one of their requests, the therapist should not permit such manipulation. If a patient's request is inappropriate from the perspective of rehabilitation and therapy or is not in the patient's best interest, the therapist should communicate this determination directly to the patient. Recognizing that a helpful service is being offered, the therapist should not be influenced by a patient's threats to resume former behavior if the requests are not honored.

Sometimes a request for treatment must be refused. Violent individuals may refer themselves to treatment (or be referred by a lawyer) after they have broken the law and fear prosecution. For example, the therapist may learn that an individual requesting treatment is awaiting a court hearing related to that person's recent violent behavior. Under such circumstances, especially when the therapist believes that the would-be patient can be helped, there may be a temptation to begin treatment. In the author's experience, however, this type of entrance into therapy is usually unsuccessful. Quite often, such patients disappear as soon as they no longer feel under threat of prosecution. As a general rule, the beginning of therapy should be delayed until after the court hearing and a decision by the court about referring the individual for evaluation and treatment.

Some patients offend again while in treatment. In such cases, the therapist may be called upon to provide the court with information about the patient's recent psychological state, response or nonresponse to previous treatment, and motivation for treatment. Patients typically hope that the therapist will present a sympathetic picture of their behavior and amenability to treatment. Here again, honesty is the only course to follow. The therapist can and should indicate to the court what previous attempts the patient has made to control violent behavior, what treatment has taken place, why treatment appears to have failed, and what might be done next. In such circumstances, it is always a mistake to promise the court that there will be a "cure" if the patient is returned to treatment.

Therapist Burnout

Prolonged work with violent patients, especially with those who are characterologically disordered, can be quite draining. Therapists who work exclusively with violent patients easily become discouraged, cynical, and exhausted. A diversified practice is the best means to prevent burnout and maintain quality of service. Treating nonviolent patients sharpens clinical skills while providing the therapist with new ideas about treating the violent patient. Case consultation with other therapists about the most difficult patients is also helpful. In the author's experience, clinical research on violent patients has been an important mechanism for sustaining interest in these patients, in the basic phenomenon of violence, and in the improvement of service delivery. Some of the ideas and approaches presented in this chapter could be useful topics for future clinical research on violent patients.

EFFECTIVENESS OF TREATMENT

The ability of a violent person to change psychologically often depends on the ego strength the patient brings to or develops during treatment. Over time, some violent patients grow in their ability to appreciate how external and internal stresses cause them to act violently or impulsively. Patients with ego strength learn to delay, to verbalize rather than act out, and to seek support when it is needed. Unfortunately, however, the personality of many violent persons greatly limits the hopes for radical change that some therapists bring to treatment. In working with violent patients, the therapist often must settle for less than optimal goals. If patients who formerly assaulted others succeed in getting out of stressful or provocative situations without striking out, this is a major accomplishment. If impulsive patients learn to modulate their behavior to the extent that they can hold a job, this also is a major accomplishment. Even patients who seek periods of "cooling off" in the hospital as a way of avoiding violence should be assessed as having made a therapeutic gain.

It is, of course, appropriate for clinicians and behavioral scientists to seek empirical verification of the effectiveness of treatment, evidence beyond the types of general statements and impressions that have been presented thus far. Unfortunately, well-structured evaluations of the efficacy of psychological treatments for violent patients either have not been performed or have produced results that are difficult to evaluate or replicate. Most of the existing outcome studies regarding psychological treatments of violent persons have been concerned with institutional programs such as those at the Patuxent Institute in Maryland and Bridgewater State Hospital in Massachusetts. Although these programs have been criticized (e.g., National Institute of Mental Health 1976; Roth 1980) and have been extensively modified in recent years, there are some encouraging reports.

Carney (1974) found that after patients had been released from outpatient supervision on the recommendation of the institution, the recidivism rate among a fully treated group of 135 Patuxent patients was only 7 percent. Such a success rate is quite dramatic, especially when compared with much greater reported failure rates for men released from supervision by the courts and against the advice of the institution. The Patuxent data suggest, however, that the major reduction in recidivism rate was achieved not through "inhouse psychological treatment" but, instead, because of the effectiveness of parole supervision.

Kozol et al. (1972) report a reoffense rate of only 6 percent for dangerous persons released on staff recommendation from Bridgewater State Hospital, but their study is a difficult one from which to generalize. The staff at Bridgewater apparently pursued an indepth approach that included an extended period of institutional diagnosis, evaluation, and treatment. Methodological questions have also persisted about Bridgewater criteria for recidivism and about the duration of followup (see, for example, Dix 1980 pp. 536–39).

Followups have been disappointing from other well-known institutional treatment programs for characterologically disturbed persons, such as the program at the Herstedvester Detention Center in Denmark (Sturup 1968). In 1975, a blue-ribbon British committee on mentally abnormal offenders visited Denmark in the hope of "discovering answers to our problems." They found, instead, that the treatment program at Herstedvester had been modified, chiefly as a result of objections to the principle of indeterminate sentences. Research had also shown no significant difference in reconviction rates between offenders released from Herstedvester and ordinary offenders, except that offenders released from Herstedvester had, on average, been reconvicted after a longer interval than those released from other prisons (British Home Office, Department of Health and Social Security 1975, p. 91).

The work of Yochelson and Samenow, who worked with a number of offenders, some violent, at St. Elizabeths' Hospital in Washington, D.C., has not gained general acceptance. Yochelson and Samenow recommend a kind of therapy in which the therapist attempts to correct the offender's cognitive distortions, which are abnormal and exploitative "thinking patterns" (Yochelson and Samenow 1976, 1977). The authors present data concerning only a relatively small number of persons, and the work was uncontrolled. Furthermore, they report long-term personality change in only about 15 of the 60 or more men with whom they worked (Martin et al. 1981).

More encouraging is the recently reported work of Frederiksen and Rainwater (1981), who, through a "skill development" approach involving cognitive and behavioral therapy, decreased the angry explosive behaviors of hospitalized veterans. The treatment program was designed in part to correct the patients' mistaken psychological expectations about social situations and to help patients gain new social skills, thereby providing response modes other than anger or violence. This approach is not for everybody. Of the patients who began treatment, 50 percent dropped out, and many other patients were lost to followup once discharged. Nevertheless, this therapeutic approach seems promising for some types of violent persons.

Negative, controversial, and partial findings from studies of institutional programs for violent offenders do not end the matter. Nor should these results discourage future research. Recent conclusions of a National Academy of Sciences Panel on Research on Rehabilitative Techniques seem highly relevant to the problem of evaluating treatment effectiveness for violent persons. As noted by the panel:

> Although there is little in the reported literature that demonstrably works, the conclusion that "nothing works" is not necessarily justified. It would be more accurate to say that nothing yet tried has been demonstrated to work. This is because many plausible ideas have not been tried and because the research done so far, even when theoretically informed, has not been carried out satisfactorily. The research has been flawed by limitations in the evaluation of programs, the questionable degree to which treatments are actually implemented, and the narrow range of approaches actually attempted (Martin et al. 1981, p. 3).

Similar conclusions were reached by LeVine and Bornstein (1972) in their review of 295 citations from the literature dealing with the effectiveness of various treatments for antisocial personality disorders. Only 10 of the studies (comprising 13 citations) met the minimum standards for evaluation. Most of the studies lacked adequate controls and/or followup.

More adequate research designs should be developed for future study of treatment strategies for violent persons such as those summarized in this chapter. Studies of both community and institutional treatment programs are needed, in contrast to the former interest in institutional programs only. Insufficient research attention has been given thus far to the design, implementation, and evaluation of community programs of care for patients released from institutional treatment programs. The author's experience, and that of other contributors to this volume, has been that the development of "holistic" systems of community care is vital if treatment gains made with violent persons are to be maintained.

REFERENCES

American Psychiatric Association. Clinical Aspects of the Violent Individual. Task Force Report 8. Washington, D.C.: The Association, 1974.

British Home Office, Department of Health and Social Security. Report of the Committee on Mentally Abnormal Offenders. London: Her Majesty's Stationery Office, Oct. 1975.

Carney, F.L. The indeterminate sentence at Patuxent. Crime and Delinquency 20(2):135–143, 1974.

Carney, F.L. Treatment of the aggressive patient. In: Madden, D.J., and Lion, J.R., eds. Rage, Hate, Assault, and Other Forms of Violence. New York: Spectrum Publications, 1976. pp. 223–248.

Carney, F.L. Inpatient treatment programs. In: Reid, W.H., ed. The Psychopath: A Comprehensive Study of Antisocial Disorders and Behaviors. New York: Brunner-Mazel, 1978. pp. 261–285.

Chawst, J. Control: The key to offender treatment. American Journal of Psychotherapy 19(1):116–125, 1965.

Child, I.L. Socialization. In: Lindzey, G., ed. Handbook of Social Psychology. Vol. III. Reading, Mass.: Addison Wesley, 1954. pp. 450–859.

Clark, K.B. Empathy: A neglected topic in psychological research. American Psychologist 35(2):187–190, 1980.

Dix, G.E. Clinical evaluation of the "dangerousness" of "normal" criminal defendants. Virginia Law Review 66(3):523–581, 1980.

Frederiksen, L.W., and Rainwater, N. Explosive behavior: A skill development approach to treatment. In: Stuart, R.B., ed. Violent Behavior: Social Learning Approaches to Prediction, Management and Treatment. New York: Brunner-Mazel, 1981. pp. 265–288.

Halleck, S.L. Psychiatry and the Dilemmas of Crime. New York: Harper & Row, 1967.

Harbin, H.T. Episodic dyscontrol and family dynamics. American Journal of Psychiatry 134(10):1113–1116, 1977.

Itil, T.M., and Wadud, A. Treatment of human aggression with major tranquilizers, antidepressants, and newer psychotropic drugs. Journal of Nervous and Mental Diseases 160(2):83–99, 1975.

Kalogeriakis, M. Homicide in adolescents: Fantasy and deed. In: Fawcett, J., ed. Dynamics of Aggression. Chicago: American Medical Association, 1972. pp. 93–103.

Kozol, H.L.; Boucher, R.J.; and Garofalo, R.F. The diagnosis and treatment of dangerousness. Crime and Delinquency 18(4):371–392, 1972.

Kozol, H. The diagnosis of dangerousness. In: Pasternack, S.A., ed. Violence and Victims. New York: Spectrum, 1975. pp. 3–13.

LeVine, W.R., and Bornstein, P.E. Is the sociopath treatable? The contribution of psychiatry to a legal dilemma. Washington University Law Quarterly 2:693–711, 1972.

Lion, J.R.; Bach-y-Rita, G.; and Ervin, F.R. Violent patients in the emergency room. American Journal of Psychiatry 125(12):1706–1711, 1969.

Lion, J.R., and Pasternack, S.A. Countertransference reactions to violent patients. American Journal of Psychiatry 130(2):207–210, 1973.

Lion, J.R.; Azcarate, C.; and Christopher, R. A violence clinic. Maryland State Medical Journal 23:45–48, Jan. 1974.

Lion, J.R. The development of a violence clinic. In: Pasternack, S.A., ed. Violence and Victims. New York: Spectrum, 1975, pp. 61–88.

Lion, J.R.; Madden, D.J.; and Christopher, R.L. A violence clinic: Three years' experience. American Journal of Psychiatry 133(1):4, 1976.

Lion, J.R.; Christopher, R.L.; and Madden, D.J. A group approach with violent outpatients. International Journal of Group Psychotherapy 27(1):67–74, 1977.

Lion, J.R. Outpatient treatment of psychopaths. In: Reid, W.H., ed. The Psychopath: A Comprehensive Study of Anti-Social Disorders and Behaviors. New York: Brunner-Mazel, 1978. pp. 286–300.

Madden, D.J. Psychological approaches to violence. In: Madden, D.J., and Lion, J.R., eds. Rage, Hate, Assault, and Other Forms of Violence. New York: Spectrum, 1976. pp. 135–151.

Madden, D.J.; Lion, J.R.; and Penna, M.W. Assaults on psychiatrists by patients. American Journal of Psychiatry 133(4):422–425, 1976.

Madden, D.J. Voluntary and involuntary treatment of aggressive patients. American Journal of Psychiatry 134(5):553–555, 1977.

Madden, D.J., and Lion, J.R. Clinical management of aggression. In: Brain, P.F., and

Benton, D., eds. Multidisciplinary Approaches to Aggression Research. Elsevier, Holland: Biomedical Press, 1981. pp. 477–488.

Martin, S.E.; Sechrest, L.B.; and Redner, R., eds. New Directions in the Rehabilitation of Criminal Offenders. Washington, D.C.: National Academy Press, 1981.

Meichenbaum, D. Cognitive-Behavior Modification: An Integrative Approach. New York: Plenum Press, 1977.

National Institute of Mental Health. Criminal commitments and dangerous mental patients: Legal issues of confinement, treatment and release, by Wexler, D.B. Washington, D.C.: DHEW Pub. No. (ADM) 76–331, 1976.

National Institute of Mental Health. The clinical prediction of violent behavior, by Monahan, J. Washington, DC: DHHS Pub. No. (ADM) 81–921, 1981.

Novaco, R.W. The functions and regulation of the arousal of anger. American Journal of Psychiatry 133(10):11241128, 1976.

Quen, J.M. A history of the Anglo-American legal psychiatry of violence and responsibility. In: Sadoff, R.L., ed. Violence and Responsibility. New York: Spectrum, 1978. pp. 17–32.

Rappeport, J.R. Enforced treatment—Is it treatment? The Bulletin of the American Academy of Psychiatry and the Law 2(3):148–158, 1974.

Roth, L.H., and Meisel, A. Dangerousness, confidentiality, and the duty to warn. American Journal of Psychiatry 134(5):508–511, 1977.

Roth, L.H. Correctional psychiatry. In: Curran, W.J.; McGarry, A.L.; and Petty, C.S., eds. Modern Legal Medicine, Psychiatry, and Forensic Sciences. Philadelphia: F.A. Davis, 1980. pp. 677–719.

Rothenberg, A. On anger. In: Pasternack, S.A., ed. Violence and Victims. New York: Spectrum, 1975. pp. 201–211.

Saul, L. Personal and social psychopathology and the primary prevention of violence. American Journal of Psychiatry 128(12):1578–1581, 1972.

Schmideberg, M. Re-evaluating the concepts of "rehabilitation" and "punishment." International Journal of Offender Therapy 12:25–27, 1968.

Shah, S. Dangerousness: Some definitional, conceptual and public policy issues. In: Sales, B., ed. Perspectives in Law and Psychology. Vol. 1. New York: Plenum Press, 1977. pp. 91–119.

Sturup, G.K. Treating the "Untreatable." Chronic Criminals at Herstedvester. Baltimore: Johns Hopkins Press, 1968.

Symonds, M. The accidental victim of violent crime. In: Pasternack, S.A., ed. Violence and Victims. New York: Spectrum, 1975. pp. 91–99.

Toch, H. Violent Men: An Inquiry Into the Psychology of Violence. Chicago: Aldine, 1969.

Wolfgang, M.E. Family violence and criminal responsibility. In: Sadoff, R.L., ed. Violence and Responsibility. New York: Spectrum, 1978. pp. 87–103.

Yochelson, S., and Samenow, S.E. The Criminal Personality. Volume I: A Profile for Change. New York: Jason Aronson, 1976.

Yochelson, S., and Samenow, S.E. The Criminal Personality. Volume II: The Change Process. New York: Jason Aronson, 1977.

4

Psychopharmacology and Aggression

Joe P. Tupin, M.D.

Violence committed by individuals is most often a consequence of multiple, interacting phenomena. Occasionally a single factor will make a major contribution, but rarely will it be sufficient by itself to cause violent behavior. Throughout this chapter, multiple etiologic factors will be assumed, so that psychopharmacologic intervention will be viewed as usually representing only one part of a complex management strategy. For the clinician, psychopharmacologic intervention is appropriate only in cases in which violence is of medical-psychiatric origins. It is <u>not</u> indicated for administrative-punitive purposes or for patients whose violence is clearly of a volitional, manipulative, or political nature.

This chapter will consider only psychopharmacologic interventions and will be divided into two parts. The first concerns evaluation and management strategies for emergency, short-term management of violent behavior. The patient's diagnosis may be unknown, and a complete physical and psychiatric evaluation is impossible. This situation is usually, but not exclusively, encountered in emergency rooms, crisis clinics, and admitting wards. Violent patients may also be found in many criminal justice settings. The second part of this chapter focuses on evaluation and management for long-term purposes. In the latter situation, accurate diagnosis is essential. Since multiple factors exist, all need to be identified and appropriately managed.

Additional discussions of the pharmacologic interventions mentioned in this chapter can be found in such excellent reviews as those by Sandler and by Lion (Sandler 1979; Lion 1983).

SHORT-TERM USE OF
PSYCHOPHARMACOLOGIC AGENTS

Medication Choice and Administration

When the subject is acting in an immediately dangerous or seriously threatening manner, there is concern for safety of staff and others, and the patient's history is unknown, medication may be used for short-term control until a psychiatric diagnosis, if any, can be established. Then a specific choice of management can be made for patients with a significant medical-psychiatric condition.

A comment on the techniques used for humane, effective, appropriate restraints and seclusion would be beyond the scope of this chapter (see chapters 6 and 11). However, the subject must be under physical control before medication can be safely given. Safe treatment must include the capacity to give as well as to monitor all effects of the medication.

The following specific principles will guide the choice and administration of medication:

1. The medication must have a rapid onset of action.
2. The medication must be effective.
3. The drug of choice must be available in dosage form suitable to the skills of the personnel and to the urgency of the situation.
4. Side effects or potential for adverse interactions with medical conditions or other drugs must be anticipated, and the staff must have the knowledge, training, and equipment to diminish any risk of untoward effects.

The question of rapidity seems obvious, but a few comments may illustrate the point. For example, chlordiazepoxide and diazepam are both poorly absorbed when given intramuscularly. Other medications such as oxazepam are slowly absorbed when given orally. Long-acting, injectable antipsychotics (fluphenazine enanthate, for example) are a poor choice because they are designed to have a slow release with gradually increasing blood levels. Thus, onset of action must be considered.

In an emergency situation, the drug must be effective; i.e., the medication should give reasonable assurance that it can effectively calm, tranquilize, or sedate a patient. The goal is to gain control, reduce risk of harm, and allow the diagnostic process to begin. Repeated administration of medication should take place only for these purposes, since it is not appropriate to initiate long-term treatment without adequate evaluation. An emergency room situation provides little opportunity to do a formal assessment or acquire a history or laboratory information that will aid in the choice of medication. Nonetheless, the clinician must be alert to brain injury, toxicity, particular disease, and physical problems in general.

Route of administration of medication is important. Patients who are out of control or seriously combative are unlikely to cooperate with the administration of oral medication. The delay in onset of action attendant to oral administration is usually unacceptable, and it may not be known whether the person has taken other medications, such as anticholinergics, which delay gastric emptying and absorption. Oral administration is therefore not recommended∞tramuscular administration is the route of choice. Intravenous administration of medications is acceptable only when violent behavior is very serious and the institution and staff members can safely manage the potential side effects.

Medical interactions and interactions between multiple drugs must be assumed to be possible in patients with unknown medical, psychiatric, and drug histories. All medications that can be suggested for emergency management of violence may cause serious side effects or interact with medical conditions and other drugs. It is important, therefore, to choose medications with known side-effect risks and minimal life-threatening potential. Because some of these problems are inevitable, however, they must be anticipated and be reflected in staff training, equipment, and the availability of contra-active medication.

These principles of drug choice are central to an effective program for emergency psychopharmacologic management of violence.

Choice of Medication

Three classes of medication can be considered to generally satisfy the preceding criteria. Each has advantages and disadvantages. None is specifically "antiviolent," but each has a beneficial, short-term effect on agitation and excitement and may be useful for long-term use.

ANTIPSYCHOTIC MEDICATIONS

Antipsychotics are generally used for schizophrenia and mania. However, they are also effective for short-term control of aggressive, agitated, combative, paranoid, or nonspecific psychotic behavior. They may be used cautiously, and in low doses, for short periods with patients suffering from dementia or delirium. As a class, these medications

Table 1
Antipsychotic Medications

Potency	Examples	Single Intramuscular Dose	Maximum per 24 hours
High-potency	Trifluoperazine (Stelazine)	2.5–5 mg	20–40 mg
	Fluphenazine (Prolixin)	2.5–5 mg	40 mg
	Haloperidol (Haldol)	2.5–10 mg	40–60 mg
	Thiothixene (Navane)	4 mg	16–20 mg
Low-potency	Chlorpromazine (Thorazine)	25–75 mg	400 mg
	Thioridazine (Mellaril)	Not available	
	Mesoridazine (Serentil)	25 mg	25–200 mg

can cause problems with side effects and routes of administration. Some medications are not available in intramuscular form, and none have yet been introduced in this country for intravenous use. Since oral administration is not suitable in the emergency situation, some antipsychotics, such as thioridazine, are excluded.

Side effects and the potential for adverse interactions are moderate problems with antipsychotics. All of these drugs exhibit some anticholinergic effects and orthostatic hypotension, the low-potency phenothiazines (see table 1) more so than the high-potency drugs. When used for brief emergency situations, long-term effects such as tardive dyskinesia are unlikely. Antipsychotics act synergistically (additively) with any central nervous system depressants and narcotics. They are widely available, and most mental health facilities are well aware of their problems, assets, and administration.

In the short-term situation, high-potency drugs are more suitable than the more sedating, low-potency ones (Zavodnick 1978). The sedating quality of the low-potency drugs has not proved to be of significant clinical importance in controlling symptoms of excitement and agitation (Man and Chen 1973). High-potency drugs have less anticholinergic effect, are not as likely to induce seizures, have minimal impact on blood pressure and heart rate, are rapidly absorbed, are available in appropriate dosage forms, and have been extensively studied (Donlon et al. 1979). Among the high potency drugs, haloperidol, trifluoperazine, thiothixene, and fluphenazine are all reasonable choices.

The type of medication administration called "rapid neuroleptization" has been fairly well studied and would appear to be useful in this population (Donlon et al. 1979). Basically, the strategy is to give repeated doses of medication (e.g., haloperidol 2.5 to 10 mg intramuscularly every 20 to 30 minutes) until the target behavior (agitation) is controlled. Dosage levels up to 60 mg in 24 hours have been found to be safe and effective. Acute dystonias (muscle spasms) are fairly common; they may very rarely involve the larynx and thus potentially produce respiratory distress. Dystonia can be reversed quickly with intramuscular or intravenous diphenhydramine 50 mg (Benadryl).

ANTIANXIETY MEDICATIONS

Antianxiety medications have been used for the anxious, agitated patient (Bond and Lader 1979). As noted earlier in the chapter, the intramuscular administration of chlordiazepoxide (Librium) or diazepam (Valium) is characterized by inconsistent and delayed absorption, and thus is not recommended. Diazepam, available for intravenous use, is widely used as an immediate and effective control for seizures. However, unless staff members are well trained and capable of dealing with respiratory depression, intravenous administration should not be used even though complications are very rare.

Antianxiety medications have been found to aggravate violence in some patients and, in rare cases, to produce paradoxical excitement (Bond and Lader 1979). Their efficacy even in adequate doses is not great for combativeness unless sleep is induced. Because antianxiety medications interact additively with other central nervous system sedatives or disease, they may increase central nervous system depression. However, they are considered to be extremely safe when used appropriately, and their side effects are generally not life threatening. Abuse and withdrawal occur only after long-term, high-dosage use. Where there is little capacity to manage serious side effects and where anticholinergic, serious sedation, and blood pressure problems are to be avoided, antianxiety medications may be a reasonable choice in spite of their marginal effectiveness with combativeness.

SEDATIVE MEDICATIONS

Sedatives offer yet another choice for managing violence pharmacologically. Barbiturates are widely used and reliably produce sedation, although the margin of safety between a sedating dose and one that may seriously depress respiration is relatively narrow. Nonetheless, the wide availability, rapid effectiveness, and various dosage forms of barbiturates warrant their consideration. They are available in intravenous, intramuscular, and oral forms, and they are rapidly absorbed.

Sedation is the end point with these drugs: with inadequate doses, they may only aggravate agitation through disinhibition. Thus, larger doses are required and risk of respiratory depression increases. Main side effects are problems with central nervous system depression and the potential for interaction with other central nervous system depressants. Intermediate-acting barbiturates such as Sodium Amytal have been advocated and can be a useful choice. Sodium Amytal is available for both intravenous and intramuscular administration; intramuscular administration is preferred for safety. Doses of 150–300 mg are generally adequate for most cases.

MONITORING

It is essential to monitor violent patients carefully after the administration of any medications. Regular checks on blood pressure, respiration, level of consciousness, and pulse rate are imperative. Any evidence of deepening sedation, alterations in respiration, or drop in blood pressure must be managed rapidly and effectively. It is thus important that institutions be prepared to manage whatever side effects of the chosen drugs are most likely to be encountered.

Laboratory tests and other evaluation procedures can begin while the patient is being monitored. It is important to perform a quick physical examination to assess coexistent problems and to obtain additional history from medical records, family, or acquaintances as soon as possible. Another important step in the initial evaluation is to assess the patient's neurological status, including drug use and level of consciousness. Toxicological screens on urine and blood should be obtained at the earliest possible moment because some drugs disappear rapidly; unless an early determination is made, valuable information will be lost. Should the medication aggravate the situation, an immediate reassessment is necessary. If no further history or laboratory tests can be obtained, another medication from a different category should be chosen.

LONG-TERM USE OF PSYCHOPHARMACOLOGIC AGENTS

Principles

The major issue regarding principles is the question of adequate diagnostic assessment. While nonspecific, broad-spectrum strategy is appropriate for short-term emergency situations, long-term management requires a different approach. In such cases diagnostic certainty with specific indications is the basis for effective treatment. Many patients who may have required medication initially for short-term control may not need it for long-term management or may need a different medication. Specific psychotherapeutic or other interventions may be more useful, so careful evaluation is essential.

Evaluation

The initial task is to determine whether the subject has a condition that requires medical-psychiatric intervention. Since many persons are violent for criminal, cultural, or political reasons and are not suitable for psychiatric treatment, the assessment should be thorough and include biomedical, developmental, family, psychiatric, and extrinsic factors (Tupin 1975; National Institute of Mental Health 1981; American Psychiatric Association 1974; Lion 1972).

A detailed history should be taken to determine the pattern, focus, and precipitants of the violent behavior. Developmental antecedents, including family dynamics and structure, early childhood behaviors, perinatal brain injury, seizure phenomena, etc., must all be examined. Neurologic evaluation should include assessment for "soft signs." Psychiatric evaluation must include attention to personality structure, impulse control, inter-episode behavior, mood, guilt, evidence of psychosis, and substance abuse. Laboratory studies might include an electroencephalogram (EEG), CAT scan, electrolytes, and other measures of metabolic state. The EEG should include nasopharyngeal leads and sleep. Finally, psychological tests can elucidate evidence of subtle brain injury not recognized by neurologic examination.

All these data can then lead to a specific medical and/or psychiatric diagnosis with a subsidiary set of identified factors that may be relevant to the behavior itself. For example, a person with a paranoid psychosis might also experience drug abuse, alcohol abuse, and brain disturbance.

Diagnostic considerations that are important for medical or psychopharmacological intervention follow. Studies of murderers find paranoid psychosis and schizophrenia to be the most frequently recognized psychoses. However, only about 20 percent of incarcerated murderers are diagnosed as psychotic; the remainder is diagnosed as having a personality disorder, if anything. Other psychoses include organic brain syndrome, mania, and depression. Nonpsychotic depression is infrequently linked to violence; psychotic depression is a more common, but still rare, finding among violent persons.

Personality disorders, particularly antisocial, borderline, schizotypal, passive aggressive, and histrionic, have been identified in murderers. Other clinical diagnoses include intermittent explosive disorder (Monroe 1970) and various sexual abnormalities. The clinician must also consider the setting and victim relation to the aggressor to gain a full understanding.

Behavior disturbances induced by drugs—specifically alcohol, amphetamines, PCP, cocaine, hallucinogens, and sedatives—are of unequal importance. Alcohol, amphetamines, and other central nervous system stimulants are the best studied and most consistently have a potential for promoting violence (Ellinwood 1971). Marijuana, heroin, and other narcotics rarely directly cause violent behavior. It is important to remember that barbiturate and sedative withdrawal may be associated with delirium, seizures, and combative behavior. Anticholinergic drugs and any other cause of delirium should be considered.

Of the other biomedical problems, central nervous system damage is certainly the most important (Monroe 1978). Whether violence should be seen as a seizure phenomenon is controversial. Brain injury and disease may, however, increase the risk for violent outburst by mechanisms other than seizures.

Some investigators have suggested that testosterone plays an important role in increasing the severity of assaults (Mattsson et al. 1980), while others have stressed the need for further research (Rubin et al. 1981). Irritability, impulsiveness, and combativeness have been associated with various metabolic disturbances, including increased levels of corticosteroids, hypercalcemia, hepatic encephalopathy, hypertensive encephalopathy, and other causes of delirium. These are but a few examples. Obviously, diagnostic precision is a necessary prelude to choosing a pharmacologic intervention.

Management

Treatment is directed to the underlying psychiatric or medical condition that is the basis of violence. Simple suppression of symptoms without an adequate, relevant diagnosis is rarely acceptable for long-term management.

ANTIPSYCHOTIC MEDICATIONS

Antipsychotics are not generally indicated for long-term treatment of nonpsychotic violent behavior but are indicated in a variety of psychoses. Their most obvious use is the long-term treatment of schizophrenia, paranoid psychosis, and the initial management of mania. Antipsychotics may also be helpful in the short-term control of delirium and some symptoms of dementia, particularly paranoid, agitated behaviors. Antipsychotics have been used to reduce agitation and anxiety in psychotic behavior associated with central nervous system stimulants and hallucinogens. Borderline personality disorder symptoms may respond to these medications for intermittent use at low doses, e.g., 5 mg of thiothixene once or twice a day.

Use of antipsychotics for the long-term management of schizophrenic psychosis and paranoid psychosis is well accepted (Klein et al. 1980), but side effects include extrapyramidal, anticholinergic, and metabolic effects. Although these are generally benign and reversible, changes in liver function, bone marrow suppression, and cardiac arrhythmias may be more serious. Shader (1975) has also identified reduction in seizure threshold and reduction in blood pressure as problems. The general trend among authorities is to use low-dose, high-potency drugs because of their more benign side effects and reduced sedation.

The long-term risk of developing permanent neurologic complications (tardive dyskinesia) remains serious with all antipsychotics. Therefore, the long-term use of these drugs must be tempered with careful continued assessment of diagnostic indications and the risk-benefit ratio of treatment. The dose with the lowest effect should be used. After a single initial episode of psychosis, patients who respond well may be considered for a trial period off medication.

Mania, often characterized by hostility and aggressiveness, must be suspected when adolescents and young adults with good premorbid adjustment develop "atypical schizophrenia." Although further research about emotionally unstable adolescents is needed (Rifkin et al. 1972), antipsychotics may help control violent outbursts.

ANTIDEPRESSANT MEDICATIONS

Surprisingly, some depressed patients may act in a violent way. Seriously depressed patients may be delusionally concerned about future risk to themselves and family for financial, health, or other reasons. They may harbor thoughts of killing family members and then themselves. Occasionally, depressed parents who are nondelusional may respond with violent outbursts because of irritability. Tricyclic antidepressants play an important role in the management of individuals with serious depression, whether bipolar or unipolar. Atypical depression, reactive or neurotic depression, or dysthymic disorder may respond to tricyclics; monoamine oxidase (MAO) inhibitors may also be useful (Klein et al. 1980). Because psychotically depressed patients may not respond well to antidepressants alone, antipsychotics may also be required (Glassman et al. 1977).

There seems to be little difference among the major tricyclic antidepressants in terms of their beneficial effect. When used in adequate dosage, they produce a 60 to 70 percent remission rate. Side effects do differ: some medications are more sedating, others have more anticholinergic effects, while others are associated with cardiovascular phenomena. In high doses, e.g., greater than 250 mg of amitriptyline, these drugs may produce or enhance seizure tendencies. Doxepine and amitriptyline are the more sedating and have high anticholinergic effects. Amoxapine may act more quickly. Like other new antidepressants, amoxapine, maprotiline, and trimipramine seem to have less anticholinergic, sedation, and cardiovascular effects.

Studies have suggested that the more reactive, neurotic, or atypical depressed patients may respond to MAO inhibitors (Klein et al. 1980). Like the tricyclics, these medications are slow to act and require 2 to 4 weeks before an adequate stable dose is achieved. Since they block MAO, and since this enzyme system is partially responsible for the metabolism of various bioactive amines, these medications produce a different set of side effects. A patient using MAO inhibitors should avoid the ingestion of compounds that can increase blood pressure and lead to potential cerebral hemorrhage. These compounds, typified by tyramine, can be found in various cheeses, wines, pickled foods, and some fermented foods. Similar chemicals (such as phenylephrine) occur in some preparations for colds and asthma (Klein et al. 1980).

Antidepressants are best monitored through clinical response and side effects. Some recent work also suggests that blood level determinations may be a useful way of estimating the clinical effectiveness of tricyclics. As of this writing, however, a close correlation between blood level and clinical effectiveness has not been established for all of the tricyclics.

LITHIUM

Lithium, originally introduced for the treatment of mania, was subsequently demonstrated to be effective in the prophylaxis of both manic and depressive episodes of bipolar disorder. Lithium has been used for numerous other clinical psychiatric states and for various other medical problems (Tupin et al. 1973b; Jefferson and Greist 1977). In addition to controlling violence that stems from bipolar disorder, lithium may contribute to the control of certain kinds of episodic violent behaviors (Tupin et al. 1973b). Such behaviors need not be associated with manic depressive illness or any other psychiatric condition; they may be associated with personality disorders or other psychopathology or simply appear in apparently normal people.

Violent individuals responsive to lithium include those characterized by the following disorders (Tupin et al. 1973b):

1. Special sensitivity to provocation: These individuals respond with violence to innocent, accidental, or serious provocation. This sensitivity seems to vary from time to time and may be influenced by some underlying psychological state, alcohol ingestion, or fatigue.

2. Lack of cognitive review: These individuals report that they are unable to make an instant assessment of the circumstances and nature of the provocation. They seem to have a "short circuit" between stimulus and action and may not reflect on the seriousness of the provocation, accidental nature, risk of punishment, danger to themselves, etc. This inability varies over time.

3. Lack of control: These individuals have little control of their rage once it is provoked. They are as likely to engage in serious assault because of minor provocation as they are because of major provocation. Once the assault has started, they seem to have little control over their behavior, which is often therefore characterized by "excessive" violence and brutality.

It is unclear whether or not these individuals are remorseful. In Diagnostic and Statistical Manual III (DSM III), the diagnosis of explosive personality disorder emphasizes the ego dystonic quality of these assaults, and consequently the patient feels guilt and remorse following an episode of violence. However, if the sample is drawn from a prison population, one might expect to find less guilt and remorse.

A diagnosis of schizophrenia does not preclude the possibility that lithium could be useful for an explosive component. Studies have also suggested that similar behavior patterns may be responsive to anticonvulsants (Monroe 1975). The management of lithium is essentially the same as in the prophylaxis of manic depressive illness.

ANTIANXIETY DRUGS

Clinical observations suggest that anxiety may be an antecedent to assault. In these cases, antianxiety drugs may have a role (Lion 1979). Serious panic, particularly associated with psychosis, may be more appropriately treated with antipsychotic drugs. Antianxiety drugs may be a useful adjunct in the treatment of borderline personalities. Whether these drugs can serve as a useful long-term strategy remains to be proved. They may expose the patient to abuse and withdrawal problems. Furthermore, there are reports that long-term use of antianxiety drugs can cause paradoxical excitement or increased aggression.

ANTICONVULSANT MEDICATIONS

Although there seems to be little evidence that aggressive behavior is a true ictal phenomenon, there certainly is evidence of abnormal EEG findings and other neurologic abnormalities in violent individuals. Goldstein (1974), Monroe (1978), and others (DeLong 1980) have suggested that there may be underlying epileptiform abnormalities in some episodically violent subjects.

Researchers have used activation techniques to activate EEG abnormalities (Monroe 1978). Anticonvulsants may be useful for some patients with abnormal EEG readings. Brain abnormality may adversely alter controls or intensity of affect rather than induce seizures. A number of anticonvulsants have been suggested, including phenytoin, carbamazepine, primidone, chlordiazepoxide, and valproic acid (Monroe 1978).

The use of anticonvulsants without specific findings of brain injury, EEG abnormalities, or epilepsy would not seem to be justified at this point (Lion 1981).

HORMONES

A few studies suggest that hormone intervention may be useful (Blumer and Migeon 1975; Mattsson et al. 1980; Berlin and Meinecke 1981; Gagne 1981; and Halleck 1981). This premise is predicated in part on the controversial view that elevated testosterone may be associated with the seriousness of assault by males or may be related to sexual crimes. Drugs with an antiandrogen property may control certain intractable violent sexual deviations. Medroxyprogesterone acetate has been used (Gagne 1981). This drug may diminish sexual preoccupation and urges, making self-control easier (Berlin and Meinecke 1981). Major side effects reported include weight gain, lethargy, sweats, nightmares, shortness of breath, hyperglycemia, hypogonadism, and leg cramps. Circulation disorders have also been reported.

The use of drugs in the hormonal treatment of sexual offenders has recently been comprehensively reviewed by Bradford (1983). Because medroxyprogesterone acetate suppresses sexual desire in general (and not only deviant sexuality), caution is required to ensure that the violent person provides an understanding consent to the drug's use. The suppression of sexual desire reverses once the drug is stopped.

Birth control pills have been associated with increased depression in women and, consequently, with potentially increased aggressiveness. Increased irritability and aggression have also been associated with the premenstrual period.

STIMULANTS

Increasing interest has been taken in adult manifestations of minimally brain dysfunctional (MBD) children (Cole 1978). As these children grow up, their behavior has been characterized by irritability, antisocial behavior, social instability, etc. Some studies have suggested that the use of stimulants may be indicated in these individuals, as well as tricyclic antidepressants and antipsychotics (Wender et al. 1981; Cole 1978). Multiple murderers have reported a high incidence of childhood hyperactivity (Tupin et al. 1973a).

MISCELLANEOUS MEDICATIONS

Propranolol has been suggested in a few studies as a potentially effective agent in the control of serious assault and aggression. The research is inconclusive, and propanolol does not seem to be appropriate for clinical use at this time (Yudofsky et al. 1981).

CONCLUSION

Pharmacologic treatment for human aggression is divided into two strategies: one for short-term emergency control, the other for long-term management. Diagnostic and management approaches differ for the two situations. Emergency treatment is limited to a few selected medications. Long-term management requires careful clinical assessment before appropriate medication can be chosen. Virtually all types of psychoactive medications can be used in the effort to establish effective long-term control of violence.

REFERENCES

American Psychiatric Association. Clinical Aspects of the Violent Individual. Washington, D.C.: the Association, 1974.

Berlin, F.S., and Meinecke, C.F. Treatment of sex offenders with antiandrogenic medication: Conceptualization, review of treatment modalities, and preliminary findings. American Journal of Psychiatry 138(5):601–607, 1981.

Blumer, D., and Migeon, C. Hormone and hormonal agents in the treatment of aggression. The Journal of Nervous and Mental Disease 160(2):127–137, 1975.

Bond, A., and Lader, M. Benzodiazepines and aggression. In: Sandler, M., ed., Psychopharmacology of Aggression. New York: Raven Press, 1979. pp. 173–182.

Bradford, J.M.W. The hormonal treatment of sexual offenders. Bulletin of the American Academy of Psychiatry & the Law 11(2):159–169, 1983.

Cole, J.D. Drug therapy of adult minimal brain dysfunction (MBD). McLean Hospital Journal 3(1):37–49, 1978.

DeLong, R. Violent Behavior Disorders in Children. Presented at: American Psychiatric Association 133rd Annual Meeting, San Francisco, 1980.

Donlon, P.T.; Hopkin, J.; and Tupin, J.P. Overview: Efficacy and safety of the rapid neuroleptization method with injectable haloperidol. American Journal of Psychiatry 136(3):273–278, March 1979.

Ellinwood, E.H. Assault and homicide associated with amphetamine abuse. American Journal of Psychiatry 127(9):1170–1175, 1971.

Gagne, P. Treatment of sex offenders with medroxyprogesterone acetate. American Journal of Psychiatry 138(5):644–646, 1981.

Glassman, A.H.; Perel, J.; Shostak, M.; Kantor, S.; and Fleiss, J. Clinical implications of impramine plasma levels of depressive illness. Archives of General Psychiatry 34(2):197–204, 1977.

Goldstein, M. Brain research and violent behavior. Archivesof Neurology 30:1–35, 1974.

Halleck, S.L. The ethics of antiandrogen therapy. The American Journal of Psychiatry 138(5):642–643, 1981.

Jefferson, J.W., and Greist, J.H. Primer of Lithium Therapy. Baltimore: Williams & Wilkins, 1977.

Klein, D.F.; Gittelman, R.; Quitkin, F.; and Rifkin, A. Diagnosis and Drug Treatment of Psychiatric Disorders: Adults and Children. 2nd ed. Baltimore: Williams & Wilkins, 1980.

Lion, J.R. Evaluation and Management of the Violent Patient. Springfield, Ill.: Charles C. Thomas, 1972.

Lion, J.R. Benzodiazepines in the treatment of aggressive patients. The Journal of Clinical Psychiatry 40:70–71, 1979.

Lion, J.R. Medical treatment of violent individuals. In: Hays, J.R.; Roberts, T.K.; and Solwag, K., eds., Violence and the Violent Individual. New York: Spectrum, 1981. pp. 343–351.

Lion, J.R. Special aspects of psychopharmacology. In: Lion, J.R.; and Reid, W.H., eds., Assaults within psychiatric facilities. New York: Grune and Stratton, 1983. pp. 287–296.

Man, P.L., and Chen, C.H. Rapid tranquilization of acutely psychotic patients with intramuscular haloperidol and chlorpromaine. Psychosomatics 14(1):59–63, 1973.

Mattsson, A.; Schalling, D.; Olweus, D.; Low, H.; and Svensson, J. Plasma testosterone, aggressive behavior, and personality dimensions in young male delinquents. American Academy of Child Psychiatry 19(3):476–490, 1980.

Monroe, R.R. Episodic Behavioral Disorders. Cambridge: Harvard University Press, 1970.

Monroe, R.R. Anticonvulsants in the treatment of aggression. The Journal of Nervous and Mental Disease 160(2):119–126, 1975.

Monroe, R.R. Brain Dysfunction in Aggressive Criminals. Toronto: Lexington Books, 1978.

National Institute of Mental Health. The Clinical Prediction of Violent Behavior, by Monahan, J. Crime and Delinquency Issues Monograph. DHHS Pub. No. (ADM) 81–921, 1981.

Rifkin, A.; Quitkin, F.M.; Carrillo, C.; Blumber, A.G.; and Klein, D.F. Lithium in emotionally unstable character disorders. Archives of General Psychiatry 27:519–523, 1972.

Rubin, R.T.; Reinisch, J.M.; and Haskett, R.F. Postnatal gonadal steroid effects on human behavior. Science 211(4488):1318–1324, 1981.

Sandler, M., ed. Psychopharmacology of Aggression. New York: Raven Press, 1979.

Shader, R.I., ed. Manual of Psychiatric Therapeutics. Boston: Little, Brown, 1975.

Tupin, J.P.; Mahar, D.; and Smith, G. Two types of violent offenders with psychosocial descriptors. Diseases of the Nervous System 34(7):356–363, 1973a.

Tupin, J.P.; Smith, D.G.; Clonon, T.L.; Kim, L.I.; Nugent, A.; and Groupe, A. The long-term use of lithium in aggressive prisoners. Comprehensive Psychiatry 14(4):311–317, 1973b.

Tupin, J.P. Management of violent patients. In: Shader, R.I., ed., Manual of Psychiatric Therapeutics. Boston: Little, Brown, 1975. pp. 125–136.

Wender, P.H.; Reimherr, F.W.; and Wood, D.R. Attention deficit disorder (minimal brain dysfunction) in adults. Archives of General Psychiatry 38(4):449–456, 1981.

Yudofsky, S.; Williams, D.; and Gorman, J. Propranolol in the treatment of rage and violent behavior in patients with chronic brain syndromes. The American Journal of Psychiatry 138(2):218–221, 1981.

Zavodnick, S. A pharmacological and theoretical comparison of high and low potency neuroleptics. The Journal of Clinical Psychiatry 39(4):332–336, 1978.

5

Behavioral Approaches to Treatment of the Violent Sex Offender

Gene G. Abel, M.D.
Judith V. Becker, Ph.D.
Linda J. Skinner, Ph.D.

Sexual assault continues to be a serious societal problem. For every rape reported to the police, at least 2.2 rapes are actually committed (Curtis 1975). Estimates of incest and child molestation are no less alarming. Woodbury and Schwartz (1971) report that 10 percent of all Americans have had incestuous experiences. When conducting a comprehensive 5-year study of sexual crimes against children in Brooklyn, DeFrancis (1969) found that the molestation rate was 149.2 per 100,000 children.

The authors collected data from sexual aggressives assured of the confidentiality of their records. These data reveal that the frequency of rape and/or child molestation by sexual aggressives is much higher than that reported in the literature. For example, 207 men reported having committed a total of 796 rapes or attempted rapes ($\underline{M}$ = 3.85) and a total of 14,950 child molestations or attempted molestations ($\underline{M}$ = 72.22). When the frequency of these assaults was examined in relation to the men's primary arousal patterns, the mean number of adult and child victims was enormous (see Table 1). The data presented in table 1 also indicate that some chronic sexual aggressives commit multiple types of sexual offenses. Unless effective intervention helps them gain control over their deviant behavior, they are highly likely to continue committing sexual offenses.

A recent survey of treatment programs for sexual aggressives in-

Table 1
Frequency of Sex Offenses by Primary Arousal Pattern

		Type of Assault			
	Number of Subjects Seen	Attempted or Completed Rape of Adult Female		Attempted or Completed Child Molestation	
Primary Arousal Pattern		Total	Mean	Total	Mean
Heterosexual pedophilia	26	4	.2	3,120	120.0
Heterosexual incest	24	50	2.1	2,634	109.8
Homosexual pedophilia	31	0	0	6,364	205.3
Homosexual incest	2	0	0	470	235.0
Rape of adult females	25	517	20.7	14	.6
Exhibitionism to adult females	31	20	.7	123	4.0
Exhibitionism to female children	4	0	0	80	20.0
Sadism	4	184	46.0	0	0
Homosexuality	18	1	.1	1,998	111.0
All other	42	20	.5	147	3.5
TOTAL	207	796	3.9	14,950	72.2

dicated that there were only 70 such programs in existence in the United States (Treatment of Sexual Aggressive News, 1981). The paucity of treatment programs for sexual aggressives is discouraging in view of the magnitude of the problem. It is encouraging, however, that research and existing programs demonstrate that this population is, in fact, amenable to treatment. In the last 10 years, behavioral approaches have been used with increasing success in assessing and treating sexual aggressives (Abel 1976; Abel and Blanchard 1976; Abel et al. 1976, 1977; Barlow 1974; Barlow and Abel 1976). This chapter will review issues and procedures associated with the treatment of sexual aggressives.

ESTABLISHING AND OPERATING AN OUTPATIENT PROGRAM FOR SEXUAL AGGRESSIVES

Treating sexual aggressives poses many complicated problems. Anticipating and preparing for these possible problems is critical when establishing and operating an outpatient treatment program.

Political Considerations

Anticipating political problems is critical, since politics can destroy a program before it is begun. Using police statistics, a detailed assessment of the potential locality of the treatment facility should ascertain the crime patterns of the immediate vicinity and surrounding communities. The availability of treatment facilities, including mental health centers, private practitioners, religious groups, and self-help groups should be determined. Collaborative and cooperative relationships should then be established with all of these groups.

It is crucial to establish and maintain an open dialogue with institutional personnel and community residents. In educating a community about the need for a treatment program, the emphasis should not be that a new program for sexual aggressives is being brought into the area. Rather, it should be pointed out that a specific program to combat sexual assault will be brought to bear on an already existing community problem.

It is particularly advantageous for a program to have an advisory board composed of community leaders. Keeping community leaders informed of the program's workings will enable the leaders to educate residents and allay their anxiety.

Without institutional and community support, a treatment program can be doomed to failure. Providing information, asking for others' input, giving feedback regarding a program's progress, and incorporating community members into an advisory board will help to ensure a successful program.

Staffing the Program

It is essential to the success of a treatment program for sexual aggressives that the staff be as comfortable as possible in their work. Sexual aggressives are a difficult population. Not everyone can work with them, therefore, staff members must be carefully selected.

Potential employees' comfort should be addressed during the initial interview. Strong emotional responses to sexual assault may prevent an individual from being objective when working with sexual aggressives. Applicants should be carefully interviewed to determine their attitude toward this population. When interviewing and considering an applicant, it is important (1) to be very open and frank about the philosophy of the program and how patients are evaluated and treated; (2) to allow the applicant to read the program's protocol or statement of policy; and (3) to ask the applicant why he or she is seeking employment with a treatment program for sexual aggressives. If penile measures are used as part of the assessment procedure, a potential laboratory technician should be given an opportunity to observe other technicians conducting such evaluations. The applicant will then have a clear idea of exactly what the technician's responsibility is and what the nature of contact with the offender will be.

Working with sexual aggressives involves the use of sexually explicit language, which makes many people uncomfortable. In addition, case histories often include descriptions of physical violence, torture, or mutilation. It is helpful to present applicants with typed or audiotaped samples of the language and descriptions of activities they will encounter so they can make an informed decision regarding their ability to handle this aspect of work with sexual aggressives. It is particularly important to consider this factor when hiring secretaries, since they will have to deal with sexually explicit materials.

There is some risk of physical or emotional trauma when working with sexual aggressives. Applicants should be apprised of this fact during the hiring process. They should be informed that safeguards have been taken, but that the possibility of trauma or injury still exists. The extent of legal and/or psychological counseling available to staff members should also be discussed. Before being hired, staff members should be required to sign an informed consent form that outlines staff risks and protective measures.

Since most people have not actually worked with sexual aggressives, only time will reveal a person's ability to work with this population. However, careful interviewing will aid in better staff selection and will improve the competency of those working with this population.

Male or Female Staff Members

Mental health professionals establishing programs for sexual aggressives must determine whether the staff should consist of males only, females only, or both males and females. No research has yet been conducted on this issue, but authors can share their experiences. A number of male patients have reported that it is easier to talk to a female therapist. On the other hand, some male patients, particularly Hispanic clients, report extreme discomfort in discussing their deviant behavior with a female therapist.

When an interviewer feels that a patient is having difficulty relating because of the interviewer's sex, a second interview should be conducted by a therapist of the opposite sex to ensure that a complete history has been obtained.

Until controlled studies have been conducted to document the effectiveness of male versus female therapists in working with sexual aggressives, a conservative position would be to hire both male and female staff members.

Staff Cohesiveness

A cohesive staff is imperative to effective work with sexual aggressives. Program personnel will be confronted with problems both from the patient and from their work with sexual aggressives. Since sexual aggressives are not an easy population with which to work, all staff members will be faced with a variety of patient problems. Regular meetings, during which staff members discuss such problems, can provide a forum for learning to handle the problems.

There may also be problems with family, friends, and other professionals who may feel that the staff members are "sick" or "perverted" because they work with sexual aggressives. Acquainting staff members with the possibility of these reactions and training them in coping methods may lessen the possibility of these reactions and training them in coping methods may lessen the possibility of trauma if such reactions occur.

The lines of communication between senior and supporting staff members should always be open so that problems can be dealt with immediately. It might be helpful to develop a questionnaire to check periodically the staff members' adjustment to working with sexual aggressives.

Lack of Immediate Reward

When working with sexual aggressives, staff members would like to see an immediate reduction of deviate behavior. However, most of these patients show a gradual rather than sudden diminution in such behavior, and this can often prove frustrating and demoralizing to the staff members. Since immediate reinforcement is rare, staff members must be trained to accept delayed gratification, and they should receive constant praise and reinforcement for the work that they do.

Staff Burnout

Staff burnout, common in members of the helping profession, can be a major problem in programs for sexual aggressives. Staff members whose primary function is to interview patients or conduct laboratory sessions may be exposed to brutal stories without ever seeing changes in the patient; this tends to be demoralizing. Methods that are extremely helpful in dealing with this issue include (1) having support groups for staff; (2) having staff meetings, during which each patient's progress is tracked; (3) having staff members observe therapy sessions so that they can see treatment progress; and (4) having staff members observe followup interviews.

Staff Protective Measures

Since there are risks inherent in working with sexual aggressives, measures should be taken to maximize staff members' safety. Personal information such as telephone numbers, addresses, types of cars owned, and last names should not be discussed with the patients. While therapists may give their telephone numbers to specific patients for use in times of crisis, all staff members should be required to have unlisted telephone numbers, and staff members should be instructed to have no contact with the patients outside of therapy. Finally, at least two staff members should be present on the unit whenever a patient is being seen.

To ensure the safety of treatment staff and other staff, patients should be given a specific route to follow when entering and leaving a building in which the treatment program is located. When a patient is accepted into the treatment program, part of the consent form should detail this route to and from the clinic and indicate that deviation from that route may result in termination from the treatment program.

Patient Protection

Protecting the privacy of patients is of paramount importance. Curiosity and fear may prompt efforts by others to identify sexual aggressives who are receiving treatment. Criminal justice personnel may try to keep a program under surveillance to identify suspects.

One way of dealing with these problems is to omit phrases such as "sexual aggressive" or "sexual offender" when naming the program. Instead, a more general title such as "Sexual Behavior Clinic" or "Special Problems Unit" can be used. Another solution is not to limit the services of the program only to sexual aggressives. Other staff and criminal justice personnel can be made aware that both sexual aggressives and nonaggressives are seen at the clinic so it would be erroneous to label all people seen entering the clinic as sexual aggressives.

Security of Patient Records

Confidentiality of records is a crucial issue in treating sexual aggressives. If a patient is charged with a sexual crime in the future, prosecuting attorneys and police will want access to information about previous evaluation and treatment. Patients will not cooperate with treatment unless they are assured that the information they reveal is truly confidential.

Several procedures are recommended to make a breach of confidentiality extremely unlikely:

1. The patient should be told not to reveal specific information about any illegal acts. If no such information is given, staff members cannot be forced to reveal it.
2. The patient's file should contain no identifying information,

such as name, address, birth date, telephone number, place of employment, and records of previous arrests or hospitalizations.

3. All patient files should be kept in locked cabinets.

4. If patients are participating in group therapy, they should use a false name in the group and not discuss the specifics of their deviant behavior during group meetings.

5. Formal reports of a patient's evaluation or treatment progress should be issued only to the patient. The patient then can make the decision whether to provide the information to a third party.

The importance of these procedures to protect the records of the patient cannot be overestimated. While implementation of these procedures requires time and effort, the safeguards are necessary for the success of a treatment program. Without these safeguards, a sexual aggressive may decide to avoid the program.

Public Relations

Publicity is essential in recruiting patients for an outpatient treatment program, but it must be handled with caution. To the greatest extent possible, care should be taken to ensure that the publicity presents the program clearly and avoids the sensationalism that the media frequently use in describing such programs.

Before a program representative agrees to an interview with a member of the media, it is important to assess the interviewer's previous record to ascertain how he or she has dealt with sensitive issues. To avoid misinterpretation, interviews should not be given over the phone but in person. The program representative should also have the right to read and approve the news story prior to release. A senior staff person should approve all releases to the media.

Informational brochures describing the services, referral procedures, and eligibility requirements of the treatment program should be prepared and sent to potential referral sources. Whenever possible, a staff member should distribute these brochures personally.

In general, establishing and operating an outpatient program for any population requires considerable planning. When the program is designed for those who commit sexual assaults, the task is even greater. Time and effort spent in dealing with the sensitivities and attitudes of staff, patients, and the community can yield significant rewards.

OVERVIEW OF CURRENT TREATMENT

All sexual deviations can be viewed as encompassing a number of behavioral excesses and deficits that can be quantified (Abel 1976; Abel et al. 1978; Barlow and Abel 1976). Treatment needs are defined when an aggressive's scores fall outside the normal range. The goal of treatment is to bring the aggressive's behavior within normal limits. This model allows the use of treatment procedures derived from any theoretical orientation and quantitative evaluation.

One treatment component common to all theoretical backgrounds is considered necessary in any total treatment program for sexual aggressives: establishing an empathetic relationship between the aggressive and the therapist so that information can be obtained from the aggressive, treatment needs can be identified, treatment can be implemented, and response to treatment can be evaluated.

In addition to the client–therapist relationship, five other components should be considered in any total treatment program designed specifically for sexual aggressives. These components are decreasing deviant arousal, increasing nondeviant arousal, skills training, correcting cognitive distortions, and sex education and sex dysfunction therapy. Assessment results determine which and how many of the treatment components a patient should receive.

Decreasing Deviant Arousal

Sexual arousal caused by inappropriate objects (such as children) and/or activities (such as rape) is a defining characteristic of the sexual aggressive. All such patients need treatment to reduce this arousal, since it is acting out deviant sexual arousal that results in harm to the victim and exposes the aggressive to possible arrest and imprisonment. Treatment agents should have extensive training in procedures to reduce deviant arousal. Despite the obvious need to include this component in a treatment program for sexual aggressives, however, many programs fail to develop procedures to reduce deviant arousal.

Group therapy relies on a variety of self-control methods, such as confrontation, catharsis, and testimonials, while biologically oriented programs rely on chemical or surgical castration to eliminate sexual drive entirely (Abel et al. 1970; Money 1970; Hoffet 1978; Ovesey et al. 1963; Rado 1949; Sturup 1968). (See chapter 4.) Behavioral approaches represent another alternative and will be discussed later in this chapter.

Increasing Nondeviant Arousal

Excessive deviant arousal may be associated with a deficit in nondeviant arousal. For example, pedophile aggressives may lack arousal to mutually consenting sexual activity between adults and, therefore, be unable to relate sexually with adult partners. A second component that should be available in a total treatment program, therefore, is specific treatment to increase nondeviant sexual arousal. Some of the behavioral procedures that have been used to increase nondeviant sexual arousal to adult partners are masturbatory conditioning, exposure, fading, and systematic desensitization. These and other procedures have been the focus of several literature reviews (Abel and Blanchard 1974, 1976; Abel et al. 1978).

Skills Training

A third component that should be available in a treatment program for sexual aggressives deals with deficits in social, assertive, and/or empathic skills necessary to interact effectively with adult partners. The sexual aggressive may lack skills to establish communication, initiate conversation, maintain the flow of conversation, learn about the interests of others, share intimacies about one's own life with others, empathize with others, and ask for a change in another person's behavior. These deficits make it exceedingly difficult for a sexual aggressive to establish and maintain a social relationship that might lead to a closer bonding with an adult partner. Training in social, assertive, and empathic skills to correct these deficits have frequently been an element of treatment programs for sexual aggressives (Abel 1976; Abel et al. 1976, 1978; Peters and Roether 1972; Peters et al. 1968). Procedures for assessing these skills have been described in the literature (Barlow et al. 1977; Eisler et al. 1973, 1974; Hersen et al. 1973). Abel et al. (1978) present a detailed clinical example of social skills training.

Correcting Cognitive Distortions

A fourth treatment component focuses on the sexual aggressive's cognitive distortions surrounding the deviant sexual behavior. Some sexual aggressives, particularly exhibitionists, rapists, and child molesters, develop bizarre cognitions to explain their deviant behavior. For example, an exhibitionist may believe that a woman stares at him while exposing himself because she is sexually interested in him. Similarly, a child molester may label sexual interaction with a child as sex education or claim that children are fully able to refuse sexual advances by adults. By maintaining these false beliefs, a sexual aggressive avoids realistically facing up to the deviant behavior. While strongly believing in these irrational cognitions, the aggressive does not communicate them to other adults and, therefore, lacks opportunities to test the beliefs' acceptability.

Group therapy with sexual aggressives is an excellent vehicle for correcting cognitive distortions. The most obvious advantage is that the group's challenge of a person's irrational beliefs can be very potent. A second advantage is that, after hearing some of the irrational beliefs of other group members, some sexual aggressives realize that they use the same or similar beliefs to rationalize their own deviant behavior. Finally, in a group setting, each member serves as a kind of therapist for the other participants. When sexual aggressives help other patients restructure their beliefs, it is easier for them to accept that they, too, have irrational cognitions.

Sex Education and Sex Dysfunction Therapy

A large number of sexual aggressives do not have much sexual knowledge (Quinsey 1977). Some lack adult sexual interactions altogether or have poor relationships because of a limited knowledge about adult sexuality. As a result, deviant behavior can result from avoidance of mutually consenting, sexual interactions with an adult partner. Other aggressives may have a specific sexual dysfunction that prevents them from entering into sexual relationships with adult partners. Thus, a fifth component of a total treatment program for sexual aggressives involves traditional sex education and/or sexual dysfunction treatment.

In summary, although treatment needs of sexual aggressives vary, all patients require treatment to reduce deviant arousal. A thorough behavioral assessment of each patient will reveal which, if any, of the remaining four components should be included in the patient's treatment plan. Any total treatment program for sexual aggressives must have available the five treatment components outlined above to meet the potential needs of patients.

TREATMENT ISSUES

Fostering Valid Patient Reports

The treatment of sexual aggressives demands an ongoing assessment of the patient's deviant urges and behaviors. Since approximately 50 percent of these patients have multiple deviations, the therapist should ask initially and during the course of treatment and followup not only about the occurrence of the identified deviant sexual behavior but also about other sexual deviance in which the patient may have participated.

Sexual aggressives are frequently reluctant to report their true arousal patterns and frequency of deviant behavior for fear of legal consequences. To increase the likelihood of valid reporting, patients should be told to provide only the types of general information that the therapist needs to know about their arousal pattern and frequency of deviant behavior. The therapist should model this type of information reporting until the patient becomes proficient at it. For example, if the patient molested a 10-year-old female in a specific location 5 days prior to coming in for treatment, the therapist should demonstrate for the patient to say, "I molested a girl less than 13 years of age sometime in the last 2 months." In this way, the therapist obtains needed therapeutic information on the frequency of the behavior and the relative age of the victim without the patient divulging specific information. If the patient does provide more specific information than is needed for therapy, the therapist should not write it down.

Psychophysiological Assessment

Some sexual aggressives either cannot or will not accurately report their arousal pattern or the frequency of their deviant acts. Fortunately, psychophysiological methods can address this problem and serve as an adjunct to clinical evaluation. The most accurate means of psychophysiological assessment is direct measurement of the patient's penile circumference while presenting various sexual stimuli to him. Abel et al. (1978) discuss the use of erection responses in the assessment of sexual aggressives. The following case illustrates how such measures can be used in outlining treatment needs.

CASE EXAMPLE

Charles, 45 years old, was referred for treatment after having impregnated his 15-year-old daughter. He had been sexually involved with her for a year. Prior to entering a treatment program, the patient had been placed on probation. He denied having any ongoing sexual arousal toward his daughter or other children and believed that he needed no treatment.

In the laboratory, Charles was presented with 2-minute descriptions of sexual encounters with 8 to 10-year-old girls, a description of sex with his own daughter, and sex with an adult female. His erection responses to these types of descriptions were 94 percent, 63 percent, and 32 percent of a full erection, respectively. When these erection responses were shown to the patient, he rapidly agreed that he needed treatment, since there was clear evidence of his arousal to his own and other children.

Repeated clinical experience has shown that patients who otherwise persist in denying their deviant sexual arousal will accept the evidence presented by direct recording of their erection responses to various sexual stimuli. Psychophysiological assessment thus is an excellent means of helping a patient recognize sexual deviance and augmenting a patient's clinical history to arrive at a clear understanding of sexual arousal patterns and treatment needs.

Depression Resulting From Arrest

A common misconception about sexual aggressives is that they have little concern about their deviant behavior and are primarily hedonistic individuals whose deviant behavior is but one expression of an antisocial personality. Some sexual aggressives are antisocials and feel little guilt about their deviant behavior. Others, however, are aware of the inappropriate nature of their behavior and are devastated by their own loss of control. Depression may be particularly serious when the patient's deviant behavior has remained unknown until it suddenly becomes public knowledge following arrest, as is illustrated in the following case.

Case example. Frank, 50 years of age, was referred for treatment following his arrest for attempting to pick up a 13-year-old boy in a local amusement center. He reported that since the age of 12 he had been involved sexually with young males, and had had sexual relations with more than 200 boys. At the age of 19, he was arrested for molesting a young boy and was incarcerated overnight. Shortly thereafter, he joined a monastery in an attempt to control his deviant urges. He left the monastery after approximately a year and, at the age of 22, he married in an attempt to control his deviant urges. However, his sexual involvement with boys continued.

Three months prior to referral for treatment, Frank had been drinking at home and had an argument with his teenage daughter. He eventually blew up, left the house, and attempted to pick up the 13-year-old boy. He was arrested and charged with endangering the morals of a minor.

When initially seen, Frank felt tremendous guilt over the assault. Since the arrest, he had developed signs and symptoms of depression, including crying spells, difficulty concentrating, depression, terminal sleep disturbance, decreased sexual drive, and suicidal thoughts. Agitation and rumination about his poor self-worth had resulted in loss of appetite, a 10-pound weight loss, and marked anxiety that he treated by excessive drinking.

Although upsetting to him, Frank's lifelong deviant behavior had not produced the severe depression. Instead, the depression resulted from his recent arrest and fears that he would be publicly exposed in his own small community as a child molester. Treatment included antidepressants to control the depressive symptomatology, family therapy to help him gain control over his excessive drinking, and a specific treatment intervention to decrease his arousal toward young boys.

The Dangerous Period Following Arrest

Sexually deviant fantasies and urges that were high prior to arrest normally decrease markedly after a sexual aggressive has been arrested. When patients note the drastic reduction in their deviant fantasies, they erroneously conclude that the arrest has had a major impact on deviant arousal and that treatment is not needed because the urges and fantasies about deviant behavior have stopped.

Arrest itself, however, has never been documented to be effective in permanently changing arousal patterns. As the time following arrest increases, the patients' deviant urges return, their control begins to diminish, and they eventually reoffend unless treatment has been instituted.

The time immediately following arrest is one of the most dangerous periods for sexual aggressives since it is during this time that they make critical judgments about the importance of therapy. Unfortunately, these judgments are frequently based on a temporary reduction in deviant arousal. In addition, sexual aggressives' pressure to escape the negative experience of confinement may lead them to request release on bail at the very time that arousal is quite volatile and recommission of the crime is very likely.

During this critical time, the therapist needs to clarify to the patient that the decrease in deviant arousal is only an illusion of improvement. Furthermore, the patient should be encouraged not to seek release from jail unless treatment has been initiated and the patient has already undergone a number of sessions to decrease deviant arousal. The following case illustrates the importance of protecting patients by not allowing them to make decisions that place them in jeopardy.

Case example. James, a 23-year-old college student, had been living with Cynthia, with whom he had a satisfactory sexual relationship, for 6 months. He had had urges to rape for a year, and these urges were becoming progressively stronger.

One weekend, he waited outside a university parking lot and entered the car of a female student leaving the campus in the evening. He commandeered the car, drove into the country, and raped her. He was arrested the following day.

The patient denied to his relatives that he had raped the victim, but he did tell his attorney that he had committed the crime. Aided by his family's adamant belief that he had not committed the crime, he was released on bail. James was initially extremely relieved, but within 24 hours his urges to rape had returned. Within 48 hours following his release, he had returned to the same parking lot where he commandeered another car and raped a second female student.

Alcohol and Sexual Assault

A therapist must be particularly sensitive when working with a patient who reports that alcohol makes deviant urges more difficult to control. For most other categories of patients, the consequences of alcohol consumption are not as devastating as they can be for the sex offender. If breakdown of control results from alcohol abuse, the net result may be child molestation or rape with years of resultant incarceration, devastation to the victim, and losses to all concerned.

It is strongly recommended that a therapist consider using disulfiram for sexual aggressives who abuse alcohol. Taken internally, this drug remains in a person's system for 3 to 5 days, interacting with any alcohol consumed by forming an acid aldehyde reaction, including severe tachycardia, diaphoresis, hypotension, and severe anxiety. Use of disulfiram affords the patient greater control over urges to act out sexually, since it prevents use of alcohol at least 3 to 5 days after ingestion of the medication. The therapist and someone in the patient's environment should monitor disulfiram use. The spouse or a relative can observe oral intake of the drug and keep appropriate records to be checked by the therapist. Many therapists may be alarmed at the disruption of the "trusting" patient-therapist relationship implied by checking on the patient. However, not checking on disulfiram use ignores the reality that failure to use the drug may lead to failure to stop drinking and an increased likelihood that a sexual crime will be committed. Under these circumstances, drug compliance is essential.

Incest

A therapist treating an incest offender is faced with the issue of knowing the identity of a patient's victim. In such a situation, the therapist is ethically bound to behave in a way that protects the potential victim as well as the offender. Such protection can be provided by bringing together the members of the family to discuss how incest crimes damage the victim, offender, and family unit. Behavioral rehearsal should be used to teach each family member how to report suspicions about incest to other members of the family and to an agency providing protective services for children. Special attention should be paid to the usual methods offenders use to conceal their deviant acts. The entire family, including the potential victim, should be made very aware of what an offender might tell a victim as a justification for not reporting the sexual interactions. The therapist should then ask why such statements might be ignored by the potential victim. This interaction should be role-played until all family members are capable of generating the appropriate responses.

Inappropriate Patient Attempts at Control

Sexual aggressives, their families, and their doctors frequently view a patient's recurrent urges to commit sexual crimes as a moral issue or as an issue of will power. This position generally takes the form: "if he really wanted to stop, he would." As a result, some patients attempt to control their deviant urges by repressing all sexual thoughts or by relying exclusively on their religion to help them.

Patients who have made such decisions are difficult to treat because their self-imposed repression can isolate the therapist from the very information—knowledge of the patient's deviant urges and fantasies—

necessary to implement treatment. Other patients may report that they do not want to discuss their deviant thoughts or urges because such discussion would be contrary to their attempts at religious control. The following case is a prime example of the outcome of one of these self-imposed treatment strategies.

Case example. Sam was seen 1 month after his release from prison following his second incarceration for rape. Subsequent to his first release, he raped on three occasions but was arrested for only one of these rapes. During the last 4 years of his 8-year incarceration for this second arrest, he developed his own treatment plan. He reasoned that since he intermittently had urges to rape, had used these urges and fantasies during masturbation, and had eventually acted on these urges, he would eliminate sex completely from his life. Sam reported that he had not masturbated for the last 4 years prior to his release. Psychophysiological assessment revealed that he still had considerable arousal to thoughts of rape. Attempts to involve him in therapy were unsuccessful, and he had reoffended within 5 years of his release into the community.

A similarly perplexing problem involves individuals who rely exclusively on their religious convictions to control deviant fantasies. These persons often view any examination of their deviant arousal patterns as sinful, since discussion of deviant thoughts and behaviors runs counter to their religious beliefs. This places the therapist in a most difficult situation since the very act of examining the individual's need for treatment is viewed as countertherapeutic by the religious approach which the patient espouses. The patient may also be supported in this approach by his own church.

Case example. Alan gave an extensive history of multiple deviations, including exposure, voyeurism, pedophilia, and, more recently, rape. He had been arrested on two occasions for sexual crimes. At the time of his first arrest, he became deeply involved in his church and decided that he should rely upon his religious convictions and faith in Jesus Christ to control his urges. Indeed, this was highly effective for approximately 7 months, at which time he began exposing himself again. He interpreted the resumption of this deviant behavior as a loss of faith in Christ.

Alan's exhibitionism and voyeurism accelerated. While window peeping one evening, he entered a woman's apartment and raped her. He turned himself into the police a day later because of his guilt feelings about the rape. To his surprise, he was released within 8 months because of a legal technicality. He interpreted his release as a sign from God that he should be given another chance.

Alan was next referred to the authors for treatment. During his initial evaluation, he reported that he no longer had sexual difficulties and was reluctant to undergo any assessment for fear that the devil would enter his mind. After some discussion, he did allow a brief psychophysiological assessment that showed that he had high arousal to child molestation stimuli. When these results were discussed with the patient, he viewed them as essentially evil thoughts that must be controlled through his religious convictions. He refused therapy, only to return 5 months later for having exposed himself; he reported having increasing urges to molest young girls.

It is sometimes helpful in such cases to involve a patient's minister or priest in the therapeutic decision regarding treatment. Sometimes the patient's church is not as opposed to treatment as the patient might suggest. At other times, it can be suggested to patients that the referral for treatment may be an expression from God that they should seek outside help.

Immediate Availability of the Therapist

Sexual aggressives usually attempt to deal with their deviant urges and fantasies entirely by themselves. They are frequently appalled, embarrassed, and guilty about their urges to commit sexual crimes. Furthermore, since there are strong community and personal sanctions against individuals who commit sexual offenses, they often have no one to turn to for help during emergency situations, when urges to offend become exceedingly difficult to control. This dilemma is very similar to that faced by alcoholics who become aware that their control over their drinking is breaking down and that they need immediate access to an empathic person who can provide assistance.

It is imperative to provide the therapist's hotline numbers to sexual aggressives in treatment or followup so the patient can request immediate consultation. In addition, the therapist should explain to the patient the importance of asking for immediate help when it is needed. Patients having such numbers relieves them of considerable anxiety, since they know emergency assistance is available. Fears of obscene phone calls or harassment of the therapist have proved unwarranted. In the authors' experience, the therapist is not overwhelmed with phone calls; when emergency calls are received, immediate effective treatment intervention can be provided.

Recurrence of Deviant Urges or Fantasies

The concept that deviant urges or fantasies may return after successful treatment is alien to most sexual aggressives. However, since multiple factors may impinge upon the patient and lead to the return of urges to commit sexual offenses, a patient needs to be taught that, while the primary objective of treatment is to curb deviant arousal and urges, there may be times in the future when such urges recur.

The therapist should instruct the patient in treatment techniques that can be used during periods when deviant arousal recurs. Treatment should never be viewed as having been completed. Instead, during the period traditionally viewed as followup, treatment continues at a lower frequency. Until there is a better understanding of assessment techniques to delineate treatment effectiveness, indefinite followup appears to be the most prudent course for the sexual aggressive and for society as well.

TREATMENT APPROACHES

Various treatment approaches have focused on decreasing deviant arousal. Traditionally, major tranquilizers have been used to suppress the patient's sexual drive in the hope that the general suppression will control deviant sexual arousal. Although temporary, this therapy may frequently be effective by immediately reducing the patient's drives in general. This approach does not allow selective reduction of sexual arousal, however; appropriate nondeviant arousal is reduced while deviant arousal is reduced.

Drugs such as medroxyprogesterone have also been used to eliminate deviant arousal. Although more effective at reducing the patient's sexual drive than drives in general, this drug and similar drugs cannot be expected to reduce the patient's deviant sexual drive while preserving nondeviant sexual drives (see chapter 4).

Behavioral interventions of various kinds have been used to decrease deviant arousal. For example, aversive conditioning has been used to associate mild pain delivered to the fingertips with thoughts of deviant sexual behavior. The expectation is that, over time, this procedure will reduce the patient's deviant urges. Unfortunately, this treatment is easily ethically abused, and its effectiveness is yet to be demonstrated.

Covert sensitization offers considerable promise for reducing deviant arousal. This technique involves helping the patient associate deviant sexual fantasies with fantasies that are socially aversive. For example, the patient may be told to imagine urges to rape a woman. Once the image is in his "mind's eye," he is instructed to switch immediately to thoughts of aversive consequences, such as being incarcerated because of the rape or being beaten up in prison after arrest. These pairings occur frequently within the therapy session until the patient develops the skill to recall immediately the aversive scene when he has urges to rape or fantasies of rape.

Currently, the most effective behavioral intervention to reduce deviant arousal is masturbatory satiation. This treatment is based on analytic and behavioral understanding of the development of sexual arousal (Abel and Blanchard 1974). Sexual arousal develops as the patient fantasizes various images during masturbation. Throughout one's lifetime, repeated pairings of orgasm and the patient's fantasy lead to a welding of a specific fantasy and the pleasure of orgasm. In the case of a sexual aggressive, this welding is based on fantasies of deviant sexual behavior being paired repeatedly with orgasm.

Masturbatory satiation severs the relationship between deviant fantasy and pleasurable masturbatory orgasm by having the patient use deviant fantasies repeatedly over time during the postorgasmic phase of masturbation. The patient is instructed to masturbate to ejaculation as rapidly as possible using nondeviant fantasies, or to masturbate until the usual latency to ejaculation period plus 2 minutes has passed. Once the patient has ejaculated or the latency period has been exceeded, the patient immediately switches to the use of deviant fantasy, using the most erotic deviant material possible, and continues to masturbate for a total masturbatory time of 1 hour. The patient audiotapes fantasies while masturbating. These tapes are spot checked by the therapist, who then gives the patient feedback about how to alter both the nondeviant and deviant fantasies. The spot check also ensures compliance with the treatment procedure.

Case example. Jack, a 22-year-old graduate student, had a lifelong history of sadomasochistic fantasies, attraction to girls 8 to 10 years of age, and, more recently, strong urges to rape. His family history was replete with violent confrontations among various family members during family drinking bouts.

Because Jack was exceedingly tall and self-conscious about his height, he found it difficult to date throughout high school. His referral to treatment was precipitated by his accelerating use of sadomasochistic fantasies and his fears that he could no longer control his sadomasochistic urges. On two occasions he had purposely gone out while intoxicated to rape a female acquaintance, but he was unable to gain entry into her apartment.

Jack was taught about the development of deviant arousal, its relationship to masturbation, and its elimination by the satiation procedure. Treatment proceeded by having him tape record his sexual fantasies during masturbation. He was instructed to masturbate using fantasies of mutually consenting sexual activity with an adult. He was told that, once he had ejaculated, he was to switch immediately to his sadomasochistic fantasies and to continue to masturbate using the most erotic deviant material possible for a total masturbatory time of 1 hour. This treatment procedure was conducted by the patient in his own home. The 1-hour masturbatory audiotapes developed by Jack were spot checked by the therapist, who then gave him feedback about how to alter both his deviant and nondeviant fantasies. (A complete transcript of an actual masturbatory satiation session is available from the first author.)

The role of a therapist using masturbatory satiation is twofold. First, the therapist teaches patients how to incorporate greater warmth, tenderness, and caring to their nondeviant fantasies. Second, patients must be encouraged to use their most erotic deviant fantasies during the postorgasmic phase of masturbatory satiation. The goal is for patients to repeat those deviant fantasies that are the most erotic, which frequently requires them to repeat the same phrase 10 to 15 times during the post-orgasmic phase. Through the repeated use of such deviant fantasies when orgasm and pleasurable masturbation is impossible, the very stimuli that used to evoke erotic responses become satiated. As the masturbatory satiation proceeds, without sexual arousal, the deviant fantasies become boring and eventually become aversive.

Masturbatory satiation has several advantages over other behavioral techniques:

1. It is exceedingly effective.
2. It incorporates the powerful pairing of physiological sexual arousal to sexual fantasies.
3. The therapist can spot check numerous masturbatory satiation sessions to ensure treatment compliance.

4. Treatment is cost effective because for each hour of therapy with the patient, the therapist can spot check 5 hours of the patient's masturbatory satiation sessions.

The major difficulty most therapists have when using masturbatory satiation is their disgust with the violent and deviant fantasies voiced by many patients. Although it would be less anxiety producing for the therapist, it is not in the patient's best interest for the therapist to avoid hearing such fantasies and later discussing them with the patient. Direct discussion of the fantasies by the therapist conveys to the patient that deviant fantasies, like other elements of the patient's life, can be dealt with effectively.

CONCLUSION

Assessment and treatment of sexual aggressives have therapeutic, ethical, and legal problems similar to those associated with treatment of other aggressive patients. The stigma assigned to those who commit sexual crimes and those who work with sexual deviates, however, is greater than the stigma attached to other types of deviates and treatment programs. Society's reluctance to support adequate treatment programs for sexual aggressives is probably the most significant factor preventing the stopping of sexual assaults at the source—i.e., the known or admitted individual sex offender. It is hoped that increased knowledge about preventing sex offenses will lead to a change in these societal attitudes.

REFERENCES

Abel, G.G.; Levis, D.; and Clancy, J. Aversion therapy applied to taped sequences of deviant behavior in exhibitionism and other sexual deviations: A preliminary report. Journal of Behavior Therapy and Experimental Psychiatry 1(1):58–66, 1970.

Abel, G.G., and Blanchard, E.B. The role of fantasy in the treatment of sexual deviation. Archives of General Psychiatry 30(4):467–475, 1974.

Abel, G.G. Assessment of sexual deviation in the male. In: Hersen, M., and Bellack, A.S., eds. Behavioral Assessment: A Practical Handbook. New York: Pergamon Press, 1976. pp. 437–458.

Abel, G.G., and Blanchard, E.B. The measurement and generation of sexual arousal in male sexual deviates. In: Hersen, M.; Eisler, R.M.; and Miller, P.M.; eds. Progress in Behavior Modification. Vol. 2. New York: Academic Press, 1976. pp. 99–136.

Abel, G.G.; Blanchard, E.B.; and Becker, J.V. Psychological treatment of rapists. In: Walker, M.J., and Brodsky, S.L., eds. Sexual Assault: The Victim and the Rapist. Lexington, Mass.: Lexington Books, 1976. pp. 99–115.

Abel, G.G.; Barlow, D.H.; Blanchard, E.B.; and Guild, D. The components of rapists' sexual arousal. Archives of General Psychiatry 34(8):895–903, 1977.

Abel, G.G.; Blanchard, E.B.; and Becker, J.V. An integrated treatment program for rapists. In: Rada, R., ed. Clinical Aspects of the Rapist. New York: Grune and Stratton, 1978. pp. 161–214.

Barlow, D.H. The treatment of sexual deviation: Towards a comprehensive behavior approach. In: Calhoun, K.S.; Adams, H.E.; and Mitchell, K.M., eds. Innovative Treatment Methods in Psychopathology. New York: Wiley, 1974. pp. 121–147.

Barlow, D.H., and Abel, G.G. Sexual deviation. In: Kazdin, A.; Mahoney, M.; and Craighead, E., eds. Behavior Modification: Principles, Issues and Applications. Boston: Houghton Mifflin, 1976. pp. 341–360.

Barlow, D.H.; Abel, G.G.; Blanchard, E.B.; Bristow, A.; and Young, L. A heterosexual skills checklist for males. Behavior Therapy 8(2):229–239, 1977.

Curtis, L.A. Present and future measures of victimization and forcible rape. In: Walker, M. ed. Rape: Research, Action, Prevention. Report #29. Tuscaloosa, Ala.: Center for Correctional Psychology, Department of Psychology, University of Alabama, 1975. pp. 20–30.

DeFrancis, V. Protecting the Child Victim of Sex Crimes Committed by Adults. Denver: American Humane Association, 1969.

Eisler, R.N.; Miller, P.M.; and Hersen, M. Components of assertive behavior. Journal of Clinical Psychology 29(3):295–299, 1973.

Eisler, R.N.; Hersen, M.; Miller, P.M.; and Blanchard, E.B. Situational determinants of assertive behavior. Journal of Counseling and Clinical Psychology 43(3):330–340, 1974.

Hersen, M., and Eisler, R.N. Components of assertive responses: Clinical, measurement, and research considerations. Behavior Research and Therapy 11(4):505–521, 1973.

Hoffet, H. On the application of the testosterone blocker cyproterone acetate (SH 714) in sex deviants and psychiatric patients in institutions. Praxis 57:221–120, 1978.

Money, J. Use of androgen-depleting hormones in the treatment of male sex offenders. Journal of Sex Research 6(3):165–172, 1970.

Ovesey, L.; Gaylin, W.; and Hendin, H. Psychotherapy of male homosexuality. Archives of General Psychiatry 9:19–31, 1963.

Peters, J.; Pedigo, J.; Steg, J.; and McKenna, J. Group psychotherapy of the sex offender. Federal Probation 32(3):35–41, 1968.

Peters, J., and Roether, H. Group psychotherapy for probationed sex offenders. In: Resnik,

H.L., and Wolfgang, M.E., eds. Sexual Behavior: Social Clinical and Legal Aspects. Boston: Little, Brown, 1972. pp. 255–266.

Quinsey, V. The assessment and treatment of child molesters: A review. Canadian Psychological Review 18(3):204–220, 1977.

Rado, S. An adaptational view of sexual behavior. In: Hoch, P., and Zubin, J., eds. Psychosexual Development in Health and Disease. New York: Grune and Stratton, 1949. pp. 159–189.

Sturup, G.K. Treatment of Sexual Offenders in Herstedvester, Denmark: The Rapists. Copenhagen, Munsgaard, 1968.

Treatment of Sexual Aggressives News, 4:1–7, 1981. (Published by the Sexual Behavior Clinic, Research Foundation for Mental Hygiene, Inc., 722 W. 168th Street, New York City, NY 10032.)

Woodbury, J., and Schwartz, E. The Silent Sin. New York: New American Library, 1971.

6

Physical Controls: The Use of Seclusion and Restraint in Modern Psychiatric Practice

Paul H. Soloff, M.D.

In an era of psychodynamic sophistication and pharmacologic advances, discussing physical control of the mentally ill may seem distinctly anachronistic. To some, the discussion may suggest regression to the methods of a less enlightened era. Memories may be evoked of the nonrestraint movement of the last century, which challenged the legitimacy of physical controls as a form of treatment for the mentally ill.

Despite such reservations, however, seclusion and physical restraint remain important treatment techniques in the management of violent and disruptive psychiatric patients. In some form or other, seclusion and restraint continue to be used in most clinical settings. Recent public exposure and judicial review have increased awareness of such controls and highlighted the paucity of systematic studies concerning this practice. It is apparent, though, that the persistence of physical controls as a treatment method in the modern era warrants objective assessment and review.

This chapter will discuss the continued relevance of seclusion and physical restraint from a clinical and theoretical perspective. In addition, some general guidelines will be provided to assist hospital administrators, psychiatric staff, and others in assessing the use of these methods in treatment settings.

RELEVANCE OF PHYSICAL CONTROLS

The rising concern regarding the use of physical controls in modern psychiatric practice seems to be, in large part, the result of increased visibility. Changes in social policy, philosophy, and funding have resulted in larger numbers of violent and disruptive patients being referred to treatment facilities at the community level (Edelman 1978). Instead of being treated in State hospitals as in the past, many severely disturbed chronic mental patients are now being managed in front-line facilities, such as community mental health centers and full-service general hospitals. The intense controversy over the propriety of admitting aggressive and involuntary patients to general hospital psychiatric units reflects the problems that have developed (Leeman 1980; Crowder and Klatte 1980).

Changes have also occurred in the composition of the population served by the practice of psychiatry. Alcohol-related offenses and public drunkenness have been redefined as symptoms of illness that should be referred to the local mental health center rather than the criminal justice system. Many minor offenders are referred to the mental health system for evaluation and treatment of psychosocial factors involved in deviant behavior. In an ironic turn of events, excessive violence in the jail setting has come to be viewed as possible indication of a need for referral to a local mental health facility. While such referral is fully warranted in some cases—e.g., violence associated with psychosis or homosexual panic—the practice has also increased the amount of violent behavior being treated by local mental health practitioners.

Still another development of major importance is the epidemic of drug abuse—e.g., LSD, amphetamines, PCP—that has created new disorders of chemically associated violence in the community. For example, the National Institute on Drug Abuse (NIDA) reported in 1979 that the abuse of PCP had reached "epidemic" proportions in 1978 and was responsible for 200 deaths and 10,000 emergency room visits (NIDA 1979). PCP is associated with a high incidence of paranoid reactions and violent behavior that can include suicide and homicide (Burns and Lerner 1978). According to the same NIDA report, 32 percent of clients under the age of 19 who were seen in drug abuse counseling settings used PCP. The result is a greater number of violence-prone individuals in the community, a greater influx of such individuals into community mental health facilities, and a greater visibility of the physical controls that may be needed in their treatment.

The most forceful critics of physical controls—both in the past and in the modern era—are persons who have worked with chronically ill patients in long-term care settings. In the 19th century, Robert Hill, William Tuke, and John Conolly viewed the philosophy of nonrestraint as the very cornerstone of humane care of the mentally ill. Conolly's famous admonition embodies the moral ideology of his age: "Restraint and neglect are synonymous. They are a substitute for the thousand attentions needed by a disturbed patient" (Knoff 1960). In support of their position, Conolly and others demonstrated the feasibility of systematically abolishing use of mechanical constraints through humanistic treatment of patients.

In the modern era, Greenblatt reaffirmed the value of nonrestraint in his efforts to change the Boston Psychopathic Hospital from a custodial to a therapeutic care facility. He wrote eloquently about the "evils" that characterized locked seclusion in the 20th century: "over routinization of use, lack of knowledge concerning the patients' feelings, poor communication about these feelings among staff, and lack of adequate motivation for serving the basic psychological needs of the patient" (Greenblatt 1955, p. 84).

In opposition to these views, at the founding meeting of the Association of Medical Superintendents of the Insane in 1844, Isaac Ray defended the practice of restraint in the treatment of the mentally ill (Deutsch 1949). More than a century later, the Massachusetts Psychiatric Society supported this view, advising a Federal court that restraint is "a highly respected form of treatment, of great value to many severely disturbed patients, and essential to the preservation of order and safety during psychiatric emergencies" (Rogers v. Okin 1979).

One may agree with Greenblatt that the "evils" he described are a significant indictment of the use that has often been made of physical controls in long-term care facilities. Theoretically, at least, this is a type of setting in which conditions are relatively favorable for carefully assessing a patient's problems and establishing a therapeutic relationship. Within such settings, psychodynamic understanding and pharmacologic strategies can have a major therapeutic impact. Yet even here, violence associated with psychosis can erupt episodically and unpredictably, resulting in the continuing need for availability of physical controls.

The long-term treatment setting is far removed from the realities of the psychiatric emergency room or acute admissions ward, in which the absence of an established relationship with the patient and the overwhelming pathology of many patients creates an even greater need for the availability of physical controls. Some clinicians nonetheless cling to the belief that, even in psychiatric emergency settings, resort to physical restraint is evidence of staff members' failure to make effective use of other means to calm a patient. For example, in his review of psychiatric emergency services, Barton advanced the view that "dynamic understanding in experienced hands can render a potential combatant quickly cooperative" (Glasscote 1966, p. 30). A philosophy that one should try to "talk down" a violent patient is still common in psychodynamically oriented facilities. Similarly, a strong professional prejudice against the use of force provides support for the clinician who tries to contain or control violent behavior entirely through verbal or voluntary chemical means (Lion 1972; Lion and Pasternak 1973; Guirguis 1978).

The position that resorting to physical restraint indicates staff members' "failure" has had unfortunate consequences. If, as Barton suggests, violence and impulsive behavior are not so much the product of autistic process as a defensive response to "ambiguous, confusing, belligerent, or threatening treatment," staff members share responsibility for whatever violent outcomes occur (Glasscote 1966, p. 30). In effect, staff members bear not only the physical brunt of the violent behavior but the added burden of "countertransference responsibility." Views and prejudices such as these delay the preventive use of physical controls, reinforce denial of potential danger, and ultimately contribute to the underreporting of assaults on staff.

Wide disparities do, in fact, exist between recorded assaults on staff members and actual clinical experience. In one study of assaultive behavior in a State mental hospital, Lion et al. (1981) noted that 203 assaults on staff members had been officially recorded during the survey year, but that a detailed review of 3 months of daily nursing notes at the hospital suggested a true annual incidence of 1,108 assaults. In another survey of 101 psychiatrists, psychologists, and social workers employed in a wide variety of settings, Whitman et al. (1976) reported that 43 percent of the respondents had been personally threatened and 24 percent actually assaulted in the course of 1 calendar year. The authors concluded that "attacks on a therapist are infrequent but almost inevitable" (Whitman et al. 1976, p. 426). In a third survey, Madden et al. (1976) found that 41 percent of clinical psychiatrists had been assaulted by patients at least once in their careers. Data such as these, as well as the toll of physician and staff member injuries resulting from violence in mental health settings, seem to require reconsideration of the practical limitations and consequences of relying on passivity and nonrestraint in the treatment of the potentially violent patient.

Perhaps the most obvious and important reasons for the persistence of physical controls are the inability to predict or prevent episodic violence and the time required to diagnose and treat its underlying cause. Violent behavior in psychiatric patients must be viewed as symptomatic of underlying disorders, some of which are responsive to medication, others not. Following an acute outburst of violent behavior, most patients can be brought under temporary control through neuroleptic or sedative-hypnotic drugs, after the patient has been physically secured (see chapter 4). Treating the underlying cause of the violence requires time, however, during which the violence commonly recurs. Violent or disruptive behavior based on psychotic thought process or hallucinatory experience may require days to weeks of treatment before the psychotic process is resolved. With new neuroleptization techniques reducing the time delay to hours or days, the time required to reverse the underlying cause still provides a clear rationale for continued availability of physical controls. Even with disorders responsive to pharmacotherapy, medication has its limits. At some point, the risk to the patient of aggressive pharmacologic treatment must be weighed against the potential benefit of buying time with physical controls. For example, total chemical control is always available through narcosis, but seclusion and restraint provide the time needed for less drastic measures.

Not all violent behaviors arise from disorders that are responsive to simple pharmacologic approaches. Episodic violence based on psychodynamic issues, such as defense of self-esteem, cultural masculinity, or other character conflicts, is frequently seen in nonpsychotic patients. Where interpersonal psychotherapy is the treatment of choice, physical controls must remain available to contain extreme behavior during the time needed to establish a therapeutic alliance if such patients are to be treated in a hospital setting. Short of suppressing acute episodes, chemical controls have no well-proved value in preventing recurrent episodic violence arising out of primitive impulsive character pathology, yet the incidence of such disruptive behavior is quite high (Soloff 1979).

There are many special circumstances in which medication should not or cannot be given, despite the presence of violent or disruptive behavior. For example, a period of observation may be needed to follow a patient's sensorium (as in a suspected drug overdose) or to establish an accurate diagnosis, or when medical factors such as impaired hepatic, cardiac, or renal function complicate the clinical picture. Where neuroleptic medication is contraindicated, physical controls must remain an essential clinical option.

CLINICAL USE OF SECLUSION AND RESTRAINT

Theory and Practice

The proper clinical indications for seclusion and restraint have not changed greatly. Physical controls must be employed when violent or agitated behavior does not respond to verbal or chemical intervention. While the definition of what constitutes "violent" or "agitated" behavior varies widely with the social tolerance of each setting, all treatment facilities define a set of ultimately unacceptable behaviors that may require the imposition of physical controls because of ethical, legal, and clinical considerations.

Gutheil (1978) and Rosen and DiGiacomo (1978) have recently reviewed the therapeutic indications for use of seclusion and restraint. Containment of violent impulses and behavior, isolation from distressing external stimuli, and definition of disrupted ego boundaries are the therapeutic principles that underlie the use of physical controls as a legitimate form of treatment. Since these indications for treatment apply to target symptoms found in a wide range of psychiatric disorders, the use of seclusion and restraint is independent of diagnosis. Physical controls have been recommended for the acute management of patients who are violent, schizophrenic, manic, or brain-damaged; patients with intoxication, personality disorders, or episodic dyscontrol; and patients requesting restraint to assure control over disruptive or frightening impulses (Lion 1972; Bursten 1976).

Empirical Studies

Recent legal challenges to the use of seclusion and restraint have stimulated interest in systematic studies to define the parameters of this type of treatment, indications for its use, actual patterns of use, and patient characteristics. Five retrospective and two prospective studies provide a good overview of some current patterns of use.

The first recent effort to define patterns of seclusion was done by Wells (1972). In a retrospective survey of seclusion practice on a short-term unit of a university hospital, Wells found that 4 percent of the patients required seclusion. The unit had an average length of stay of 3 1/2 weeks and a mixed private and clinic population. The unit policy dictated that seclusion be reserved for "violent behavior unresponsive to verbal interaction, the presence of helpful others, or injection of tranquilizing drugs." Among 15 secluded patients, 7 carried a diagnosis of schizophrenia, while 3 were diagnosed as hypomanic. In contrast, only 23 percent of the patients in the overall ward population had received these diagnoses. Although events precipitating seclusion were not studied, the association of psychosis with violent behavior was strongly implicated as the critical factor in the Wells study.

Soloff (1978) examined the use of physical restraint on two acute psychiatric wards of a military teaching hospital. The clinical management of the wards was structured along the lines of a formal community milieu, with patient government and community meetings three times a week. Patients were drawn from an adjoining military base where basic training was conducted, and from active and retired military personnel and their dependents in the surrounding community. A chart review revealed that 3.6 percent of the patients had required restraint on at least one occasion. (This facility used leather restraints that confined patients to their own beds in preference to locked isolation rooms.)

Patients requiring physical controls in the Soloff study were predominantly psychotic (64.3 percent) and differed significantly from a randomly selected control group (18.3 percent psychotics). Precipitating factors leading to restraint were studied and classified as violent or nonviolent behaviors. The two leading causes of restraint were nonviolent behaviors, such as violation of community or administrative limits (elopement, screaming at night, etc.), which were cited in 35.1 percent of the episodes; and nonspecific rationales ("patient escalating," "unable to control behavior," "inappropriate," etc.), cited in 16.3 percent of the episodes. The third leading cause of restraint was physical attack or threat to staff, cited in 14.4 percent of the episodes. Overall, violent behavior of any type was a precipitating factor only 40.5 percent of the time.

As expected, Soloff found that the psychotic patient was most likely to provoke restraint, usually during the first half of the hospital stay before the milieu and medication began to work. Contrary to expectation, violence was not a predominant cause of restraint episodes for psychotic patients, despite the broad definition of violence that Soloff used in the study. Moreover, when days at risk for restraint were considered (controlling for length of stay), nonpsychotic patients were found to have a higher incidence of restraint than psychotic patients. Soloff concluded that the heavy use of involuntary restraints in nonviolent situations found in his study raised some serious ethical and legal questions (Soloff 1978).

Mattson and Sacks (1978) reviewed experience with seclusion on a 104-bed, private, voluntary psychiatric ward of a general hospital in

New York City. Secluded patients were compared to randomly selected, nonsecluded controls. During the study period, 7.2 percent of the patients required seclusion. The predominant diagnoses among secluded patients were schizophrenia (63 percent) and manic-depressive illness, in the manic phase (17 percent), both significantly disproportionate to representation of these diagnoses in the nonsecluded control group (38 percent and 4 percent, respectively). Behavior leading to seclusion was also studied. The primary cause of seclusion was "behavior disruptive to therapeutic environment," accounting for 34.4 percent of the episodes, and defined in nonviolent terms as behavior "not usually threatening to either the patient or others." Violent behavior ("assaultive to others") was the second most frequently cited precipitant, accounting for 25.5 percent of the seclusion episodes.

In a large university-affiliated municipal hospital in the same city, Plutchik et al. (1978) reported a much higher incidence of seclusion. Their chart review yielded an incidence of 26 percent of the patients requiring seclusion. Again, schizophrenic diagnoses differentiated secluded patients from nonsecluded controls and far outranked other disorders in incidence of seclusion. Among secluded patients, 64 percent were schizophrenic, compared to 45.8 percent in a nonsecluded control group. In a pattern similar to the studies previously cited, nonviolent behavior precipitated the largest number of seclusion episodes. "Agitated, uncontrolled behavior" was cited as a reason for seclusion in 21 percent of the episodes, followed by a violent behavior ("physical aggression toward other patients"), in 15.3 percent. Limit-setting activities of staff members accounted for over 60 percent of the precipitants cited in this study. These activities included seclusion for "loud, noisy behavior," "prevention of AWOL behavior," "inappropriate sexual behavior," "disruptive verbal abuse," "refusal to participate," "refusal to take medications," and even "waking other patients at night."

In the only study reported from a university hospital crisis intervention unit, Binder (1979) found that 44 percent of the admissions required seclusion. The unit was an 11-bed facility with an average stay of "just over 6 days" and an average of 30 admissions per month. Half of the patients admitted during the survey period were brought to the unit by police. Schizophrenics were disproportionately represented in the secluded sample (68 percent), compared to the overall admissions experience (56 percent). The most common precipitants were "agitation" (cited 16 times), "uncooperativeness" (14 times), "anger" (12 times), and a "history of violence" (9 times). Actual violent behaviors ("physically resistive," "striking out at staff or property," "throwing water or urine at staff") were cited only 14 times in total. Binder suggests that the unit's list of reasons for seclusion "offers some evidence that seclusion at times is used as a weapon of retaliation and control" (Binder 1979, p. 268).

In each of the five retrospective surveys, the investigators derived precipitating factors from recorded notes and approximated them to summary categories. Multiple precipitants were cited for single episodes of seclusion in some studies, there being no way to assess the precipitants' relevance to the actual clinical decision. The importance of time at risk in determining a relationship between diagnosis and incidence of seclusion was controlled only in the military study. Finally, the degree of physical restriction and social isolation involved in seclusion or restraint practices varied widely among settings. Seclusion in the Wells study meant restriction to "a locked 10-room portion of the floor." In the Mattson and Sacks study, seclusion referred to an individually locked isolation room, while Soloff found in his military study that restraint was preferred to seclusion and consisted of leather restraint that was "generally accomplished in the patient's own bed in an open small ward" (Soloff 1978).

Prospective studies offer a better means than record searches to determine the factors most responsible for clinical decisions to seclude a patient. In one such study, Schwab and Lahmeyer (1979) examined the use of seclusion on the psychiatric ward of a university teaching hospital, which advocated a long period of drug-free observation to establish correct diagnosis. Over a 6-month period, the charge nurse was requested to record the date, time, patient's name, nurse's name (by code number), and reason for initiating seclusion, as well as whether restraints were necessary and whether security officers were called. Following the pattern of the retrospective designs cited earlier, the charts of all patients were subsequently reviewed. The often multiple reasons for initiating seclusion were derived from the information contained in the charts.

Schwab and Lahmeyer found during their study period seclusion was used at some point during the hospitalization of 36.6 percent of the admissions. The reasons for seclusion most frequently cited in the charts were to remove the patient from the stimulation of the unit milieu (28 percent of all reasons given), agitation or acute excitement (17 percent), and poor impulse control (15 percent). Relatively few cases of seclusion cited threats to assault others (6 percent) and actual physical assaults (4 percent). No correlation was found between years of nursing experience in psychiatry and frequency of instituting seclusion or restraint, which suggests a high degree of consensus among staff members regarding when physical controls were indicated in this particular setting. Patients with manic-depressive illness in the manic phase had the highest incidence of seclusion. Schizophrenics were not secluded more often than controls.

Soloff and Turner (1981) also used a prospective design to clarify reasons for seclusion over an 8-month period on two inpatient units of a large university-operated psychiatric hospital with an extensive lower-class catchment area. At the time of seclusion, the nurse most responsible for initiating the decision completed a forced-choice questionnaire describing the patient and defining a presumptive diagnosis (Diagnostic and Statistical Manual II), mental status, and reason for seclusion. The list of behavioral precipitants for seclusion was derived from chart reviews of seclusion events reviewed in the study conducted in a military hospital (Soloff 1978). The list of precipitants was randomly arranged to avoid creating an apparent choice between groupings of violent and nonviolent patient behaviors. The responding nurse was directed to select the single item in the list that best described the patient behavior leading to seclusion. Incidence, frequency, duration, precipitating event, and type of seclusion (open door vs. locked door) were documented for 59 patients through 107 episodes of seclusion and compared to 159 nonsecluded controls on a wide variety of demographic, diagnostic, and legal variables.

Soloff and Turner found that 10.5 percent of all admissions during the study period required seclusion on at least one occasion. Contrary to all of the other previously cited studies, Soloff and Turner also found that a violent behavior ("physical attack on staff with physical contact") was responsible for the largest number of seclusion episodes (34.6 percent). A nonviolent behavior described as "patient escalating, unable to control behavior, or inappropriate behavior, etc. (as a preventive measure)" was the second most frequent precipitant, cited in 24.3 percent of the episodes. In this particular setting, it was also found that schizophrenic and manic-depressive patients were not disproportionately secluded when compared to controls. Similarly, seclusion rates for patients described as psychotic were not significantly different from those for nonpsychotics.

Comparisons among studies of seclusion are hampered by differences in method, patient population, and treatment philosophy within different treatment settings, but some general patterns in the literature can be discerned. Public facilities with unrestricted access and large clinic populations use seclusion more than private, voluntary facilities and military facilities. The highest seclusion rates are associated with programs that serve patients admitted to the hospital under emergency commitments and high concentrations of acute care patients. Philosophy of treatment was acknowledged as a reason for the high seclusion rate reported in a university teaching hospital that preferred to manage newly admitted patients without using pharmacotherapy until assessment was complete (Schwab and Lahmeyer 1979). Another high seclusion rate is reported on a research ward at the National Institute of Mental Health, where carefully selected schizophrenic patients were studied without the use of medication (Wadeson and Carpenter 1976).

Systematic bias in the use of seclusion that is not related to the therapeutic principles of the method suggests it is being used as a sanction. A majority of the studies previously reviewed in this chapter show that young schizophrenic and manic patients are at highest risk for seclusion but are also clinically most in need of external controls. Most research to date indicates that sex and race are not significantly related to incidence of seclusion. Soloff and Turner (1981), however, found a greater incidence of seclusion of black patients in their study. This finding was not compatible with treatment indications, since the black patients were not more prone to violent behavior than were white patients. The seclusion instead appeared to reflect failure of communication between the predominantly white medical staff members and the black patients. Flaherty and Meagher (1980) raised similar concerns in their recent study of the differential treatment of black and white male schizophrenics in an inpatient setting. They also found that seclusion and restraint were more likely to be used with black patients.

The study by Soloff and Turner (1981) is the only one to date that has examined the impact of chronicity and commitment on seclusion. Chronic patients, frequently admitted to the hospital in an advanced stage of decompensation, were found to be secluded more frequently for assaultiveness and loss of control than were first-admission patients. The researchers concluded that staff members' anticipation of problem behavior, based on prior experience with these patients, may have increased their readiness to use seclusion. With respect to commitment, Soloff and Turner found no disproportionate violence among committed patients as compared to voluntary patients, but they found a higher incidence of seclusion for those admitted under emergency commitment. The researchers' view of likely significance of this finding is that "patients admitted to the hospital under emergency commitment are usually presumed dangerous to self or others on admission. Although their behavior does not differ from secluded voluntary patients, the fact of commitment exerts a bias toward the use of physical controls. These patients may be secluded as much for their status as for their acts" (Soloff and Turner 1981.)

Duration of seclusion has been found to vary widely from setting to setting, from a mean of 4.1 hours reported by Plutchik et al. (1978) to a mean of 15.7 hours reported by Binder (1979). Seclusion times ranged from 10 minutes to 120 hours. It is noteworthy that staff members' estimates of average duration (2.1 hours) in the Plutchik et al. (1978) study and their estimates of ideal seclusion time (1 hour) were below the actual mean (4.1 hours). Soloff and Turner (1981) found that seclusion was employed for very specific therapeutic reasons but that duration of seclusion bore no statistical relationship to the reason. Amount of time spent in seclusion proved to be independent of demographic, legal status, mental status (psychotic vs. nonpsychotic), and diagnostic variables. Duration of seclusion and degree of restrictiveness did not change significantly with repeated seclusion episodes.

These findings of the independence of cause and duration of seclusion, as well as the wide range of seclusion times found across treatment settings, suggest a relationship to staff or unit factors that is independent of patient behavior. If an element of arbitrariness exists in the practice of seclusion, it may well be duration of seclusion rather than the precipitating event. The statistical bias toward greater use of physical controls with younger, schizophrenic, manic, chronic, and committed patients indicates a need for greater scrutiny of staff members' interactions with such patients. Soloff and Turner's (1981) finding that race is a relevant variable suggests that attribution of violent traits, cultural prejudice, fear, and distrust compromise the quality of interaction between patient and staff, ultimately contributing to a systematic bias in the use of seclusion.

Seclusion in Defense of the Milieu

It is quickly apparent that seclusion and restraint can be used both as treatment for impulsive, violent, and disruptive behavior and as a form of social control. Few would argue with the need to contain and control individual patient's destructive behavior and gross physical agitation. There is, however, heated debate over the use of seclusion and restraint as a form of social control on psychiatric units.

Defense of the therapeutic milieu and preservation of order are important staff responsibilities. Clinically and legally, the treatment team has a duty to each patient to provide a treatment atmosphere that is both safe and conducive to recovery and rehabilitation (Youngberg v. Romeo 1982). Each psychiatric ward or unit is a complex social system that overtly (or covertly) defines its own limits for tolerance of deviant, bizarre, or regressed behavior. As these limits are reached, staff members may resort to physical controls to restore social order and defend the therapeutic milieu from disruption. The Soloff and Turner review of the research literature on actual precipitants to seclusion has also shown that physical controls are often used to deal with unwanted patient behaviors that do not involve patient violence or aggression. Seclusion for reasons other than patient violence is a widespread and accepted practice.

When bizarre or deviant behavior—e.g., fecal smearing, public masturbation, uncontrolled screaming (especially at night)—stems from psychosis, physical controls can serve the needs of both the patient and the milieu. The issue of legitimacy of physical control is properly raised only when seclusion and restraint are imposed independently of the patient's clinical need, i.e., purely in defense of the social order. The issue is most frequently, though not exclusively, encountered in relation to "limit testing" on the ward by nonpsychotic character-disordered patients. When seclusion is used to deal with problems such as swearing at staff and refusal to participate, the setting of limits becomes an administrative sanction. At this point, legal analogies between seclusion in mental hospitals and administrative isolation in prison gain validity.

How may one deal with the limit-testing behaviors characteristic of impulsive character-disordered personalities? Seclusion and restraint can be legitimate measures of social control for such individuals when a prior agreement or "behavioral contract" exists between the patient and the staff members as part of a voluntary treatment plan. This agreement can define mutually acceptable ways in which seclusion and other forms of behavior modification can be used as a treatment modality in response to specified target behaviors.

In the absence of such informed consent on the part of the patient, the use of seclusion for purely social control is symptomatic of a mismatch between the patient and the treatment milieu. Where such a mismatch exists for a psychotic patient, a more tolerant treatment milieu should be found. Where it exists for the limit-testing patient with an impulsive character disorder, "therapeutic discharge" or transfer to a less intense treatment setting are recommended (Friedman 1969). Such alternatives are always preferable to the use of seclusion or restraint as punitive sanctions.

PROCEDURES

The psychiatric literature is strangely silent regarding the actual techniques of properly applying seclusion and restraint. Psychiatric residents are rarely prepared for managing violent or disruptive patients, and nurses, attendants, and security staff fare little better in their training. The theory and practice of seclusion and restraint must be effectively taught to front-line mental health personnel.

To meet this need, experienced persons have developed workshops to teach physical methods of nonaggressive confrontation and noninjurious control (Samuels and Moriarity 1981). While this chapter cannot include a detailed exposition of techniques, several general principles governing the use of physical controls are worthy of review.

1. Each unit should establish clear guidelines and procedures for the use of seclusion and restaint (see chapter 11 of this volume). Typically, a member of the nursing staff initiates the process by reporting behavior that exceeds accepted limits for the unit. The head nurse or charge nurse assumes responsibility for deciding that physical controls are or are not needed and directs implementation of the procedure. Whenever possible, the staff members discuss a plan of action prior to actual confrontation with the patient. This discussion should include a review of the options that will be offered to the patient, a clear definition of the goals of the intervention (e.g., medication, isolation, locked seclusion, or restraint), and direction regarding the physical methods to be employed.
2. A "show of force" must be available from the beginning of any confrontation with patients. Even if force is not ultimately employed, it is important for patients to perceive clearly that there is sufficient force to control their behavior and achieve the staff members' goals. Sufficient personnel must be present to overwhelm the patient safely, with minimum risk to all.
3. The patient should be given few and clear behavioral options without undue verbal threat or provocation. When control of behavior is the predetermined goal of the confrontation, psychodynamic negotiation is superfluous and defeats the purpose of setting limits. Staff should make every effort to allow the patient a safe retreat into control without provoking a violent defense of self-esteem. The time allotted for the patient's decision should be brief—seconds rather than minutes.
4. Physical force commences at a given signal from the directing

clinician. Through staff members' use of noninjurious tech-niques, the patient is physically controlled, brought to the ground, restrained, medicated, and moved to the seclusion room. The patient's release from the physical hold (in the case of locked seclusion) follows a prearranged pattern.

5. Whenever possible, a noninvolved monitor should observe the procedure and debrief participants on technique and execution following the event.

6. The use of noninjurious technique is critical from both a prac-tical and clinical perspective. The use of force to contain violent behavior early in a hospital course must not be so traumatic that it precludes a therapeutic alliance with the patient once the issue of violence is resolved. Restraint without undue pain or injury preserves hope for a therapeutic alliance.

7. Clearly prescribed nursing procedures should govern the mainte-nance of seclusion and restraint. Patients must be kept under close observation, ideally under visual inspection, at all times or, as a minimum, they should be visually inspected every 15 minutes. The patient must be examined by an attending psychiatrist at least daily for a reveiw of the continuing indications for this type of treatment. Release from physical control should follow a prede-termined pattern. As behavioral goals are achieved—e.g., dimin-ished psychotic thinking, improved behavioral controls—the pa-tient should be "weaned" from seclusion by graded steps. If the patient fails to maintain behavioral controls at a particular step in the weaning process—e.g., when the door to the seclusion room is left open or when the patient is allowed to begin using the toilet or shower outside the seclusion room—restriction should be re-sumed until patient improvement is sustained.

8. Reentry into the patient population from seclusion should be a slow and measured process, with each step contingent on patient behavior.

9. The meaning of the seclusion/restraint experience for a partic-ular patient should be openly discussed among staff members and between staff members and the patient when physical con-trols are terminated.

RISKS OF SECLUSION AND RESTRAINT

A great deal has been written on the complex countertransference issues evoked in staff members by violent confrontations with patients.

The impact of physical controls on staff members' attitudes, ward atmosphere, and the therapeutic efficacy of the milieu as a whole has received less attention. Greenblatt (1955) noted that "routinization" of seclusion as a means of behavioral control evokes a predictable host of "evils," primarily the progressive dehumanization of patients subjected to repeated or prolonged restraint or seclusion. As a defense against fear and anger, staff members focus on the techniques of managing the secluded patient rather than on the factors requiring the continued use of physical controls. Staff members can become so entrenched in the automatic processes of management that they lose meaningful interchange with the patient. Seclusion then becomes a means of avoiding contact with the patient rather than an intensive care treatment. One must always suspect this "routinization" when duration of seclusion exceeds several days despite aggressive pharmacologic treatment.

The use of seclusion and restraint exacts a psychological toll on the patient as well. The possible adverse effects and risks include the patient's rage, bitterness, and fear—often persisting up to a year following the event (Wadeson and Carpenter 1976). In some cases, seclusion has been found to foster hallucinations in patients. The stigma of seclusion can follow the patient through future admissions in which staff's readiness to use physical controls is conditioned by earlier experience. The use of seclusion can become progressively easier with each repetition, resulting in a progressive drift toward intolerant and authoritarian management of patients.

The more feared physical risks of seclusion and restraint are typically less significant than the psychological impact. Repeated confrontation in the seclusion room to administer medication, feed, and toilet the patient exposes staff (and patient) to physical injury. The use of leather restraints always raises the possibility of dislocated joints, compromised circulation, and pressure sores on the skin. Hyperthermia is a rare but well-described risk of cold wet pack restraints, especially in conjunction with phenothiazine medication (Greenland and Southwick 1978). The danger of missing important changes in the patient's medical condition and the potential for self-inflicted injury are additional risks of seclusion. Proper management techniques, including close observation and careful choice of physical method, can reduce these risks.

The two most common methods of physical control are locked seclusion and leather restraints. Each has its own advantages and disadvantages. Advocates of the seclusion room cite the greater isolation from overwhelming stimuli, the relative physical freedom of movement, and preservation of personal dignity. Patients are able to feed, toilet, and even sponge bathe themselves in this setting. The patient's greater physical freedom, however, becomes the chief liability of seclusion when the patient is impulsively violent toward self or others. The author's experience shows that violent patients in seclusion are likely to experience neglect as staff members seek to minimize injury by reducing the number of entries to the seclusion room and completing each entry procedure as quickly as possible. Seclusion can delay staff response to patients who are impulsively self-destructive (e.g., head banging). Leather restraints may be used with or without seclusion. Four-point leather restraints may be used in the patient's own bed when isolation from external stimuli is not desired. At the cost of personal dignity and considerable additional nursing effort (e.g., to bathe, toilet, and feed), leather restraints allow easy access to the patient and can assist in establishing interpersonal rapport. Staff can be less fearful of contact with the patient and more willing (and able) to meet the patient's needs. Medication can be administered to the patient in restraints at little risk to staff. The safe management of leather restraints requires that staff be familiar with the physical risks of the method and the techniques for "weaning" the patient without undue exposure to injury.

The choice of method of physical control should depend upon the patient's individual needs. Unfortunately, allowable methods are often legislated rather than prescribed.

CONCLUSION

Seclusion and restraint are valuable forms of treatment for acutely agitated, violent, or disruptive patients. To treat these patients safely and effectively, psychiatrists must overcome their professional disdain for physical controls, recognize and accept the limitations of psychodynamic understanding and pharmacologic management, and develop a pragmatic balance of treatment approaches to the violent patient. In the current era of psychological and pharmacologic management, use of physical controls can and should be limited primarily to the acute treatment of violent patients.

REFERENCES

Binder, R.L. The use of seclusion on an inpatient crisis intervention unit. Hospital & Community Psychiatry 30(4):266–269, 1979.

Burns, R.S., and Lerner, S.E. Causes of PCP related deaths. Clinical Toxicology 12(4):463–481, 1978.

Bursten, B. Using mechanical restraints on acutely disturbed psychiatric patients. Hospital & Community Psychiatry 26(11):757–759, 1976.

Crowder, J.E., and Klatte, E.W. Involuntary admissions to general hospitals: Legal status is not the issue. Hospital & Community Psychiatry 31(5):325–327, 1980.

Deutsch, A. The Mentally Ill in America. 2nd Ed. New York: Columbia University Press, 1949.

Edelman, S.E. Managing the violent patient in a community mental health center. Hospital & Community Psychiatry 29(7):460–462, 1978.

Flaherty, J.A., and Meagher, R. Measuring racial bias in inpatient treatment. American Journal of Psychiatry 137(6):679–682, 1980.

Friedman, H.J. Some problems of inpatient management with borderline patients. American Journal of Psychiatry 126(3):299–304, 1969.

Glasscote, R. The Psychiatric Emergency: A Study of Patterns of Service. Washington, D.C.: American Psychiatric Association and National Association for Mental Health, 1966.

Greenblatt, M.; York, R.; and Brown, E. From Custodial to Therapeutic Patient Care in Mental Hospitals. New York: Russell Sage Foundation, 1955.

Greenland, P., and Southwick, W.H. Hyperthermia associated with chlorpromazine and full sheet restraint. American Journal of Psychiatry 135(10):1234–1235, 1978.

Guirguis, E.F. Management of disturbed patients: An alternative to the use of mechanical restraints. Journal of Clinical Psychiatry 39(4):295–303, 1978.

Guthiel, T.G. Observations on the theoretical basis for seclusion of the psychiatric inpatient. American Journal of Psychiatry 135(3):325–328, 1978.

Knoff, W.F. Modern treatment of the "insane." A historical view of nonrestraint. New York State Journal of Medicine 60(14):2236–2243, 1960.

Leeman, C.P. Involuntary admissions to general hospitals: Progress or threat? Hospital & Community Psychiatry 31(5):315–318, 1980.

Lion, J.R. Evaluation and Management of the Violent Patient, Springfield, Ill.: Charles C. Thomas, 1972.

Lion, J.R., and Pasternak, S.A. Countertransference reactions to violent patients. American Journal of Psychiatry 130(2):207–210, 1973.

Lion, J.R.; Snyder, W.; and Merrill, G.L. Under-reporting of assaults in a state hospital. Hospital & Community Psychiatry 32(7):497–498, 1981.

Madden, D.J.; Lion, J.R.; and Penna, M.W. Assault on psychiatrists by patients. American Journal of Psychiatry 133(4):422–425, 1976.

Mattson, M.R., and Sacks, M.H. Seclusion: Uses and complications. American Journal of Psychiatry 13(10): 1210–1213, 1978.

National Institute on Drug Abuse. Diagnosis and treatment of phencyclidine (PCP) toxicity. In: Drug Abuse Clinical Notes. Washington, D.C.: U.S. Supt. of Docs., U.S. Govt. Print. Off., 1979.

Plutchik, R.; Karasu, T.B.; Conte, H.R.; Siegel, B.; and Jerrett, I. Toward a rationale for the seclusion process. Journal of Nervous and Mental Disease 166(8):571–579, 1978.

Rogers v. Okin, 478 F. Supp. 1342 (D. Mass. 1979). Brief of the Massachusetts Psychiatric Society as Amicus Curiae, 1976.

Rosen, H., and DiGiacomo, J.N. The role of physical restraint in the treatment of psychiatric illness. Journal of Clinical Psychiatry 39(3):228–233, March 1978.

Samuels, M., and Moriarty, P. One Step Ahead Series, 1981 (4 training films). Cricon (Crisis Control) MTI, 3710 Commercial Street, North Brook, IL 60062. Cricon workshop, 200 McAlister Drive, Pittsburgh, PA 15235.

Schwab. P.J., and Lahmeyer, C.B. The uses of seclusion on a general hospital psychiatric unit. Journal of Clinical Psychiatry 40(5):228–231, 1979.

Soloff, P.H. Behavioral precipitants of restraint in the modern milieu. Comprehensive Psychiatry 19(2):179–184, 1978.

Soloff, P.H. Physical restraint and the non-psychotic patient: Clinical and legal perspectives. Journal of Clinical Psychiatry 40(7):302–305, 1979.

Soloff, P.H., and Turner, S.M. Patterns of seclusion: A prospective study. Journal of Nervous and Mental Disease 169(1):37–44, 1981.

Wadeson, H., and Carpenter, W.T. Impact of the seclusion room experience. Journal of Nervous and Mental Disease 163(5):318–328, 1976.

Wells, D. The use of seclusion on a university hospital psychiatric floor. Archives of General Psychiatry 26(5):410–414, 1972.

Whitman, R.M.; Armao, B.B.; and Dent, O.B. Assault on the therapist. American Journal of Psychiatry 133(4):426–431, 1976.

Youngberg v. Romeo, 457 U.S. 307 (1982).

7

Special Diagnostic and Treatment Issues Concerning Violent Juveniles

Dorothy Otnow Lewis, M.D.

The psychiatrist who agrees to evaluate a violent delinquent child or adolescent has a special responsibility, greater than that of the child guidance clinic psychiatrist or of the private practitioner. The evaluation usually is conducted at the request of a judge, an attorney, or the administrator of a detention or correctional facility. The report may be used to establish competence to stand trial, to assign responsibility for given acts, or to recommend disposition of the case, and will often weigh heavily in determining whether a child is sent home, placed in a treatment setting, or incarcerated. Even after being informed of the purpose of the evaluation, the youngster may have little understanding of its consequences. Therefore, psychiatrists should approach their task with caution and humility based on their own understanding of the gravity of the task. The customary brief psychiatric interview with delinquent youngsters in court clinic settings is rarely, if ever, an adequate assessment of the psychiatric status of violent young offenders.

What is known about juvenile offenders as a group that can guide evaluation and treatment plans? Multiple diverse factors usually influence violent behaviors. Social, familial, medical, cognitive, and psychiatric factors often combine to contribute to a particular act of violence.

It takes little skill or sophistication to recognize the social deprivation experienced by most delinquents. Unfortunately, adverse social conditions are often so overwhelmingly obvious that they tend to obscure subtler, less apparent factors affecting delinquent behavior. The inexperienced evaluator easily assumes that a lack of material goods motivates robbery and that any ensuing violence is attributable to "tough" subcultural values. The diagnostician must therefore be mindful that most individuals raised in the same sociocultural environment do not behave violently; it is important to look beyond purely sociological factors. Moreover, some of the psychobiological vulnerabilities the psychiatrist is likely to encounter are concomitants of social deprivation. In brief, a thorough evaluation will often reveal a history of perinatal insult, severe central nervous system injury, past physical abuse, a psychotic parent, or psychotic and organic symptomatology. Any or all of these factors may contribute to violence.

FAMILY HISTORY

It has long been recognized that delinquents come from chaotic family situations, and delinquency has often been associated with broken homes. According to Offord and his colleagues (1978), it is not so much the breakup of the home as the preceding family discord that fosters delinquency.

In the past, primarily psychodynamic explanations were used to explain the association of parental psychopathology and delinquency in their children. The concept of superego lacunae (i.e., the parents' communicating their own unconscious antisocial impulses to their children, who then act them out), formulated by Johnson and Szurek (1952), was invoked to explain children's antisocial behaviors. Others (West and Farrington 1973; Glueck and Glueck 1950) attributed delinquent behaviors to parents' failure to supervise and discipline their children properly.

More recent studies have attempted to ascertain the type of parental psychopathology in the families of delinquents that is associated with marital discord, broken homes, and inability to supervise and discipline adequately. Recent evidence suggests that the parents of delinquents are significantly more likely than parents of nondelinquents to have been psychiatrically hospitalized (Lewis et al. 1976; Lewis and Balla 1976). Similarly, delinquency has been reported to be more prevalent in children of schizophrenic parents than in these of nonschizophrenics of the same socioeconomic status (Lewis and Shanok 1978). Family studies of hyperkinetic children also suggest familial and environmental factors associated with antisocial behavior (Cantwell 1978). Others have reported learning and behavior problems in the fathers of especially antisocial children (Mendelson et al. 1971).

What relevance do these studies have to diagnostic evaluation of violent delinquents? Psychiatrists are now beginning to appreciate the hereditary predisposition to certain kinds of psychiatric disorders. Family members can furnish valuable clues to the understanding of certain aberrant childhood behaviors. Schizophrenia (Heston 1966, 1977; Rosenthal et al. 1968), manic-depressive illness (Rosenthal 1971; Winokur et al. 1969), and even minimal brain dysfunction (Cantwell 1978) are now thought to be influenced in part by hereditary factors. The discovery that a child has a paranoid schizophrenic parent may shed light on the physiological underpinnings of the child's inordinately suspicious, sometimes violent and bizarre behaviors. Similarly, the knowledge that an adolescent who is periodically out of control, destructive, and verbally and physically abusive has a manic-depressive parent should encourage the psychiatrist to explore the possibility that such a disorder contributes to the behavior that brought the child to the attention of the police. Most important, knowledge of heritable psychiatric disorders in family members has implications for possible effective treatment for the child. Behaviors previously dismissed by the psychiatrist as simply characterologic may, with the benefit of an accurate family history, be recognized as manifestations of other kinds of effectively treatable psychopathology.

In child guidance clinics and juvenile courts, parents are frequently interviewed by probation officers; only the child is seen by a psychiatrist. As already noted, many parents of children who come to juvenile court suffer from serious psychopathology. In addition to furnishing information regarding other relatives, interviews with parents permit skilled clinicians to assess parents' medical and psychiatric status. It is, therefore, advisable for the individual who interviews the parents to have expertise in psychiatric interviewing and diagnostic evaluation. Otherwise, there is the real danger that the seriously disturbed parent who, for example, has been incarcerated will be dismissed as merely sociopathic, or that the extremely depressed parent who frequently drinks to excess will be dismissed as simply alcoholic. On the other hand, recognizing the nature of parental psychopathology has implications not only for understanding and treating the child but also for arranging effective treatment for the parent. Such treatment enables the parent to function more appropriately and provide a supportive environment for the child. Improving parental functioning can be as important to the rehabilitation of a delinquent child as any direct service to the child.

VIOLENT DELINQUENCY
AND HISTORY OF PHYSICAL ABUSE

The common assumption that violence begets violence has recently been documented with violent juvenile offenders (Lewis et al. 1979b). In a study of 97 incarcerated male juveniles over 75 percent of the more violent boys in the group had experienced severe physical abuse, usually at the hands of parents or parent surrogates. For example, one boy was thrown downstairs by his father, another was chained and burned, another had all of his fingers broken by a psychotic mother, and yet another had a leg broken by a mother wielding a broomstick.

For many reasons, it is essential to the understanding of violent behaviors to know whether the violent child has been physically abused. Children tend to imitate behaviors they have witnessed or experienced. Whether called "modeling" or "identification with the aggressor," there are behavioral manifestations of a child's having grown up in an atmosphere of violence. Knowledge that family members have treated a child brutally will also often help to explain the child's suspiciousness of, indeed, rage toward, other adults. Many violent delinquent youngsters evaluated by the author have actually been protective of their abusing parents; they seem to displace their rage at having been mistreated onto others in their environment, children and adults alike. Finally, physical abuse often leads to injury to the central nervous system and the kinds of problems with impulse control characteristic of brain-damaged individuals. For example, the youngster previously described as having been thrown down a flight of steps by his father had a seizure immediately after the injury. He was later found to suffer from a variety of learning and behavioral problems often associated with brain damage.

To treat these patients effectively, both psychodynamically and medically, it is vital to obtain a history of any physical abuse that has occurred. How does one obtain such a history without thoroughly alienating the child or the parents? The author has found that an empathic stance with the parents is most likely to elicit honest information. Therefore, the inquiry regarding abuse usually begins with a statement such as, "I know Johnny has really been a handful to raise. When he's really acting up, have you ever lost your cool?" The parents are then asked, "What did you do? Did you ever go further than you meant to? What happened?" When interviewing a mother, the author will ask such questions as, "How about Johnny's father? Does he have a temper? Have you ever had to get him to stop hitting Johnny?"

· Children are usually reluctant to "tell on" a parent, no matter how abusive the parent has been. Questions regarding abuse are therefore phrased in terms of how a parent has responded when the child has misbehaved. One might ask, "When you do something your mom (dad) doesn't like, does she (he) ever really let you have it? What does she (he) do?" If the response is positive, the evaluator must try to learn just how seriously a child has been injured at the hands of the parents: "Were you ever knocked out?" "Did you ever have to go to a doctor or to the emergency room when your dad hit you?" The actual medical records of violent children, documenting multiple apparent accidents and injuries, suggest that a parent-inflicted injury is often reported as a fall out of bed or a bicycle accident. In the course of a psychiatric evaluation, delinquent children will sometimes admit that they lied to emergency room doctors about the true cause of their injuries.

MEDICAL HISTORY OF VIOLENT DELINQUENTS

Many delinquent children, particularly those who have committed numerous and serious antisocial acts, have extremely poor medical histories. Medical problems of violent juveniles are often characteristic of their entire lives, beginning with perinatal problems and continuing throughout childhood (Lewis and Shanok 1979; Lewis et al. 1979a). Head and face injuries and child abuse are particularly common among violent delinquents. The multiplicity of biopsychosocial factors affecting the lives of delinquent children often makes it impossible to determine the contribution of particular medical events. Sometimes, however, it is possible to document the onset of deviant behaviors following particular trauma to the central nervous system. For example, one boy who had remained out of trouble with the law became extremely violent and paranoid, actually raping and assaulting several women following a car accident in which he sustained a severe head injury. Another boy became assaultive and unmanageable following an episode of encephalitis when he was 5 years old. Yet another youngster, a teenage girl who had been considered her "mother's angel," became involved in a multiplicity of antisocial acts and began to experience episodes of violent behaviors that she could not remember; this behavior followed an episode of meningitis.

All these children came from families with many problems. Prior to central nervous system trauma, they had coped adequately with their environments. Following the described trauma, the first child became overtly psychotic and violent, the second became hyperactive and destructive, and the third developed episodic violence with no memory about the violent acts. In each case, discovery of the medical factors preceding the antisocial behaviors led to further diagnostic assessments and eventually to trials of specific therapeutic interventions. The child who had suffered encephalitis at age 5 and who had continued to be unmanageable throughout childhood was found to respond well to low-dosage amphetamine and barbiturate medication. He could function well in a therapeutic setting where, without medication, he had previously been unwelcome. The teenage girl, after it was found that she had an epileptiform electroencephalogram, responded well to Dilantin and, on antiepileptic medication, suffered no further violent episodes. The paranoid youngster who raped and assaulted women functioned well in an open setting at a correctional school where he was provided with weekly psychotherapy and minimal dosages of phenothiazine medication.

So-called "routine" physical examinations performed in detention or correctional settings cannot be assumed to reveal the kinds of medical problems that have been discussed. Such physical examinations are usually directed toward finding current disorders that might affect participation in athletic programs or infectious diseases that might be transmitted. Little attention is given to perinatal factors or previous accidents, injuries, or illnesses that might have longstanding effects on behavior and functioning. In spite of a child's having had a recent physical examination resulting in a clean bill of health, it is wise for psychiatrists to conduct evaluations as though they were the only ones responsible for determining the youngster's past and present state of health.

Since perinatal complications are so frequently found in the histories of violent delinquents, it is appropriate to ask children (and, of course, their parents, when available) what they know about their births. Many youngsters have been told by their parents how small they were or how long they had to stay in the hospital. Several court-involved youngsters have reported being told that their mothers had almost died at birth, information subsequently confirmed by hospital records.

In addition to inquiring about accidents and injuries, the evaluator must obtain a history of consciousness loss, dizziness, headaches, and the effect of alcohol and drugs. The author has found that questions relating to altered states of consciousness must be asked in several different ways. For example, a youngster who denies ever having been unconscious may readily describe blackouts or falling episodes. One individual with obvious signs of organic dysfunction denied ever having been knocked unconscious or having suffered a head injury or illness of the central nervous system. Toward the end of the interview, however, she voluntarily reported an incident at age 15 when she had received a near-fatal electric shock from a faulty floor lamp, had fallen to the floor, and had been bedridden for 6 months afterward. She simply had never associated this event with being knocked unconscious. One will ask, "Have you ever been unconscious? How about blackouts? Have you ever fainted? Ever fallen out?" One child's "blackout" is another child's "falling out."

Certain medical questions specifically relevant to violent behaviors must always be asked of violent juveniles. Do the children always remember the acts of which they are accused? Are their memories of the acts clouded or clear? Have they ever been accused of doing things or simply been told they did something they do not remember? Can they stop fighting once they have started? Can they tell in advance when they're going to get into a fight? How do they feel after the violent act—sleepy, sick, or headachey? Was the act precipitated by any particular event or did it occur spontaneously? Does alcohol increase the violence? Do they just feel mellow from alcohol? Were they taking any other drugs when the violence occurred? What drugs make them feel good?

MEDICAL HISTORY AND MENTAL STATUS EVALUATION

Often the social and psychodynamic factors associated with a youngster's violence are so flamboyantly obvious that the evaluator may be tempted to dispense with parts of the formal mental status examination. This may result in failure to identify other equally important, if less evident, factors such as hallucinations, delusions, and impaired intellectual or cognitive functioning that contribute to a child's behavior. Appearances are often deceiving. If a child appears socially appropriate during ordinary conversation, there is still the possibility that the child may hallucinate, suffer from perceptual problems, or not be of normal intelligence.

Children in conflict with the law, particularly those accused of violent acts, are often wary of psychiatrists. Most would rather be considered "bad" than "crazy" and are reticent to reveal material that might be construed as "crazy." One of the least threatening ways to gain access to information regarding such issues as hallucinations is to incorporate parts of the mental status evaluations into the medical history. For example, after discussing school, family, sports, and, of course, the problems that brought the youngster to court, the evaluator can say, "Now I'd like to ask you some medical questions." The evaluator then asks about birth, development, accidents, illnesses, and some of the symptoms already mentioned, and then inquires, "How are your eyes? Do you wear glasses?" In the same matter-of-fact tone, the questions are asked, "Do your eyes ever play tricks on you? Do things ever look very far away or really up-close? Have you ever had the experience of thinking you saw something or someone and you were mistaken? What was that like?" Similarly, the evaluator will ask about earaches, how they were treated, etc., and then, "Have your ears ever played tricks on you? Have you ever thought someone said something to you or told you to do something and you were wrong? What was that like?" Similar techniques can be used to inquire about olfactory, gustatory, and tactile hallucinations.

Many paranoid children will recount episodes in which they attacked people because they thought someone had called them an obscenity (or worse, called their mother a bad name). One such incident was actually observed on a secure unit for violent children. A small boy leaving an interview room turned suddenly and, without apparent cause, punched another youngster standing in the hall. When asked by staff members why he had done this, the boy responded in anger, "He just called me a m____ !" Not a word had been said to or about the assaultive child.

Assessing paranoid thinking is among the most difficult tasks that confront the psychiatrist evaluating delinquent children. The child's wariness of the interviewer is to be expected in light of the possible consequences of the interview. It is, however, a mistake for the interviewer to assume that carrying dangerous weapons or being ready at all times to be attacked is a normal concomitant of lower socioeconomic class existence. A child can be from a tough part of town and still not feel the need to carry a knife, crowbar, or loaded gun. The author's clinical work with violent juveniles has demonstrated the usefulness of asking in detail about feelings of endangerment or persecution. It is a fallacy to dismiss excessive suspiciousness as culturally adaptive. The examiner must understand that many violent acts by juveniles occur as a result of paranoid misperceptions and misunderstandings.

For many delinquents, the most threatening part of the mental status evaluation is not assessing hallucinations, delusions, or paranoia, but rather testing the child's ability to work with numbers and remember digits forward and backward. These aspects of the mental status examination are probably threatening both because of their association with schoolwork and because of their tendency to reveal impairments of which the child is vaguely aware.

Violent delinquents tend to be especially poor at such tasks. In fact, when samples of more and less violent delinquents were compared (Lewis et al. 1979b), 69.5 percent of the more violent youngsters could not subtract serial 7's, compared with 33.3 percent of the less violent group. Similarly, 60.8 percent of the more violent group could not recall four digits backward, compared with 13.3 percent of the less violent group. Difficulties with these kinds of tasks, while not diagnostic of any particular disorders, may suggest to the clinician possible short-term memory deficits, impulse disorders, attentional disorders, and learning disabilities (National Institute for Juvenile Delinquency Prevention 1976), all of which can then be explored further in psychological, education, and neurological assessments.

Clearly, the psychiatrist who fails to perform a detailed evaluation of mental status will miss discovering a variety of potentially treatable disorders. Many of these disorders, if left untreated, will contribute to a delinquent child's social maladaptation.

PSYCHOLOGICAL TESTING

It is erroneous to assume that even the most meticulous and sophisticated psychiatric assessment can reveal all of the personality and cognitive functioning problems addressed by psychological testing. In fact, psychotic thought processes and intellectual retardation, aspects of functioning that might be expected to be most easily recognized in a psychiatric interview, are often far from obvious and among the most difficult aspects of functioning to assess unless the psychosis or retardation is flamboyant. The wary, paranoid youngster may reveal thinking disorders on a Rorschach protocol which had been concealed easily during psychiatric interviews. Even extremely intellectually limited youngsters are often able to conduct themselves in socially appropriate ways, giving the psychiatric interviewer little indication that serious intellectual deficits, elucidated through testing, do exist. Of course, psychological testing can often reveal perceptual motor disturbances rarely discovered during psychiatric interviews.

The choice of psychological tests, their administration, and the interpretation of results are beyond the scope of this chapter. Some investigators and clinicians have found the Halstead-Reitan battery of tests to be particularly useful in the diagnosis of delinquent children. Although sophisticated instruments of this kind are most useful, much can also be learned from more commonly employed instruments such as the Wechsler Intelligence Scale for Children (WISC) and the Rorschach test. The WISC is useful not only for assessing intelligence but also for assessing many different aspects of thinking, behavior, perception, and attention. In addition to providing clues to perceptual problems and cognitive difficulties, the WISC is a valuable tool for documenting fluctuating states of attention.

Responses on the Rorschach test, in addition to contributing to the understanding of psychodynamic issues, provide very useful indicators of a child's internal controls and ability to organize thoughts coherently. Findings of perseveration, bizarre percepts, impulsivity, or marked disorganization on the Rorschach test often suggest central nervous system dysfunction or latent psychosis that may have previously been overlooked.

Psychological testing is most useful when it reveals hitherto overlooked disorders. If a child's performance during psychological testing fails to reveal any evidence of emotional or cognitive disturbance, the psychologist should report this finding but also make it clear that psychological test results have only limited value. Testing is not a substitute for complete psychiatric, neurological, educational, and social evaluations.

The results of psychological tests, like the results of individual psychiatric interviews, reveal the way in which a child is functioning at a given time. Many delinquent youngsters who at the time of psychological or psychiatric evaluation appeared well functioning later became obviously psychotic.

EDUCATIONAL ASSESSMENTS

It is well established that many delinquent children have learning disabilities (Berman and Siegal 1976; Cantwell 1978; Poremba 1975). The author's work indicates that especially violent delinquents have even more serious learning disorders than do less violent delinquents (Lewis et al. 1979b).

Educators generally use the term "learning disabilities" to connote specific learning dysfunctions that exist in the absence of detectable psychiatric or neurological problems. In the case of seriously delinquent children, however, this definition may be too restricted. For example, certain violent delinquents suffer from various neuropsychiatric disorders, such as attention deficit disorders, periodic psychotic states, and epilepsy. In such cases, medical as well as educational interventions are indicated. Such youth often, in addition, have specific learning disabilities. Some psychotic or epileptic rapists or murderers, treated appropriately with psychopharmacologic and psychodynamic therapies, have lost their psychotic or epileptic symptoms, and were able to control their aggressiveness, but still were left with specific learning disorders, such as sequencing problems and visual and auditory discrimination problems. These specific learning disorders require additional specialized educational help. Neither the treatment of psychosis and epilepsy nor the treatment of learning disabilities alone will be effective in such multiply handicapped delinquent children. Because many seriously delinquent children have learning disabilities in addition to their other neuropsychiatric disorders, a reassessment of the very definition of "learning disabilities" is required. In a recent study comparing the neuropsychiatric status of delinquents who experienced severe reading disability with that of delinquents with less severe reading disability (Lewis et al. 1980), the two groups differed more psychiatrically than neurologically; that is, the delinquents with greater reading impairment had significantly more psychotic symptoms than the better readers. Neurological symptoms did not differentiate the poorer readers from the better readers; both had a similarly high prevalence of abnormal neurological signs and symptoms. This finding is important when seeking the possible etiology of reading disorders in some delinquents. At times, confused, illogical thought processes caused by a psychotic disorder may contribute to a delinquent youngster's learning difficulties.

NEUROLOGICAL EVALUATION

Obvious current neurological deficits, such as grand mal epilepsy or hemiparesis, are rarely seen in the delinquent population (although a history of grand mal seizures in infancy or early childhood is not uncommon). The reason seems to be that seriously neurologically impaired antisocial children, like seriously psychotic youngsters, are likely to be recognized as "sick" and channeled to therapeutic facilities during early childhood. Subtle neurological impairment, on the other hand, is found when assessing seriously delinquent, violent youngsters. In a recent study comparing more and less violent delinquent boys, both major neurological impairment (such as abnormal encephalogram, history of seizures, positive Babinski sign) and minor neurological impairment (such as choreiform movements and poor coordination) were significantly more prevalent in the more violent sample than in the less violent sample (Lewis et al. 1979b).

The neurological history is often more revealing than the actual examination of coordination and reflexes. As in the psychiatric assessment, special attention must be paid to a history of central nervous system trauma and questions must be asked regarding altered states of consciousness, distorted perceptions, and sudden subjective feelings of anxiety or fear.

In the case of violent delinquents, the evaluator should ask questions about precipitants of violence, memory for violent and nonviolent behaviors, ability to cease fighting, lapses of fully conscious contact with reality, and onset of fatigue or sleep after these kinds of experiences.

Although an electroencephalogram (EEG) is an obvious component of the neurological evaluation, the results of these tests are often more confusing than helpful. It remains unclear whether sleep EEGs in children are more revealing of neuropathology than waking EEGs, but even sleep EEGs in children add little to a diagnosis such as psychomotor epilepsy, which is clinical and does not depend on the results of an EEG. The neurologist testifying in court is frequently faced with the insurmountable task of convincing a judge and jury that a normal EEG does not preclude the existence of epilepsy. Sometimes a trial of antiepileptic medication in delinquent children with psychomotor epileptic symptoms is more useful than an EEG.

A neurological evaluation is most likely to be useful diagnostically and therapeutically when the referral to a neurologist is made with care: the psychiatrist or other clinician making the referral should ask the neurologist specific questions based on a thorough psychiatric and medical history. The neurologist should be told of the child's previous head injury, particular learning disorders, or specific behaviors that have caused the psychiatrist to suspect neurological impairment. The neurologist can then be expected to pay special attention, especially while eliciting a history, to the psychiatrist's questions. Simply referring a child for a "routine" neurological examination rarely significantly contributes to the diagnostic picture. On the other hand, a well-formulated referral to a neurologist interested in the behavioral aspects of neurology often reveals helpful hitherto unrecognized neuropsychiatric vulnerabilities.

TREATMENT IMPLICATIONS

Most extremely violent delinquents suffer from a number of biopsychosocial vulnerabilities that together contribute to violent behaviors. If these behaviors are to be modified, attention must be paid to each aspect of a child's functioning. The author has found, for example, that it is useless to focus exclusively on psychodynamic factors related to having been abused and to ignore the physical damage a child has sustained. If, as a result of perinatal injury, head trauma, or central nervous system infection, a child has difficulty focusing attention on work and controlling behavior at school, the best educational intervention may fail if the child does not also receive stimulant medication. Similarly, a child whose violence is an expression of periodic paranoid psychotic states may not feel safe in the best therapeutic environment without antipsychotic medication. On the other hand, a child whose paranoid ideation, attention deficit disorder, or epilepsy is under medical control may be able to adapt to an adverse environment that was previously intolerable. The child will surely be better able to take advantage of the opportunities provided by the therapeutic milieu.

USE OF MEDICATION

The use of medication in the treatment of incarcerated delinquents raises difficult questions. Since the advent of the phenothiazines in 1954, medications have been used in institutional settings not only to relieve specific symptoms but also to sedate agitated and/or aggressive individuals. The medications have been used to keep patients quiet when adequate staff support is unavailable. Similarly, there have been reports of the misuse and overuse of stimulant medication to control unruly schoolchildren (Divoky and Schrag 1975). Delinquents, especially violent incarcerated delinquents, can become the victims of misused medication; therefore, the clinician must take special care when recommending medication for an incarcerated violent delinquent.

On the other hand, as noted, many aggressive delinquent youngsters are violent partly as a result of a variety of potentially treatable disorders: central nervous system dysfunction with hyperactivity, periodic psychosis, mania, depression, and even psychomotor seizures. It would therefore be detrimental to deprive these children of necessary and effective medication. With violent delinquents, however, as with any other psychiatrically disturbed adolescent, medication must be aimed at relieving specific symptoms. For this reason, a careful history of the exact nature of the youngster's unacceptable behavior is imperative. One youngster may be assaultive because of poor impulse control secondary to brain damage, another may be assaultive during manic episodes, another may have a seizure disorder, and another may become assaultive as a result of paranoid ideation. Each of these situations requires a different kind of pharmacologic as well as psychodynamic intervention (see chapter 4).

The use of medication with violent adolescents raises the question of how best to administer the substance in question. It is useless, except during crisis, to prescribe medication that the adolescent refuses to take. Because most violent adolescents are extremely suspicious of being given any medication at all, whenever possible the use of medication should be a joint decision of the adolescent and the doctor. For example, in the case of one extremely paranoid, psychotic adolescent rapist, the author explained that there was a medication (in this case, a phenothiazine) that might help the boy feel less anxious and suspicious. The author also noted that the youngster was very suspicious and might not take the medication if prescribed. The medication was offered, however, if the youth wished to try it. Under these nonthreatening circumstances, the adolescent shook hands on an agreement to try the medicine.

Given the suspiciousness of many delinquents, the author institutes medication slowly, making every effort to prevent the experience of side effects that might discourage the adolescent's continuing to take the medicine. The author informs the youngster what symptoms the medication should ameliorate; daily or at least several times during the first weeks of therapy, the effects of the medication are discussed. Alterations of dosage and even changes in medication become a joint decision.

Medication is highly individualized, and there is no single formula for treating violence (see chapter 4). In some cases, anticonvulsants alone have been useful; in others, antipsychotics alone have helped; and, at times, combinations of both have been beneficial. The author has also helped highly distractable, hyperactive adolescents with stimulant medication. The principles to remember are (1) that each youngster's needs are different, and (2) that medication is never the only mode of therapeutic intervention. When medication is selected and titrated carefully and is used in the context of an educational and psychotherapeutic program, the youngster neither feels nor looks medicated, but simply functions better.

EDUCATIONAL INTERVENTIONS

Most seriously delinquent adolescents have serious learning disabilities (Poremba 1975; Lewis et al. 1980). These problems may not be culturally determined, and it is a mistake to dismiss them as such. Careful individual educational assessment will reveal a sequencing problem in one child, a problem of discriminating sounds in another, and an overall intellectual deficit requiring special education in another child. The tendency simply to explain poor scores on intelligence tests or low reading scores as the result of cultural deprivation leads to neglect of many seriously handicapped delinquent youngsters. Appropriate educational treatment depends on meticulous testing procedures, and then on the ability to provide these youngsters with classes small enough to permit individualized learning programs.

PSYCHOTHERAPEUTIC INTERVENTIONS

Much has been written about milieu therapy, group therapy, and positive peer pressure in the treatment of behaviorally disturbed adolescents. Sometimes it seems as though some of these methods are tailored more to staff members' needs than to delinquent adolescents' needs. Given the almost ubiquitous shortage of trained personnel, it is not surprising to find that most programs for troubled delinquents rely heavily on group and milieu interventions.

A word should be said, however, about the individual needs of most violent, seriously delinquent adolescents. The violent adolescent, in addition to his or her other problems, generally lacks a steady, caring relationship with even one stable adult. The parents of these youngsters are usually so preoccupied with their own problems that they can give little, if any, emotional support to their adolescent youngsters. Many violent incarcerated youngsters do not even know where their parents are.

Although it would be desirable to provide family treatment for these children and families, it is usually not possible. Nevertheless, the delinquents described in this chapter need a steady relationship with at least one reliable, understanding adult. They need at least one grownup who will rejoice in their behavioral successes and be dismayed at their setbacks. In other words, they need someone who genuinely cares about them if they are to be motivated to change their behaviors. Empathy can develop from such relationships. Many youngsters pick a particular staff member with whom to have such a relationship, but something as important as an ongoing, caring relationship should not be left to chance. In addition to appropriate pharmacologic, educational, and milieu treatment, a supportive, ongoing relationship with an adult is an essential therapeutic ingredient (see chapter 3).

Recognizing the need for an ongoing caring relationship leads to the issue of length of treatment. Given the many serious neuropsychiatric vulnerabilities of violent youngsters, it is important to remember that the kinds of problems that have been noted (attentional problems, paranoid ideation, epilepsy) are often chronic. These problems and combinations of problems, while amenable to treatment, are never cured; they are controlled. Therefore, it is unrealistic to expect any program, no matter how sophisticated, to "cure" a given delinquent's violence in a limited period of time. Therapy is not expected to cure a child of heart disease, kidney disease, or diabetes; it is expected only that with good ongoing care the youngster will be able to function adequately in society. Expectations regarding the treatment of violent delinquency should be similar to those regarding other chronic disorders.

From another perspective, a violently aggressive youngster with, for example, a history of episodic psychosis and evidence of central nervous system dysfunction cannot be expected to return at the age of 16 or 18 to a chaotic depriving family after several years of residential treatment and be able to stay out of difficulty. Society does not expect middle-class, relatively neuropsychiatrically intact children to function alone at age 18. (In fact, most of the readers of this chapter will recognize that they had support in the form of institutions such as high schools, colleges, graduate schools, and medical schools, throughout adolescence and into early adulthood.) One cannot expect vulnerable, violently delinquent youngsters to require less support than ordinary middle-class adolescents. Treatment programs must therefore be planned to meet the ongoing psychological, medical, educational, and social needs of delinquent children. Although such programs will initially be highly structured, even, in some instances, secure (see chapter 9), they must allow for increasing independence corresponding to a youngster's increasing maturity and self-control. Many of these youngsters will need some kind of ongoing residential setting in the form of a specialized group home or college-type dormitory. Adequate psychiatric, medical, and educational services must afford the opportunity to create sustaining interpersonal relationships as these multiply disadvantaged young people move toward adulthood.

REFERENCES

Berman, A., and Siegal, A. A neuropsychiatric approach to the etiology prevention and treatment of juvenile delinquency. In: David, A., ed. Child Personality and Psychopathology: Current Topics. Vol. III. New York: John Wiley and Sons, 1976. pp. 259–294.

Cantwell, D.P. Hyperactivity and antisocial behavior. Journal of the American Academy of Child Psychiatry 19(2):252–262, 1978.

Divoky, D., and Schrag, P. The Myth of the Hyperactive Child. New York: Pantheon, 1975.

Glueck, S., and Glueck, E. Unraveling Juvenile Delinquency. New York: The Commonwealth Fund, 1950.

Heston, L.L. Psychiatric disorders in foster home reared children of schizophrenic mothers. British Journal of Psychiatry 112:819–825, 1966.

Heston, L.L. Schizophrenia. Hospital Practice 12(6):43-49, 1977.

Johnson, A.M., and Szurek, S.A. The genesis of antisocial acting out in children and adults. Psychoanalytic Quarterly 21:323, 1952.

Lewis, D.O., and Balla, D. Delinquency and Psychopathology. New York: Grune and Stratton, 1976.

Lewis, D.O.; Balla, D.A.; Shanok, S.S.; and Snell, L. Delinquency, parental psychopathology and parental criminality. Journal of the American Academy of Child Psychiatry 15(4):665–678, 1976.

Lewis, D.O., and Shanok, S.S. Delinquency and the schizophrenic spectrum of disorders. Journal of the American Academy of Child Psychiatry 17(2):263–276, 1978.

Lewis, D.O., and Shanok, S.S. A comparison of the medical histories of incarcerated delinquent children and a matched sample of nondelinquent children. Child Psychiatry and Human Development 9(4):210–214, 1979.

Lewis, D.O.; Shanok, S.S.; and Balla, D. Perinatal difficulties, head and face trauma, and child abuse in the medical histories of seriously delinquent children. American Journal of Psychiatry 136(4A):419–423, 1979a.

Lewis, D.O.; Shanok, S.S.; Pincus, J.H.; and Glaser, G.H. Violent juvenile delinquents: Psychiatric, neurological, psychological and abuse factors. Journal of the American Academy of Child Psychiatry 18(2):307–319, 1979b.

Lewis, D.O.; Shanok, S.S.; Balla, D.A.; and Bard, B. Psychiatric correlates of severe reading disabilities in an incarcerated delinquent population. Journal of the American Academy of Child Psychiatry 19(4):611–622, 1980.

Mendelson, W.; Johnson, N.; and Steward, M.A. Hyperactive children as teenagers: A follow-up study. Journal of Nervous and Mental Disorders 153(8):273–279, 1971.

National Institute for Juvenile Delinquency Prevention. The Link Between Learning Disabilities and Juvenile Delinquency, by Murray, C. Washington, D.C.: LEAA, 1976.

Offord, D.R.; Allen, N.; and Abrams, N. Parental psychiatric illness, broken homes and delinquency. Journal of the American Academy of Child Psychiatry 17(2):224–238, 1978.

Poremba, C.D. Learning disabilities, youth and delinquency: Programs for intervention. In: Myklebust, H.R., ed. Progress in Learning Disabilities. Vol. III. New York: Grune and Stratton, 1975. pp. 123–149.

Rosenthal, D. Genetics of Psychopathology. New York: McGraw-Hill, 1971.

Rosenthal, D.; Wender, P.H.; Kety, S.S.; Schulsinger, F.; Welner, J.; and Ostergaard, L. Schizophrenics' offspring reared in adoptive homes. In: Rosenthal, D., and Kety, S.S., eds. Transmission of Schizophrenia. Oxford: Pergamon Press, 1968. pp. 377–391.

West, D.J., and Farrington, D.P. Who Becomes Delinquent? London: Heinemann Educational Books, 1973.

Winokur, G.; Clayton, P.; and Reich, T. Manic-Depressive Illness. St. Louis: C.V. Mosby, 1969.

8

Control and Treatment of Juveniles Committing Violent Offenses

Donna M. Hamparian

The problem of the violent juvenile offender is threatening to make drastic changes in the juvenile justice system. This separate legal system has been based on the belief that juveniles are less culpable for their criminal activities than adults, and that they are more amenable to treatment than hardened adult offenders. Since the mid-1960's, however, the system has been under attack because "the juvenile court has not succeeded significantly in rehabilitating delinquent youths, in reducing or even stemming the tide of juvenile criminality, or in bringing justice and compassion to the child offender." (President's Commission on Law Enforcement and Administration of Justice 1967, p. 80). It must be stated at the outset, however, that the juvenile courts were never given sufficient resources to carry out their mission.

In the past, juvenile courts and juvenile corrections generally dealt with youngsters charged with violent offenses in much the same fashion as they dealt with any other adjudicated delinquents. Little differentiation was made in types of program, length of confinement, or supervision. The system handled most juveniles informally. The intake worker, police, or court would talk informally with juveniles and their parents, establish some informal rules, and send the juveniles on their way "to sin no more." The second largest group of juvenile delinquents were those who were placed on probation, given rules of conduct, and supervised weekly or monthly by overworked probation officers. A third group, the more serious juvenile offenders or those with longer offense histories, were committed to State training schools, where the treatment program for the status offender, property offender, and violent offender was basically the same. Case-by-case management was the key approach. The central focus was on the offender and on his or her individualized treatment and rehabilitation needs, rather than on the offense committed. "Difficult" status offenders frequently remained in the training schools longer than juveniles charged with violent offenses.

The perceived failure of the juvenile justice system to rehabilitate juvenile offenders, coupled with public concern over the increased incidence of crimes attributable to juveniles, has led many to favor a punishment model rather than a rehabilitation model as the appropriate basis for the juvenile justice system. The "purpose" clause in the 1977 juvenile code of Washington State sums up the new direction (Washington Revised Code 1977):

1. To make the juvenile offender <u>accountable</u> for his or her behavior;
2. To protect the citizenry from criminal behavior;
3. To provide punishment commensurate with the age, crime, and criminal history of the juvenile offender; and
4. To provide for a clear policy to determine what types of offenders shall receive punishment, treatment, or both.

Such recent enactments in Washington State and elsewhere specify that court dispositions are to be governed mainly by the current offense and offense history, thereby eschewing the former rehabilitative and indeterministic principles of the juvenile court in favor of the punishment assumptions of the adult criminal justice process (Fagan et al. 1981). Stated another way, the juvenile justice system is becoming an offense-based rather than an offender-based system.

Two of the most important reasons for the return to the offense-based approach are the increase in violent juvenile crime and the perceived failure of the rehabilitative model to reduce, prevent, or deter such crime.

SCOPE OF THE PROBLEM

Between 1971 and 1980, arrests of juveniles for violent offenses increased by 38 percent, from 62,302 to 86,220 arrests nationally. During the same period, total arrests for all violent crimes committed by adults and juveniles rose by 63 percent, from 273,209 to 446,373. If the data for 1975 are excluded (because of idiosyncrasies in the data available for that year), arrests for violent offenses by juveniles and adults increased steadily during the 1970's (United States Federal Bureau of Investigation 1971-1981). Between 1971 and 1977, the annual rate of increase in arrests of juveniles for violent crimes was under 10 percent. There was a striking increase in such arrests between 1977 and 1978, followed by a 9 percent decrease between 1978 and 1979, and a slight decrease (1.3 percent) between 1979 and 1980. The participation of juveniles in total arrests for violent crimes fluctuated between 21 and 23 percent from 1971 to 1979, and decreased slightly to 19.3 percent in 1980.

Some cautions are in order with regard to the above data as they pertain to juveniles. Only a very small percentage of the juveniles who come to the attention of the juvenile justice system are arrested for violent crimes; for example, only 4 percent of the juveniles arrested in 1980 were arrested for a violent crime (United States Federal Bureau of Investigation 1981). One study suggests that in stable communities, less than 2 percent of the juveniles will ever be arrested for a violent offense (Hamparian et al. 1978). A recent Rand report states that the arrest data probably exaggerate the juvenile crime threat in three ways:

> First, within any broad category of crime . . . the offenses committed by younger offenders tend to be at the less serious end of the spectrum . . . the degree of arming less lethal. Second, younger offenders are more likely to engage in group crimes than to act alone. This tendency toward group behavior leads to an overestimate of the true chance of victimization from youths . . . and the third bias is introduced by differential response by the police according to the age of the suspect (Greenwood et al. 1980, pp. vi-vii).

It is important to understand that juvenile offenders who commit violent offenses constitute a relatively small number of youngsters (Hamparian et al. 1978). Violent juvenile offenders are a very small percentage of the total juvenile population, a small percentage of the juvenile court case load, and a small percentage of the population of juvenile corrections facilities (Smith et al. 1981). Violent juveniles, however, are the critical population within the system. They are the juveniles most in need of imaginative programming unless they be lost forever as productive members of society.

PREDICTION AND REHABILITATION

Vachss and Bakal (1979) in their book, <u>The Life-Style Violent Juvenile</u>, state that a small number of violent juveniles cannot be treated outside a secure setting. The problem is how to decide or predict which juveniles require this type of treatment to prevent them from engaging in worse acts of violence in the future. A recent study of violent delinquents, The Violent Few (Hamparian et al. 1978), found no evidence to support a linear progression in severity of offenses by all such youths. When a second assaultive offense that these youths had committed was compared to their first, it was found that 25 percent of the second acts of violence were not as serious as the first, 40 percent were at the same level of seriousness, and 31 percent were more serious.

For some juveniles, an early arrest may indeed signal the beginning of a violent criminal career. Such careers, however, are relatively rare. Even though the best predictor of future violent behavior by a juvenile is a record of past violence, the past behavior does not provide an adequate basis for the prediction of future conduct. As noted by Strasburg (1978) in his study of violent delinquents: "Virtually all studies of the prediction of violence agree that it cannot be done within tolerable limits of error" (p. 7).

Despite the technical difficulties associated with prediction, the juvenile justice system has little choice but to continue its efforts to discriminate as best it can between juvenile offenders who seem more or less likely to engage in future acts of violence. After an extensive review of the literature on prediction for the Office of Juvenile Justice and Delinquency Prevention (1977c), Monahan concluded that " . . . despite its primitive state of development, it is highly unlikely that prediction will cease to play a major role in juvenile justice. One cannot attempt to rehabilitate juvenile offenders without first predicting which of them is in need of rehabilitation . . . " (p. 158).

Monahan's observation also notes the continuing focus on rehabilitation within the juvenile justice system in spite of recent tendencies in many parts of the Nation to favor punishment over a treatment approach when dealing with juvenile offenders. Much of the public, as well as many juvenile justice practitioners, still hope that treatment can succeed in diverting at least some violent juveniles from future careers in violence and crime. Even when the hope of such success is faint, the juvenile justice system is still under greater pressure than its adult counterpart to provide some treatment rather than no treatment at all. Strasburg (1978) appears to reflect a still widespread view: "Release to the community with no treatment or control may invite further violence and certainly invites a backlash of public opinion. Simply locking violent delinquents in prison . . . contradicts what we know about the destructive effects of that approach" (p. 163).

CONTROL AND TREATMENT OF JUVENILES ARRESTED FOR VIOLENT OFFENSES

The remainder of this chapter focuses on present means for the control and treatment of violent juvenile offenders, indicates some program models, and describes essential components of these programs. Juveniles officially charged with violent offenses can be handled or treated in several ways:

1. Through the criminal justice system;
2. Through the juvenile justice system;
3. Through specialized components of juvenile justice, mental health, and social service agencies.

THE CRIMINAL JUSTICE SYSTEM

Of the 95,593 juveniles arrested for violent crimes in 1978, fewer than 20 percent were handled by criminal courts (Hamparian et al. 1982). A national overview of statutory provisions in effect during that year identified four ways in which youths under 18 could be referred to adult courts for trial:

1. Judicial waiver. In all jurisdictions but four (New York, Nebraska, Arkansas, Vermont), juveniles could enter adult court through a judicial hearing in juvenile court. A judge could waive the juvenile court's jurisdiction over a youth by a finding that the youth was not amenable to treatment in the juvenile justice system and/or constituted a threat to public safety. The juvenile could then be prosecuted in criminal court.

2. Concurrent jurisdiction. In seven jurisdictions, the juvenile and adult courts shared jurisdiction for certain offenses at certain ages (Arkansas, Colorado, District of Columbia, Florida, Georgia, Nebraska, and Wyoming, not including States with concurrent jurisdiction applying only to traffic and other summary offenses). Generally, the prosecutor decided whether a youth should be charged in juvenile court or in adult court.

3. Excluded offenses. In 1978, a total of 11 States legislatively excluded some serious offenses from juvenile jurisdiction (Delaware, Indiana, Kansas, Louisiana, Maryland, Mississippi, Nevada, New Mexico, New York, Pennsylvania, Rhode Island).

4. Age of jurisdiction. By setting the maximum age of initial juvenile court jurisdiction, legislatures define who may be routinely handled as adults for any violation of the criminal law. While most States
have established this age as under 18, some (Michigan, Louisiana, South
Carolina, Texas, Illinois, Missouri, Massachusetts, and Georgia) have
set the age at under 17, and others (Connecticut, New York, Vermont,
and North Carolina) at under 16. Generally, juveniles who are tried in
criminal court under the above provisions are treated as adults for
purposes of detention, adjudication, and correctional handling. In 1978,
over 250,000 juvenile offenders under 18 were handled as adults because of a lower maximum age of juvenile court jurisdiction (Hamparian
et al. 1982).

In most States, juveniles convicted in criminal court can be placed
on probation or sentenced to the county jail or an adult prison. In a
few States, they can be placed in a juvenile facility until they reach the
age of majority in that State and then be transferred to adult prison to
serve the remainder of their sentence. In several States, youthful offender laws allow juveniles to be placed in special facilities that house
primarily first-time adult offenders and juveniles convicted in adult
court. These facilities generally provide more educational and job training programs than do adult prisons.

As a general rule, however, juveniles convicted in adult court and
sentenced to incarceration are placed in a State prison facility housing
younger adult offenders. In their book, The Life-Style Violent Juvenile,
Vachss and Bakal (1979) comment:

> We can find no evidence whatever that adult prisons offer greater
> rehabilitative possibilities than their juvenile counterparts, and we feel
> comfortable in concluding that those juveniles singled out for adult
> correctional treatment are those . . . the system considers to be "beyond
> rehabilitation" (p. 9).

Vachss and Bakal also note that juveniles placed in adult prisons can
cause serious problems as aggressors and as victims.

DETERMINATE SENTENCING

In the past 5 years, as an alternative to trying juveniles as adults,
several States have applied determinate sentencing to the juvenile justice system. For example, under a 1976 law passed in New York, family
court judges were given discretion to impose restrictive placement on

youths found delinquent for a large category of serious offenses (New York Family Court Act 1976). Youths could be placed in a secure placement facility for a minimum of 2 years, with provision that this placement could continue until a youth reached 21 years of age. In 1978, the State legislature decided to exclude all of the serious offenses named in the 1976 legislation from initial juvenile court jurisdiction, but provided for "reverse waiver" to the family court at any stage in the proceedings (New York Penal Law 1979).

In 1980, Illinois created the category of "habitual juvenile offender" as an alternative to judicial waiver (Illinois Ann. Stat. 1980). Youths in this category are tried in juvenile court and given the right to a jury trial. Youths found delinquent twice for the commission of felonies, and thereafter convicted a third time for the commission or attempted commission of one of several specified felonies, are committed to a juvenile corrections facility until the age of 21 (with time off for good behavior). The facility has no special treatment program for these youths, who are expected to have the usual training school experience.

TRADITIONAL JUVENILE COURT DISPOSITIONS

Most juveniles arrested for violent offenses are processed by the juvenile justice system with little differentiation in disposition based on the nature of the offense. The data from the dangerous juvenile offender study at the Academy for Contemporary Problems in Columbus, Ohio, showed that, within a cohort of Ohio youth, those found delinquent for aggravated offenses received State correctional sentences about 53 percent of the time. Those found delinquent for less serious offenses received such sentences about 32 percent of the time (Hamparian et al. 1978). Because violent offenses are committed less frequently than property offenses, even by a cohort of youths selected for involvement in violent offenses, the number of juvenile correctional sentences for nonviolent offenses exceeded juvenile sentences for violent offenses by a factor of nearly 2 to 1. Of the estimated national total of 16,000 juveniles sent to State training schools in 1978, fewer than 20 percent were committed because of a delinquency adjudication for a violent offense (Smith et al. 1981).

The dispositions frequently given to violent delinquents—probation or training school—appear to have little or no constructive impact on subsequent criminal behavior (Strasburg 1978). Treatment-oriented programs specifically geared to assaultive youth are just beginning to be developed in a few States. There seems to be widespread agreement, however, that secure treatment programs for repeat violent offenders have become a political and criminological necessity. The following descriptions of a few such programs are based on written materials, personal interviews, and site visits. Additional information may be found in reports from the Violent Juvenile Offender Program, established in 1981 by the Office of Juvenile Justice and Delinquency Prevention, U.S. Department of Justice. One of these reports has been published under the auspices of the National Council on Crime and Delinquency (Mathias et al. 1984).

CONTINUOUS CASE MANAGEMENT

This treatment approach for violent juvenile offenders, proposed by the Vera Institute of Justice, is designed to achieve the consistency in service delivery long advocated by the social work community but seldom accomplished because of practical difficulties and cost. Under the Vera approach, a juvenile offender would be assigned to a single responsible person who would take responsibility for the following (Strasburg 1978):

1. Assessment of the juvenile's treatment needs;
2. Development of a treatment plan;
3. Assuring that the plan is implemented;
4. Maintaining contact with the juvenile during the treatment phase;
5. Monitoring the service providers to ensure that the juvenile's needs are met;
6. Helping the juvenile reintegrate into the community if the juvenile had previously been removed for treatment or incarceration.

The following two programs illustrate the continuous case management approach.

Minnesota Serious Juvenile Offender Program

In 1978, the Minnesota Department of Corrections established a special program to provide appropriate treatment and control of delinquent 15- to 18-year-old youths who had been adjudicated for murder, first-degree arson, first- or second-degree criminal sexual conduct, first-

or second-degree manslaughter, or first- or second-degree assault, and other specified felony history criteria. The program was divided into two phases: an institutional stay and a subsequent community-based stage involving continuous case management. The program used existing secure and open juvenile corrections facilities and contracted for case managers to provide community supervision and programming.

After a youth completed an orientation at the institution, the case manager and youth developed a treatment plan covering the period of institutional stay and subsequent release into the community. While this plan was being developed, the case manager consulted with the juvenile's parents and other key actors in the community to assure that the treatment plan addressed the youth's needs. When the youth and case manager reached agreement on the treatment plan's contents, the youth signed a contract stating what he or she had agreed to do while in the institution and after release. For the period of institutional stay, the program specified the academic or vocational classes that the youth would attend and whether the youth would be involved in a chemical dependency or other special program. The contract also specified the date the youth would be released from the institution, assuming adherence to this phase of the agreed-upon treatment plan.

In the second phase, the community-based stage, the youth became involved with a network of contracted services and individuals. During the first 6 months after release from the institution, the youth lived at home, in a group home, or in a chemical dependency program under close surveillance. The last 6 months of treatment typically involved lighter supervision. The program allowed case managers and youths to adjust the individual treatment programs as changing needs and circumstances indicated.

A feature of the program was the involvement of community persons, under contract, to assist in treating the youth and in maintaining close surveillance for at least the first 6 months after release from the institution. For example, the program contracted with a member of Alcoholics Anonymous, who was an auto mechanic and race driver, to work with a youth who has a severe chemical dependency problem and a history of stealing cars and high speed driving. An evaluation of the Minnesota program found that 62 of the 76 juveniles who participated in the program during its first 25 months of operation had not been adjudicated for a new felony or gone AWOL since being admitted to the program. These youths had typically spent about 6 months in an institution prior to their release to the community. The evaluation also found that

1. The continuous case management approach appeared to improve access to the services needed by the youth and enhance accountability of service provider.
2. The designation of individual youths as serious offenders and the use of a community team of individuals to monitor these youths while in the community appeared to be useful means of establishing needed control over the youths and facilitating effective treatment.
3. Private treatment providers were willing to work with the serious juvenile offenders under the conditions established by the program.

Unified Delinquency Intervention Services Project

The Unified Delinquency Intervention Services (UDIS) Project began operation in 1974 after a year of planning by the Illinois Department of Children and Family Services in conjunction with the Illinois Law Enforcement Commission (Huff 1976; Office of Juvenile Justice and Delinquency Prevention 1977a). UDIS was originally designed to serve youths who were at risk of being committed or recommitted to Illinois juvenile institutions—for example, probation and parole violators and repeat delinquent offenders. After the program became operational, it involved the most serious juvenile offenders. Of a total of 211 youths served in the initial project year, 55 percent were offenders who had been charged with major felonies, including murder, rape, armed robbery, arson, and burglary.

UDIS utilizes a brokerage system model that utilizes purchase of services and a case management approach. Purchase of service agreements are negotiated to provide individual clients with services such as individual counseling, family counseling, educational and tutoring services, vocational testing and job placement, specialized foster care, group home care, temporary living arrangements, wilderness stress programs, and private residential treatment programs. The purpose is to maintain the offender in the community and reduce unnecessary institutionalization through coordination of existing community services. Most of the youths participate in the program as a condition of probation.

A subsequent evaluation of UDIS indicated that the program had been successful in reducing recidivism among many of its clients (Murray and Cox 1979). This finding, however, has been the subject of controversy, as described succinctly in a National Academy of Sciences report (Martin et al. 1981, p. 95):

> The controversy surrounding the UDIS report stems from the fact that the delinquents taken into the study and its various programs were those who had had high rates of offending immediately prior to getting into the study. It has been charged therefore that the study capitalizes on a regression artifact, i.e., that the delinquents would have shown lower rates of offending even if they had not been involved in any treatment program at all (McCleary et al. 1979). The authors of the original report believe, on the other hand, that the evidence supports the notion that the high-rate offenders were on an upwardly spiraling offense rate that would not have declined spontaneously for purely statistical reasons (Murray and Cox 1979).

A basic difference between UDIS and the Minnesota Serious Juvenile Offender Program described earlier is that the Illinois model favors community-based programs on a least possible restrictive basis and only includes more restrictions as needed. In contrast, the Minnesota program model begins with an institutional placement from which a youth can "graduate" to less restrictive community placements.

A JUVENILE CORRECTIONS MODEL

Green Oak Center (GOC) is a maximum security, special treatment unit for 100 males between the ages of 12 and 19. The center is located within the Institutional Services Division of the Michigan Department of Social Services (Office of Juvenile Justice and Delinquency Prevention 1977b; Michigan Department of Social Services, n.d.). Most of the youths at the Green Oak Center have been found guilty of serious crimes against persons and have been in serious trouble from an early age. The average age is over 16 at the time of placement and over 17 at the time of release. The average educational level at time of entry is lower than fifth grade.

The central treatment modality at Green Oak Center is Guided Group Interaction, which seeks to mobilize peer pressure as a means of inducing residents to show concern for others and for themselves. Basically, the program operates through assignment of residents to small groups that meet frequently for the purpose of using group dynamics to instill prosocial norms and values:

> The small group discussions at GOC involve up to ten boys, sitting in a tight circle. One boy is chosen by his peers to "have the meeting"

that day. The meetings typically last about an hour and or ninety minutes and are held four or five times a week. They focus on the boy chosen that day; his peers attempt to help him examine his behavior and improve upon it. Much confrontation accompanies these sessions, and there is constant pressure by the participants to be honest. Since the entire group may lose certain privileges when one of its members commits a serious infraction, there is considerable pressure to learn as much as one can about one's peers so as to make more informed decisions about things such as home leave or off-ground privileges. If such a decision results in an AWOL, for example, then the entire group may have to suffer the consequences (Mann 1976, p. 35).

Staff members at Green Oak Center are expected to avoid authoritarian postures so that the inmate peer culture can work effectively as a treatment tool. On the other hand, staff members are responsible for making those decisions that cannot be delegated to the peer groups and for dealing with members of the groups who become assaultive and out of control.

An evaluation of the program's impact on subsequent recidivism found that nearly two-thirds of the youths released from the program had avoided further imprisonment during the 30 months following release. This did not mean that most graduates had avoided involvement with the police, since 60 percent had been rearrested within 12 months of release. It thus appears that the program has effectively reduced the severity, if not frequency, of offenses after release.

A disturbing finding, according to program administrators, was that 60 percent of the released youths were not engaged in productive activities within 3 months after release, despite the fact that they had left Green Oak Center with a community plan approved by the Youth Parole and Review Board, that included job or school participation. Beneficial effects of special institutional programs for serious juvenile offenders are apparently not likely to persist in the absence of more effective programs of postinstitutional care (Ball 1977; Michigan Department of Social Services, n.d.).

JOINT MENTAL HEALTH-CORRECTIONS MODEL

Between 1976 and 1979, an experimental program designed specifically to treat violent, mentally ill youths was operated in New York City under the auspices of two State agencies: the Department of Mental Hygiene and the Division for Youth. The program, the Bronx Court

Related Unit (CRU) had two components: a secure 10-bed In-Patient Diagnostic Unit operated under mental health auspices, and a Long-Term Treatment Unit run by juvenile corrections. To be admitted to the program, a youth had to meet rigid criteria for mental illness and to have been adjudicated for murder, manslaughter, rape, sodomy, arson, kidnapping, robbery, or attempted murder. For evaluation purposes, the plan included a comparison group of youths who met the criteria for admission to the program but were not admitted.

Youths admitted to the In-Patient Diagnostic Unit were extensively tested, evaluated, and observed to determine the presence, nature, and degree of their mental illness. Therapeutic and remedial services included individual, group, and family psychotherapy programs; milieu therapy; pharmacotherapy; and educational and recreational activities. Three main dispositional alternatives were employed: youths evaluated as needing intensive, long-term mental health care were referred to other psychiatric facilities; youths not requiring mental health services were returned to juvenile corrections for placement; and youths assessed as suffering from "intermittent or episodic mental illness" and as potentially benefitting from treatment were placed into the long-term treatment component of the project.

The Long-Term Treatment Unit was designed as a 20-bed secure unit providing treatment for up to 18 months. The primary treatment orientation integrated behavioral principles with milieu therapy. Incorporated in the milieu treatment was a socialization program based on behavior management principles and supplemented by individual and group counseling; family therapy; remedial education; and vocational, recreational, and arts care. Major emphasis was placed on ensuring continuity of care between the Long-Term Treatment Unit and the In-Patient Diagnostic Unit.

Information on recidivism was collected on 26 CRU and 33 comparison group youths who were eventually returned to the community. It was found that

1. Somewhat fewer CRU youths recidivated (62.2 percent) than did comparison group youths (75.8 percent).
2. Of those who did recidivate, the CRU youths had a lower average rearrest rate (2.8 times) than did the comparison group (3.3 times).
3. Among those who were rearrested, the CRU youths were rearrested less often for violent crimes (38.9 percent of arrests) than were the comparison group youths (43.5 percent).

Although the recidivism differences between the two groups were slight, the results of the project may be considered encouraging in that the results were consistently in favor of the CRU youths. The project, however, was closed down at the conclusion of the experiment. The evaluation team gave four major reasons for the discontinuance (Cocozza and Hartstone 1980):

1. The high cost of the program;
2. Disagreements and strains between the two cooperating State agencies over issues of control of the program, decisionmaking power, agency allegiance, treatment orientation, etc.;
3. Underutilization of bed space because of strict enforcement of the admission criteria (seriously violent and mentally ill), misconceptions of the program, and lack of referrals; and
4. A political climate of "get-tough-and-lock-them-up," which conflicted with the treatment approach.

A PRIVATE, PROFIT-MAKING MODEL

Elan One is a private, profit-making corporation in Poland Spring, Maine, that operates a residential treatment center for "incorrigible adolescents" between the ages of 14 and 25. The center receives referrals from State agencies, "end-of-the-road" youths who have not been dealt with successfully elsewhere, and "disturbed" youths placed in Elan One by their parents. Many of the latter group have spent years in mental hospitals and psychiatric programs. As of July 1977, Elan One housed 240 residents in four separate facilities or "houses." Some of these youths were serious violent offenders, such as a girl who had murdered a child, a boy who had sniped randomly at pedestrians, and adolescents who were extremely assaultive.

Elan One is not a correctional institution or a mental hospital. Rather, it is designed to be a complete, continuous therapeutic community in which juveniles with out-of-control behavior problems come to understand the causes and consequences of their conduct and learn how to improve their lives (Cohill 1976; Davidson 1977; Levitch and Vlock 1977; Office of Juvenile Justice and Delinquency Prevention 1977b).

The treatment approach at the center emphasizes group techniques and a carefully designed reinforcing social structure that provide absolute support while promoting change. Illegal behavior is not tolerated, but is punished immediately. Three primary rules of conduct are enforced by peer pressure and staff authority: no narcotics, violence, or sex.

While leadership is shared between a psychiatrist and a program director, the program is primarily operated by paraprofessionals, many of whom are former residents.

There is a rigid hierarchical structure in each of the four houses, with promotion accorded by residents' meritorious performance. New admissions have the status of "workers," from which they can move up to "ramrods," department heads, coordinator trainees, and coordinators. Each house has six departments: business, communications, maintenance, kitchen service, medical, and expediters (the house police force). Few residents successfully "elope"; they are watched and checked at least every 10 minutes by an expediter.

To rise in this organization, a resident must justify evaluation by performance or be "shot down" (reduced in rank). Most discipline is provided in the form of the "haircut"—a confrontation session in which a youth's erring conduct and its significance are dealt with on the spot by higher ranking residents.

The four main components of the program are:

1. Group sessions—encounter, primal scream, status groups, and sensitivity sessions;
2. A structured, lawful community;
3. Paraprofessional staffing with high commitment and high turnover, resulting in low levels of burnout and disillusionment; and
4. A reentry program that prepares the youths for independent living and permits their return to group sessions on weekends if the need arises.

The program has been criticized by some observers for abusive and occasionally violent measures of behavior control. For example, some observers find it objectionable that Elan One's way of dealing with a resident who tries to use violence to intimidate others is to require that youth to enter a boxing ring and fight against the "champion of the house" until soundly drubbed (Office of Juvenile Justice and Delinquency Prevention, 1977b).

SECURE TREATMENT UNITS

Vachss and Bakal have proposed a model Secure Treatment Unit to deal more effectively with "lifestyle violent juveniles"—youths whose life is characterized by chronic violence, rather than youths who have had a single violent episode in an otherwise relatively nonviolent existence.

> Violence as a life-style is what concerns us . . . [We] wish to focus exclusively on those juveniles to whom violence is a primary means of self-expression, not those juveniles who commit any single act defined as "violent" by the legislature. This is not to say that those individual juveniles who do commit single episodic acts of violence are not fit candidates for specialized treatment. However, the purpose of the proposed Secure Treatment Unit (STU) and the purpose of the planning expressed in this work is to seriously intervene in a chronic, escalating pattern of life-style violent behavior which has implications for the future as well as for the present (Vachss and Bakal 1979).

As envisioned by Vachss and Bakal, the Secure Treatment Unit would resemble a maximum security adult corrections institution. Several distinct facilities that constitute the unit would all be surrounded "by a massive wall which is much higher than any of the structures it encloses" (Vachss and Bakal 1979, p. 163). Another purpose of the unit would be to protect society from the residents and to protect the residents from each other. "A Secure Treatment Unit that does not provide safety for its residents promotes a culture of violence that will inevitably destroy the very goals upon which the institution is founded" (Vachss and Bakal 1979, p. 67; emphasis in the original). In addition to providing security to each resident as an absolute prerequisite to treatment, the unit would provide a continuum of services to residents with a system to reward progress.

Vachss and Bakal further consider an institution such as the Secure Treatment Unit to be both a political and criminological necessity. The political reality is that

> A frightened public wants reassurance that dangerous juveniles will be off the streets and within a program that will, at least temporarily, incapacitate them. This is an area of need which cuts across all social and political philosophies: whether one believes a violent juvenile should be punished, treated, rehabilitated, or subjected to societal revenge, there is universal agreement that the price of allowing dangerous juveniles to remain at large in our communities is too high (Vachss and Bakal 1977, p. 14).

From the criminological viewpoint, a juvenile justice system has an inescapable responsibility to institutionalize violent juveniles who simply are too violent to be treated outside a closed setting. "Because such juveniles require specialized programs and specialized settings, the consequence of a failure to address these needs is the systematic destruction of all the other specialized services a proper juvenile justice network will provide for the rest of the juvenile offender population" (Vachss and Bakal 1979, p. 14).

During the 1970's, both Massachusetts and Pennsylvania embarked on major efforts to reduce the number of juveniles confined in correctional institutions. Subsequently, however, both States found it necessary to establish task forces that considered the special problems posed by seriously violent juveniles. One outcome was the establishment of secure treatment units in both States.

Massachusetts

As of 1979, Massachusetts had 10 secure treatment units for juveniles with a total of 123 beds. Admissions were screened carefully to ensure that no youth who could succeed in an open setting was placed in the secure facilities. In the view of the State Department of Youth Services, which had responsibility for the secure units, each unit needed to have strong managerial and professional leadership; clear operating guidelines; careful personnel selection; a broad range and intense program adequate to address a youth with many rehabilitative needs; a strong aftercare program, including the youth's family and community; and a setting that is as clean, efficient, pleasant as possible, given the constraints of cost and security (Commonwealth of Massachusetts, Department of Youth Services 1980).

The secure treatment units in Massachusetts have been operated primarily by private contractors on a purchase-of-care basis, with the Department of Youth Services operating other units where considered necessary. The multifaceted treatment programs include clinical, educational, vocational, recreational, and family therapies tailored to the needs and strengths of each youth. Efforts are made to incorporate day work programs into the treatment. Local gyms and swimming pools are used for recreation.

Pennsylvania

Secure treatment programs were established for serious juvenile offenders after the 1975 closure of a cell block for juveniles at the State Correctional Institution at Camp Hill (Pennsylvania Joint Council on Criminal Justice 1980). A total of seven programs for 230 youths was developed; all but two programs serve no more than 20 youths. One unit serves youths who are mentally retarded or have problems with maladaptive behavior. Another unit serves mentally ill juvenile offenders.

As of 1980, the Weaversville Intensive Treatment Unit was the only unit being operated by a private corporation (RCA, Inc.) under contract to the Pennsylvania Department of Welfare. The professional staff were serving as positive role models to the youths and were operating educational and vocational programs.

The Cornwell Heights Intensive Treatment Unit, opened in 1975, serves about 50 youths. This self-contained unit was operated by the Office of Children of the Department of Public Welfare, and located on the grounds of the Cornwell Heights Development Center. Residents were mainstreamed into the educational program established for the development center by a private contractor (RCA, Inc.). The program operated on a behavioral approach that specifies a series of stages or levels through which juveniles are expected to progress during their period of confinement.

Other Pennsylvania units are smaller and do not have all the educational and vocational resources of the larger programs. Evaluation may show, however, that the small size of the program can compensate for lack of resources.

SUMMARY AND RECOMMENDATIONS

The following conclusions can be reached about the control and treatment of juveniles committing violent crimes:

1. Relatively few juveniles are arrested for violent offenses, either in terms of total arrests of juveniles or in relation to total arrests for violence.

2. The impact of violent juvenile offenses on the juvenile justice system is far greater than the number of youths involved.

3. Fewer than half of the juveniles adjudicated delinquent for violent offenses receive probation or a juvenile corrections sentence (Smith et al. 1979; Smith et al. 1981).

4. There has been a recent trend away from the traditional practice of treating juveniles adjudicated for violent offenses in the same way as other juvenile offenders; the juvenile justice system is becoming an offense-based (rather than offender-based) system, with harsher penalties being imposed for violent offenses).

5. The criminal justice system now handles a significant percentage of juveniles arrested for violent offenses.

With much caution, the author suggests some necessary ingredients in developing effective programs for violent juvenile offenders (see also Fagan 1981; Mann 1976; Mathias et al. 1984: Office of Juvenile Justice and Delinquency Prevention 1977b; Strasburg 1978; Vachss and Bakal 1979):

1. Any program that treats violent juvenile offenders must recognize the primary need for control of these juveniles. Public safety is of crucial importance. The program must be perceived as being secure so that the cooperation of the community and the juvenile justice system can be obtained. Security should be achieved, however, without creating a jail-like atmosphere.

2. The importance of effective community reintegration programming for such youths cannot be overemphasized. The facility needs to maintain close ties with the community to which the youths will be returned. Community trips, home furloughs, and encouragement of family visits to the facility should take place while the youth is residing there.

3. Staff turnover within secure programs will probably be high, partially because of burnout. It is important to make use of young paraprofessional youth workers who can relate to the delinquent and convey a sense of hope.

4. The approach of contracting with private and community organizations for services should be explored more fully. There is no apparent reason for not providing most services to youths in secure settings on a contract basis.

5. Facilities for violent juvenile offenders must be law abiding and safe. Brutalizing of youths by staff or other inmates cannot be tolerated.

6. Treatment programs should specify realistic goals the youths are expected to attain. Youths should be rewarded promptly for meeting such goals and for other positive, prosocial behavior.

7. Programs for juvenile offenders should emphasize their helping role, which requires a staff that is committed and involved.

8. Juvenile involvement in decisionmaking should be maximized. The use of contracts or individualized treatment plans worked out jointly by staff and juveniles should be encouraged, and the contract or plan should cover the community integration period.

9. Job placement in the reintegration phase must be the focus of remedial education and job training. Followup assistance after job placement is an important facet of reintegration.

As indicated in this discussion, few treatment programs have been dedicated to the violent juvenile offender. Moreover, most of the treatment approaches described have been tried before with varying success. Some violent juveniles will benefit from these approaches; others may not be helped by any type of program. The challenge, as Mann (1976) urges, is to continue trying new approaches, keeping what seems to work, and trying again.

> Until we can give our attention to the creation of means of bringing delinquent youth into society as legitimate participants in its benefits, far too many of them will become adult criminals to scare citizens off the streets. Our inattention to the need of the system for change will produce the crime rates we deserve (Conrad 1981).

REFERENCES

Ball, D. Green Oak houses violent offenders. Detroit News, 1977.

Cocozza, J.J., and Hartstone, E. "Bronx Court Related Unit" New York State Council on Children and Families, Bureau of Research and Program Evaluation, 1980, unpublished.

Cohill, M.B. Janice's only problem is her behavior. The National Observer, Jan. 1976.

Commonwealth of Massachusetts, Department of Youth Services. Annual Report, 1978. Boston: Department of Youth Services, 1980.

Conrad, J. Crime and the child. In: Hall, J.; Hamparian, D.; Pettibone, J.; and White, J. Major Issues in Juvenile Justice Information and Training: Readings in Public Policy. Columbus, Oh.: Academy for Contemporary Problems, 1981.

Davidson, G. "Elan One." Personal communication letter to D. Hamparian describing the Elan One program, 1977.

Fagan, J.; Jones, S.J.; Hartstone, E.; Redman, C.; and Emerson, R. Background Paper for the Violent Juvenile Offender Research and Development Program. San Francisco: Ursa Institute, 1981.

Greenwood, P.: Petersilia, J.; and Zimring, F. Age, Crime, and Sanctions: The Transition From Juvenile to Adult Court. Santa Monica, Calif.: Rand Corp., 1980.

Hamparian, D.; Schuster, R.; Dinitz, S.; and Conrad, J. The Violent Few: A Study of Dangerous Juvenile Offenders. Lexington, Mass.: Lexington Books, 1978.

Hamparian, D.; Estep, L.K.; Muntean, S.; Priestino, R.; Swisher, R.; Wallace, P.; and White, J. Youth in Adult Courts: Between Two Worlds. Washington, D.C.: U.S. Department of Justice, 1982.

Huff, R. Programs based on sociology and social work. In: Mann, D. Intervening with Convicted Serious Juvenile Offenders. Santa Monica, Calif.: Rand Corp., July 1976. pp. 32–49.

Illinois Ann. Stat., Chapter 37, new par. 705–12, 1980.

Levitch, J.A., and Vlock, L.F. Violent street kids—Must it be jail? Parade, May 1, 1977.

Mann, D. Intervening With Convicted Serious Juvenile Offenders. Santa Monica, Calif.: Rand Corp., July, 1976.

Martin, S.E.; Sechrest, L.B.; and Redner, P., eds. New Directions in the Rehabilitation of Criminal Offenders. Washington, D.C.: National Academy Press, 1981.

Mathias, R.A.; DeMuro, P.; and Allinson, R.S.; eds. Violent Juvenile Offenders: An Anthology. San Francisco: National Council on Crime and Delinquency, 1984.

McCleary, R.; Gordon, A.; McDowall, D.; and Maltz, M. How a regression artifact can make any delinquency intervention program look effective. In: Sechrest L.; Philips, M.; Redner, R.; West, S.; and Yeaton, W., eds. Evaluation Studies Review Annual, Vol. 4, Beverly Hills: Sage Publications, 1979. pp. 626–652.

Michigan Department of Social Services. Information obtained from a report on the Green Oak Center. Unpublished, n.d. Also oral communication, Wolfgang Eggers, Director of the Green Oak Center, August 1977.

Minnesota Department of Corrections. Serious Juvenile Offender Program: The First 25 Months. Minneapolis: Minnesota Department of Corrections, 1981.

Murray, C.A., and Cox, L.A. Beyond Probation: Juvenile Corrections and the Chronic Delinquent. Beverly Hills: Sage, 1979.

New York Family Court Act, Sections 712 and 753-a, 1976.

New York Penal Law, Section 30.00(2), McKinney Supp., 1979.

Office of Juvenile Justice and Delinquency Prevention. The serious or violent juvenile offender—Is there a treatment response? by Goins, S. In: The Serious Juvenile Offender. Proceedings of a National Symposium in Minneapolis. Washington, D.C.: U.S. Department of Justice, Law Enforcement Assistance Administration, 1977a. pp. 115–129.

Office of Juvenile Justice and Delinquency Prevention. Who's coming to the picnic? by Hamparian, D. In: The Serious Juvenile Offender. Proceedings of a National Symposium. Washington, D.C.: U.S. Department of Justice, Law Enforcement Assistance Administration, 1977b. pp. 61–78.

Office of Juvenile Justice and Delinquency Prevention. The prediction of violent behavior in juveniles, by Monahan, J. In: The Serious Juvenile Offender. Proceedings of a National Symposium in Minneapolis. Washington, D.C.: U.S. Department of Justice, Law Enforcement Assistance Administration, 1977c. pp. 148–160.

Pennsylvania Joint Council on Criminal Justice, Inc. The Secure Care and Treatment Needs of Male Youthful Offenders in Pennsylvania, 1980.

President's Commission on Law Enforcement and Administration of Justice. The Challenge of Crime in a Free Society. Washington, D.C.: Supt. of Docs., Govt. Print. Off., 1967.

Smith, C.P.; Alexander, P.; Kemp, G.L.; and Lemert, E. A National Assessment of Serious Juvenile Crime and the Juvenile Justice System: The Need for a Rational Response. Sacramento, Calif.: American Justice Institute, 1979.

Smith, D.; Finnegan, T.; Snyder, H.; Feinberg, N.; and McFall, P. Delinquency 1978: United States Estimate of Cases Processed by Courts with Juvenile Jurisdiction. Pittsburgh: National Center for Juvenile Justice, 1981.

Strasburg, P.A. Violent Delinquents. New York: Monarch, 1978.

United States Federal Bureau of Investigation. Uniform Crime Reports for the United States. Washington, D.C.: Supt. of Docs., Govt. Print. Off., 1971–1981 annual.

Vachss, A., and Bakal, Y. The Life-Style Violent Juvenile. Lexington, Mass.: Lexington Books, 1979.

Washington Revised Code, Sec. 1340.010(2), 1977.

9

Legal and Ethical Issues in the Treatment and Handling of Violent Behavior

George E. Dix, J.D.

The delivery of mental health services increasingly addresses numerous ethical and legal concerns. These concerns are especially pertinent when the recipient is a violent or potentially violent individual. The following hypothetical case illustrates many of those concerns.

Martin K., a 27-year-old white male, has been admitted to the hospital on the basis of a 90-day "civil" court commitment. Upon initial evaluation, he is diagnosed as an explosive personality. Information available to the staff suggests that before his admission, Martin destroyed furniture in his apartment during several "fits" and threatened to beat his female roommate. He denies that he is sick and refuses to participate in any part of the unit's program. On several occasions, he has been observed arguing loudly with other patients on the unit. One patient has reported to staff that Martin poked him in the chest with his index finger during an argument concerning the ward's television programming. During informal conversations with staff members, Martin has disclosed strongly hostile feelings toward his roommate and his employer.

Staff members' legitimate concerns might include the following: What, if any, concern should or must staff members have for the safety of Martin's roommate and employer following Martin's discharge? What, if any, action should be taken on these concerns? If, at the end of the 90-day period, staff members are called to testify in proceedings to continue Martin's institutionalization, how firm and specific should they be in expressing opinions concerning the likelihood of future violent conduct? To what extent, if any, can Martin be compelled to participate in treatment programs? Under what circumstances, if any, can staff members deal with what they perceive to be an emergency situation posed by the danger that Martin will physically assault another patient? Not least, to what extent does the resolution of these matters by the staff members have potential legal consequences and, more specifically, to what extent might individual staff members be personally liable? These concerns are the subject of the present chapter, which addresses selected legal and ethical issues related to the treatment of violent persons.

LEGAL AND ETHICAL CONSIDERATIONS

"Ethics" is the consideration and determination of "right" and "wrong"—what ought or ought not to be done. In the area of professional practice, ethical considerations include not only the common sense considerations of general ethics but also matters of the nature, scope, and limits of professional expertise and judgment. A professional may be ethically justified in doing (or ethically required to do) things that a lay person is not because of the professional's training and experience. The professional has a corresponding duty, however, to recognize the limits of professional expertise and to respect those limits. Because mental health professionals deal with changing and sometimes controlling the behavior of others—matters that involve highly subjective value judgments as well as professional expertise—professional ethics are especially important to the delivery of mental health services (Roth 1979).

Legal requirements concern what must be done, given the assumption that law demands compliance only where the law is clear. Unfortunately, the legal rules relating to the delivery of mental health services are often unclear and provide little assistance to professionals who must resolve questions such as those posed by the case of Martin K. When legal requirements are not clear, professionals remain free to make decisions based on their own professional (and personal) ethical standards. Further, even if the legal requirements appear to be clear, they may contradict professional ethics. The professional may then be justified in challenging the legal requirements in an effort to change them.

Both legal and ethical concerns apply in many (if not most) of the areas of concern raised by treatment of violent persons. Perhaps the best way for the legal and ethical areas to relate is for legal requirements to impose an outer limit on what professionals must do or refrain from doing. These legal requirements should leave significant leeway in areas of special professional expertise, however, so professionals can make decisions on the basis of their own professional judgment and ethical standards.

This chapter will examine ethical and legal issues in the treatment of potentially violent persons, as illustrated by the case of Martin K. Several areas of special concern will be addressed: first, the professional's duty to protect potential victims; second, the professional's responsibility to respond to court inquiries concerning subjects' "dangerousness"; third, the question of compelling treatment; finally, the personal liability of mental health professionals.

PROTECTION OF POTENTIAL VICTIMS

The staff members in the hypothetical case of Martin K. might quite reasonably be concerned that they have an ethical or legal responsibility to other patients on the unit and to Martin's roommate and employer. Professional ethics have traditionally acknowledged that a therapist is duty-bound to consider the interest of violent patients' potential victims. The obligation of confidentiality is subject to exceptions that permit the therapist, in appropriate circumstances, to seek the patient's involuntary commitment or notify law enforcement authorities that the patient may harm others. This principle used to have minimal legal significance, because third parties were not regarded as having the legal capacity to sue a therapist even if the therapist's failure to follow professional standards resulted in a third party being injured by a patient. However, a series of cases, beginning with the California Supreme Court's decision in Tarasoff v. Board of Regents (1976), have recognized a right of third parties injured by a violent patient to sue the therapist. The slow but significant tendency of other States to recognize this right has obvious implications for treatment of violent persons.

Tarasoff Cases

Tarasoff and subsequent cases (Lipari v. Sears Roebuck & Co. 1980; McIntosh v. Milano 1979) have unfortunately been widely characterized as requiring the therapist to warn the potential victims of violent patients of the threat posed by the patient, but this is a misinterpretation of the decisions. Correctly read (Dix 1981a), the decisions impose two distinguishable "duties" on therapists; if a third party is injured as a result of a therapist's breach of either of these duties, that party may sue the therapist for financial damages. The first duty is to exercise the care and skill of a reasonable professional in identifying those patients who pose a significant risk of physical harm to third persons. The second duty is to exercise reasonable professional care in protecting third parties from those patients identified as "dangerous." Tarasoff held that meeting the second duty might include warning the potential victim of the danger, and that possibly in some exceptional cases such a warning would be the only way in which the duty could be met. Generally, however, Tarasoff holds only that in exercising reasonable professional care in seeking the safety of third persons, a mental health professional must consider (along with other options) the possibility of warning the potential victim.

The Tarasoff cases, then, can be read as merely making the therapist's existing ethical duty to potential victims a legal duty upon which an injured party can sue. Some therapists, however, believe that warning a third party of a perceived danger constitutes such a significant breach of the therapist's duty of confidentiality to the patient that professional ethics never require such a warning. The Tarasoff cases recognize that in some situations a therapist may be legally obligated to warn a third party, thus divulging information obtained from the patient in confidence. The cases therefore may be read as going beyond existing professional ethical standards.

The so-called Tarasoff duties are most frequently required during outpatient treatment. In some situations, however, they require the therapist to take action to prevent harm to a third party by a patient being treated in an institution or following the patient's release.

Compliance with Tarasoff

Compliance with the two Tarasoff duties when they apply requires only the exercise of judgment within the bounds of professional reasonableness. The therapist must exercise reasonable care in determining whether a subject presents a significant risk of violence to others. The determination is based on such factors as noting and evaluating the intensity and focus of the subject's hostility, any threats that have been made and their seriousness, and any violent past actions. In enforcing the first Tarasoff duty, courts will probably give special attention to evidence that the subject had previously acted upon violent propensities similar to those now at issue.

In complying with the second <u>Tarasoff</u> duty—responding to an identified violent patient with reasonable professional care—the therapist must consider various alternatives and the costs and benefits of each. The alternatives include (1) relying upon continued treatment to reduce the subject's violent propensities; (2) taking preventive action in the context of continued treatment, such as obtaining a weapon from the subject; (3) seeking the subject's institutionalization (or, if institutionalized, the subject's seclusion or transfer); (4) alerting law enforcement or institutional security officials; and (5) warning the potential victim.

The second <u>Tarasoff</u> duty requires only that the therapist respond reasonably, not perfectly. In choosing how to proceed, the therapist should consider several factors, including (1) the extent to which various responses would breach confidentiality (with warning probably constituting the most costly or serious breach), (2) the degree of the danger posed and the ease of identifying specific targets, and (3) the likely effectiveness of the various alternatives (Roth and Meisel 1977). In addition, the therapist's personally contributing to the risk probably increases the therapist's responsibility to take special care. In one case, for example, the patient's crisis was precipitated when the therapist left the patient, who had been referred for a drugrelated problem, alone in the office with a pad of prescription blanks.

Informing Patient of Reduced Confidentiality

A major effect of the <u>Tarasoff</u> duties on professional ethics is that a therapist might, under exceptional circumstances, conclude that his or her legal (and perhaps ethical) responsibility requires warning a third party, thus revealing at least some information obtained from the patient under assumed confidentiality. Must the therapist warn patients of this possible need to subsequently breach confidentiality before eliciting information from patients? In general practice, the likelihood of a <u>Tarasoff</u> situation arising may be so low that such warnings are not required, at least as a matter of routine. If, however, the patient is being treated in the context of a program for violent persons, the likelihood may have increased to the point that frequent, if not routine, prior warning is essential. In institutional programs, prior warning is only part of the general problem of divided loyalties and the need to inform the patient of how nontherapeutic loyalties affect the confidentiality of the therapeutic relationship. Whether a therapist's professional ethics permit functioning under divided loyalties is beyond the scope of this chapter. To the extent that such division exists, however, it seems clear that the patient must be informed.

Practical Suggestions

Few jurisdictions have explicitly adopted the Tarasoff approach at this point, and at least one has rejected it (Shaw v. Glickman 1980). It seems quite likely, however, that most courts would hold that a therapist does owe the potential victim of a patient the Tarasoff duties: to evaluate the patient for violent propensities and to respond with reasonable care whenever the patient is determined to present a significant threat of violent harm to a third person. It is less clear whether other courts will be as receptive as the Tarasoff court to suggestions that the therapist might have to respond by warning potential victims. Of course, ethical considerations may require no less.

In addition, special requirements imposed by local law may demand breaches of confidentiality without regard to Tarasoff-type case law. Child abuse provisions, for example, may require a therapist who becomes aware that a patient is abusing children to inform authorities.

It is likely that the therapist has a legal as well as an ethical responsibility to potential victims, especially in the context of programs for persons identified as violent. This responsibility suggests that therapists should exercise special care in evaluating patients who may have violent propensities. The following general practices may also be indicated:

1. Records should carefully document the assessment of risk and the reasons for it. If the patient made a focused threat or showed focused hostility that was not regarded as evidence of an actual risk, the therapist should note and explain this assessment. The therapist should take special care when there is evidence that the patient is identified as posing a significant risk to one person or a specific group of persons, especially if the patient's history includes hostile or assaultive actions directed at such persons. In these cases, the record should reflect the options considered and the reasons for the manner in which the therapist or staff members decided to proceed.

2. In questionable cases, the therapist should obtain consultations from others and include the results in the record. In many cases, courts are likely to hold that a professional fulfilled his or her duty by obtaining another concurring professional opinion.

3. Prior to treatment, the therapist should tell patients being treated

for violent propensities that the therapist's primary loyalty is to the patient, but that legal and ethical mandates require consideration of the safety of third persons. Further, the therapist should inform the patient of the possibility, albeit unlikely, that the therapist may be required to breach confidentiality to assure that no harm comes to others. In the absence of special circumstances suggesting that a warning may be necessary, the therapist need not specifically tell the patient that this breach of confidentiality might include a warning to third persons. If, however, circumstances suggest that a risk exists and that other responses may not be adequate, the patient should be specifically informed of this possibility.

TESTIMONY CONCERNING DANGEROUSNESS

In cases such as that of Martin K., members of the treatment staff may be called as witnesses in court proceedings and asked to express an opinion concerning the subject's assaultiveness. Input may also be sought less formally, such as asking for an evaluation and a report on the subject's violent propensities. If the clinician is qualified as an expert witness, the law is unlikely to place any significant limits on the level of predictive skill or specificity that the clinician can claim (Dix 1977). Unfortunately, little attention has been paid to the extent to which, if at all, professional ethics bear upon the substance of testimony in these circumstances. Because the therapist is testifying on the basis of his or her presumed skill as a mental health professional, professional ethics would seem to require that the substance of such testimony be reasonably related to the therapist's demonstrated skill in predicting violent conduct.

A major ethical concern of the mental health professional is the need to avoid assuming responsibility for decisions that are properly those of the court. Decisions regarding committing and sentencing criminal defendants and releasing certain persons are, under the legal framework, the responsiblity of the judge or, in some instances, a jury. Judges and juries often feel uncomfortable, however, when faced with the difficulty of predicting a person's future behavior, especially if the person is psychologically abnormal. Thus, they are quite often uncritically willing to defer to the judgment of a mental health professional who appears to have special and superior skill in this area. This tendency may be reflected in a willingness to accept only vague opinion testimony from the professional without requiring the sort of explanation or specificity essential to a critical consideration of whether to credit the professional's opinion.

In many cases, the type of opinion sought by the court—that the person will, if released, cause serious injury to another person—cannot be given on the basis of current predictive skill. Recent empirical evidence indicates that when mental health professionals predict that particular persons will engage in violent conduct over a long period of time, no more than (and perhaps significantly less than) half of those judgments will be established by followup to have been correct (National Academy of Sciences 1978). Monahan (1978) has also pointed out that there is virtually no useful empirical evidence on the accuracy of judgments concerning the risk of violence over short periods of time.

Intuition suggests that mental health professionals' predictions are more likely to be accurate if they concern persons with traditional mental illness, because these illnesses are the focus of the professionals' expertise (Dix 1980). The value of diagnoses in predictions, however, is problematical at best. For example, therapists need to take special care in using the diagnosis of antisocial personality in making predictions about the person's future conduct. It is uncertain how much such a diagnosis supplements the professional's ability to predict future violence on the basis of other behavioral observations (Dix 1980).

Given these considerations, the therapist called upon to provide a court with an expert evaluation of a patient's violent propensities would have the following ethical responsibilities (among others):

1. Generally, the therapist should assert only the ability to place the patient in a group of persons who pose a significantly higher than normal risk of violent conduct (American Psychiatric Association 1974). If the therapist asserts greater predictive skill (for example, by offering an opinion that the patient will, in fact, seriously assault someone if released), the therapist should be prepared to justify the assertion. Seldom—and perhaps never—can such an assertion of predictive skill be reasonably justified.

2. The therapist should take special care to avoid inaccurately implying that certain diagnoses have been demonstrated to have significant value in predicting violent conduct. This caution is particularly important with a diagnosis of sociopathy or antisocial personality.

3. The therapist should insist upon testifying in precise terms that make clear the level of predictive skills asserted. Specifically, the therapist should specify what sorts of conduct are being predicted (such

as any assaultive conduct or specifically causing serious harm to a victim), the period of time the therapist's prediction covers, and the therapist's opinion of the likelihood that the subject will engage in the conduct at issue over that period.

4. The therapist should insist as much as possible on testifying in a manner that discourages or prevents the judge or jury from shifting ultimate responsibility for the legal decision to the therapist.

TREATMENT WITHOUT "INFORMED CONSENT"

Because violent persons are often, like Martin K., enmeshed in civil commitment procedures or correctional systems and unwilling to affirmatively request treatment, therapists frequently face the ethical and legal propriety of imposing treatment without consent or over objection. Although the matter is usually discussed in terms of legal requirements, it is clear that professional ethics may be violated by providing compulsory treatment even if the law permits it (Reiser 1980). Fortunately, legal and ethical considerations in this area appear to be closely related.

Mental Patients' Right to Refuse Treatment

Several recent civil commitment decisions have held that civilly committed patients have a conditional right to refuse certain intrusive forms of treatment (Rennie v. Klein 1981; Romeo v. Youngberg 1980; Rogers v. Okin 1980). There is general agreement that a mental patient who is incompetent to make treatment decisions can be treated over objection, although some courts require the substitute consent of a guardian. The objection of a competent patient, however, can be overridden only in limited circumstances. Courts have been reluctant to override objections on the ground that treatment is necessary to reduce the risk of violence that a patient will present when ultimately discharged.

Courts are divided on whether a decision to treat a patient over objection must be made by the treating physician, the staff, or perhaps an outside mental health professional or a court. Because of the nature of the therapistpatient relationship, it can be argued that the treating mental health professional has an ethical duty to avoid assuming personal responsibility for determining whether a patient's objection can be overridden (Halleck 1974). Recent judicial decisions reflect a similar concern. Treating clinicians, it is feared, may lack the detachment required to consider factors besides the patient's best interests and may lack expertise to deal with some nonclinical matters that must be considered in overriding objections (Dix 1981b).

If responsibility for the decision is not removed from treating personnel, there is still the opportunity to structure the decisionmaking process appropriately. For example, the patient may be given a right to explain and defend objections to treatment. A decision by a group (such as the treatment team) rather than by a single individual may be required to override the decision. The court may obtain additional assurance of objective and responsible decision-making by requiring that the decision be made or approved by persons who are higher in rank than the treating clinician.

In some situations, it may be impossible or undesirable to structure the process for deciding to override a patient's objection and remove the responsibility for making that decision from treating personnel. Especially in these contexts, careful documentation of the steps taken is necessary to assure that general practice (and action taken in particular cases) can be evaluated. Such documentation will permit the staff members to identify areas where additional care needs to be taken to assure that appropriate decisions can be made to override a patient's objections.

The manner in which nonconsensual treatment is administered is also related to these concerns. Unless a treatment program is soundly based and well structured, it may improperly select subjects for the treatment or misapply the treatment. These risks, possibly acceptable for patients who knowingly consent to the treatment and the risks, are unacceptable when the treatment is administered over a patient's objections. Both legal and ethical considerations, therefore, demand that nonconsensual treatment be provided with exceptional care.

The courts will be influenced by their perception of the intrusiveness of a particular treatment in determining whether a patient has a right to decline treatment, in formulating standards and procedures for overriding that decision, and in determining whether treatment administered over objection is being adequately administered. The court will also be concerned with the nature and reversibility of any discomfort experienced as a direct effect of treatment and the nature and reversibility of side effects. These concerns will be weighed against the demonstrated effectiveness of the particular technique at issue. Thus, the courts are likely to look with increasing favor on mental patients' resistance as intrusiveness of treatment progresses from token economy wards, to medication, to electroconvulsive therapy, to aversive conditioning, to psychosurgical techniques.

Nonconsensual Treatment in the Correctional Context

Prisoners differ in at least two ways from committed mental patients with respect to compelled treatment. Because prisoners are less likely to be incompetent to make treatment decisions, the issue of compulsory treatment of competent persons is more critical in the correctional area. On the other hand, conviction for a crime may mean that prisoners have forfeited at least some of their right to personal autonomy, and therefore can more frequently be compelled to submit to treatment for social benefit. While court decisions to date are not consistent, they tend to significantly support the idea that the Government's control over prison inmates entitles it to compel them to submit to treatment for a physical condition, at least when the condition is life threatening (Commissioner v. Myers 1979).

In Vitek v. Jones (1980), the United States Supreme Court held that a prison inmate has a limited due process right to have someone other than a treating physician determine the propriety of transferring the inmate from a prison to a mental hospital. An informal hearing must be held, at which the inmate is entitled to be heard. The hearing need not be before a court (an "independent decisionmaker" is sufficient), and the "qualified" assistance to which the inmate is entitled need not be provided by a lawyer. A written statement of the reasons for and the evidence relied upon in reaching the decision to transfer the inmate is also required.

Vitek did not address the procedure necessary to place an inmate in a treatment program within the same institution. A recent lower court case, Bills v. Henderson (1980), suggests that when a decision to segregate an inmate is based upon a clinical "predictive judgment" concerning "general behavior" rather than a specific rule infraction, the only procedural requirement is that the inmate be told the reasons for the segregation. A similar approach might well be taken by a court with respect to a decision to compel inmates to participate in a prison treatment program designed to address their violent tendencies.

Despite the apparent legal ability of correctional programs to compel inmates to participate in treatment, some clinicians regard compelled treatment as totally inconsistent with the ethical requirements of their professions. Ayllon and Milan (1979), for example, have offered guidelines for ethical "behavior modification" programs in correctional settings. Their guidelines, which assume that voluntarily given informed consent is ethically essential, emphasize various ways of assuring that the consent is informed and voluntary. It remains uncertain, therefore, whether clinicians can utilize the flexibility the law provides in compelling treatment.

Consensual Treatment

Even treatment administered with the patient's consent may raise both legal and ethical concerns if the consent is obtained in a context that raises reasonable questions concerning the patient's "int elligence," "voluntariness," or "competence" to give acceptable consent. Unfortunately, there is little agreement regarding the level of impairment that renders a patient incompetent, the information necessary for a consent to be intelligent, and the pressures or influences which, if they affect the patient's decision, will render the consent legally or ethically ineffective.

The most important consent question regarding violent patients is the subject's desire to increase the likelihood of release from commitment or imprisonment by consenting to treatment. Ideally, perhaps, consent should be unaffected by such considerations, but avoiding such influences may be impossible. Legally, it is unlikely that this sort of influence will render a consent ineffective in most situations, although it may be considered in deciding whether the consent was voluntary.

A two-pronged approach may be most practical: First, treating personnel should seek to assure that releasing authorities (such as parole boards or courts) do not give undue weight to a subject's willingness to participate in a treatment program and progress through the program. Second, the subject should receive information as fully and accurately as possible regarding how participation and progress in the program will affect decisions concerning the subject's future.

Emergency Situations

When a subject is considered to pose an immediate threat of violence to others, treatment personnel have both ethical and legal flexibility. Inevitably, the treatment personnel directly involved must have substantial responsibility, but they must take care to assure that there is a sufficient need for emergency action, i.e., there is a substantial danger of imminent and serious violence. Responsibility for action should be vested in the highest possible staff level. Because the nature of

emergencies preclude anticipation of all situations in which intervention will be indicated, staff members should carefully document the
need for intervention, the choice of method, and the care used to apply
that method. This documentation will support after-the-fact scrutiny
to assure general adherence to good practice.

CLINICAL EMERGENCIES

When emergency action follows a subject's actual violent conduct
or threat or attempt to engage in such violence, the propriety of emergency action will seldom be questioned. A more difficult issue is presented when the clinician concludes, based on other types of information, that sufficient danger exists to justify emergency intervention.
The language used in recent mental health cases to define situations
justifying emergency action does not include requirements of violent
conduct by the subject. The District Court in Rennie v. Klein (1979),
for example, referred only to "sudden, significant changes in the patient's condition," resulting in the requisite danger of violent conduct.
In the correctional context, the court in Bills v. Henderson (1980) noted
the propriety of segregation following a "predictive judgment" that the
requisite danger of violence existed. The judgment was based on the
inmate's general behavior rather than on a specific rule infraction.

It might be argued that ethical considerations preclude emergency
intervention by the clinician unless some overt action of the subject
justifies the intervention. Carrying this line of argument still further, it
could be said that the emergency process is subject to minimal over-
sight, and that clinicians need to exercise special restraint. Finally, it
could be argued that since clinicians' ability to make accurate clinical
predictions of "dangerousness" is not empirically established, reasonable professional restraint requires that the evidence used in making
such a prediction include patient conduct confirming the existence of
an immediate danger of violence.

On the other hand, there is at least some indication that a requirement of overt behavior adds little or nothing to clinicians' accuracy in
predicting violence (Rofman et al. 1980). Treatment personnel have an
ethical responsibility for the safety of other subjects as well as for the
liberty of potentially violent ones, and case law is beginning to recognize a legal duty to the other subjects (Romeo v. Youngberg 1980).
(See editor's Postscript.) On a practical level, clinicians might regard
their potential liability for wrongfully taking emergency action as less
than the liability for harm done to other subjects if they do not take
such action. More significantly, perhaps, the clinicians' remaining pas-

sive may be viewed as violating the ethical duty to use clinical skills to fully perform their duties.

At this stage, it remains uncertain whether emergency action is appropriate in the absence of the subject's overt violent behavior. Present legal requirements probably do not demand such action. If clinicians are authorized to act and their actions are based on clinical judgments that do not include a patient's violent behavior or threats, they should take this type of emergency intervention only with special care and after careful evaluation of its justification.

MEDICATION

The flurry of recent litigation concerning the use of medication over objection suggests that clinicians must give special attention to the use of medications in response to emergency situations. Although it is difficult to evaluate the relative intrusiveness of various responses, the courts will probably regard the use of medication as more intrusive than other responses, such as restraint or seclusion. The case law, however, does not suggest that this judgment will result in substantially greater formal legal limitations on the use of medication. In Rennie v. Klein (1979), for example, the District Court held that 72 hours of compelled medication was permissible if the treating physician certified in the record that an emergency existed. An extension for another 72 hours was authorized when the medical director of the hospital certified that the emergency situation continued.

It is likely, therefore, that legal standards, and perhaps ethical ones as well, require that medication be regarded as more intrusive than seclusion or restraint. Medication must thus be used only when other methods are inappropriate. Further, medication should obviously be administered under the supervision of medical personnel. Directives to medicate "as needed" or similar methods of delegating much of the physician's function are questionable at best.

GUIDELINES

The absence of definitive case law complicates specific prediction of future legal requirements. The following guidelines, however, reasonably approximate the likely legal requirements.

1. Emergency medication, seclusion, or restraint should be permitted only when therapists determine that the subject poses a substantial threat of imminent and serious harm to others. The more intrusive responses to a violent subject should be used only when less

intrusive methods have been unsuccessfully tried or reasonably appear unlikely to work. Medication should generally be regarded as more intrusive than seclusion, which in turn should be regarded as more intrusive than restraint.

2. Authorization from a responsible authority (such as the physician in charge of the ward or the unit administrator) should be required before using seclusion or restraint or, if this is not practical, within a reasonable time (24 to 48 hours) after seclusion or restraint begins. (See editor's Postscript.) Staff members should be required to obtain authorization of the treating physician or, if this is not practicable, authorization of another physician before administering medication.

3. Emergency intervention of any sort should last only as long as the subject continues to present a substantial threat of imminent violence. The initial authorization for use of emergency measures should be limited to 24 to 48 hours, subject to renewal.

4. Staff members should check the subject periodically, perhaps as frequently as every 15 to 30 minutes. At least some of these checks should involve interaction with the subject to assure his or her well-being and determine whether continued emergency measures are necessary.

5. The staff members should make thorough chart entries that include: (a) a description of the behavior or condition requiring emergency intervention, (b) less intrusive alternatives (if any) to the intervention that were considered and the reasons for rejecting them, (c) the method of emergency intervention used and the means of implementation, (d) a notation concerning each periodic check and its results, and (e) the duration of the emergency intervention.

Non-Emergency Situations

Long-term treatment programs designed to address matters other than subjects' immediate violence are arguably more intrusive than emergency intervention. The absence of exigent circumstances also permits clinicians to follow more structured procedures. Not surprisingly, then, courts have been more likely to restrict overriding subjects' objections to treatment in these types of situations.

This section will consider three kinds of interventions. Several others, not addressed, are quite unlikely to be used to treat subjects' violent propensities. These rarely used treatments include psychosurgery, which Kaimowitz v. Department of Mental Health (1973) and

Wyatt v. Hardin (1972) suggest are likely to be completely prohibited in institutional programs, and milieu therapy, which is unlikely to be regarded as sufficiently intrusive to warrant legal (and perhaps ethical) concern.

A preliminary note: Perhaps without adequate consideration, courts have been critical of efforts to use nonconsensual treatment for what might be regarded as purposes of keeping internal order in institutions. Wyatt v. Hardin (1972), for example, prohibited the use of aversive conditioning programs "for the sole or primary purpose of institutional convenience." The extent to which "institutional convenience" was intended to include maintenance of order and preservation of the safety of other persons in the institution is not clear (see chapter 6). If considerations of institutional safety are significant in the decision to undertake involuntary treatment, however, clinicians should recognize that the program is likely to bear an especially difficult burden of justification.

Aversive Conditioning Programs

Aversive conditioning programs use unpleasant responses or stimuli to discourage or repress certain forms of behavior. Most programs thus far litigated or discussed in the literature have involved extremely intrusive stimuli, such as injection of apomorphine to induce vomiting in Knecht v. Gillman (1973) and succinylcholine chloride or anectine to produce respiratory arrest in Mackey v. Procunier (1973). However, the use of seclusion to discourage further antisocial behavior rather than to terminate a present episode of such conduct would also be considered intrusive.

Courts have tended to regard aversive conditioning programs as being very intrusive with minimally demonstrated effectiveness. Perhaps the procedures are regarded skeptically because the unpleasant effects are "intended," rather than constituting an unavoidable side effect: courts may tend to equate them with "punishment" rather than "treatment." Although it is not clear that the distinctions between these two categories are well developed or articulated, the case law strongly suggests that, in both the correctional and mental health context, courts will limit the use of aversive procedures to subjects who are competent and have given an effective consent. Further, this consent must be revocable even between the commission of the target conduct and the administration of the stimuli.

Aversive conditioning programs may yet prove to be permissible in extreme cases, such as with the incompetent and severely impaired subject who engages in frequent and self-destructive headbanging despite all other means of intervention. Such situations have not reached the courts, however, and are not of concern for present purposes (see also chapter 2).

If aversive conditioning techniques are limited to consenting subjects, the need for acceptable consent becomes paramount. The therapist should be assured that the subject has full and accurate information concerning how participation in and progress through the program will affect such matters as institutional assignment and release to the community. It is especially important to document the information that has been provided to the subject.

Despite such efforts, subjects may still be exposed to questionable or improper pressure to consent to participation in a program. This pressure may be offset, however, if clinicians carefully make and review in a structured manner general decisions concerning the development and implementation of the program as a whole. Care in regard to such decisions is always desirable, of course, but special care and structure are especially important—and perhaps legally essential—when, despite all reasonable precautions, there remains a risk of persons being improperly admitted into the program.

The following proposed standards for aversive conditioning programs are quite likely to be embodied in legal requirements. They might reasonably also be regarded as independently demanded by ethical considerations.

1. Each program should be carefully developed and planned in writing with objectives and means clearly stated. The program plan should be reviewed by an institutionwide or agencywide group or committee.

2. Subjects should be considered for inclusion only upon recommendation by a mental health professional who is a member of that person's treatment team. The reasons for the recommendation should be documented in the subject's record.

3. The subject's written consent should be obtained. The consent form should contain (a) full information concerning the program, its objectives, risks, etc.; (b) an explanation of the circumstances in which reports of the subject's progress (or lack of progress) will be made to others; and (c) a clear statement that the subject may withdraw from the program at any time by orally or otherwise expressing a desire to do so. During the process of obtaining consent, it would be sound policy for the subject to have access to independent advice. Providing counsel

would be one procedure, but other sources of advice might well be sufficient or perhaps even preferable.

4. A committee composed of persons not involved in planning or administering the program should review the propriety of the subject's participation in the program. The committee should also review the subject's consent to assure that it is informed and voluntary.

5. The program should be conducted under proper supervision. For example, only properly qualified persons should administer aversive stimuli.

6. Subjects' right to withdraw from the program at any time, even immediately before the stimuli, should be scrupulously honored. No particular form of withdrawal should be required; any expression of a desire to withdraw should be sufficient.

7. Each subject's record should carefully document the details of the program and the subject's progress toward his or her goals. The propriety of continuing the subject in the program should be periodically assessed. A committee should periodically review the decision to continue the subject in the program, especially after a significant period (see also chapter 2).

BEHAVIOR MODIFICATION PROGRAMS

While all of the techniques addressed in this chapter might be considered forms of behavior modification, it is useful to limit this phrase to operant conditioning programs that reward subjects for appropriate conduct by making available more attractive living conditions or other similar reinforcements (Wexler 1975). This definition would include "token economy" programs and "tier advancement" systems.

The characteristics of at least some behavior modification programs may render them legally and perhaps ethically unacceptable. The framework for rewarding the subjects often involves subjecting them to initial living conditions that fall below what they would otherwise be legally or ethically entitled to have. The programs may not be subject to ultimate objection in that they intrude only temporarily upon the subjects' right to "reasonable conditions of habitation." When there is intrusion into arguably protected interests, there must be substantial evidence of demonstrated effectiveness to counterbalance the intrusion. Wexler (1973) has argued further that some programs fail to creatively search for reinforcements that would not require severe initial deprivation. To the extent that this assertion is accurate, programs can become even more objectionable because the intrusiveness is unnecessary.

Assuming that programs are not inherently objectionable on either ethical or legal grounds, there are still limitations on their availability. The major case law consists of Clonce v. Richardson (1974) which addressed issues raised by a tier advancement program for disruptive inmates (the START program) developed by the U.S. Bureau of Prisons at the Federal Medical Center in Springfield, Missouri. The court declined to consider whether Federal constitutional considerations placed any constraints on the criteria used to include inmates in the program. The court did, however, hold that selection of inmates for inclusion required procedural due process, defined by the court as involving notice, an informal hearing, and written findings concerning the reason for selecting each inmate. Because the START program involved transferring prison inmates to a medical facility, Vitek (1980) confirms that the court was correct in its procedural holding. Moreover, even when inclusion in such a program does not require transfer to a different facility, it does dramatically alter the inmate's condition of confinement in the same way as the transfers at issue in Vitek. It is likely, therefore, that the procedural requirements imposed in Vitek and Clonce v. Richardson will apply to inclusion of subjects in tier advancement and token economy programs within the institution.

If squarely presented with the issue, most courts would probably hold that prison inmates and mental patients have a limited right to avoid participation in tier advancement or token economy programs that involve substantial initial deprivations. This almost certainly means that the courts will require somewhat restrictive criteria for inclusion of subjects. Given the likely difficulty of establishing such programs' effectiveness in changing prison inmates' long-term behavior, especially severe limits are likely to be placed on the criteria used by correctional programs to put inmates into such programs.

If compulsory participation were allowed only when a subject was determined to be incompetent, this would probably frustrate many opportunities to use these programs to address dangerousness, especially in the correctional context. If competent subjects are included in either mental health or correctional programs, however, the selection criterion should assure that each subject poses a substantial risk. Even such a limited criterion will be defensible only if the program is carefully designed to maximize effectiveness and to minimize arbitrary or otherwise improper application. Behavior modification programs should use the procedures urged above for advance approval and continuous monitoring of aversive conditioning programs when dangerous but competent subjects are compelled to participate.

Medication of Civilly Committed Patients

Recent litigation strongly suggests that the privacy interests of civilly committed mental patients will impose significant limitations on the nonconsensual administration of at least some medications. To date, litigation has focused on the major antipsychotic medications, which have been viewed by courts as significantly intrusive largely because of the nature and high risk of side effects. Rogers v. Okin (1980) specifically so limited its holding, reserving judgment on the legal status of antidepressants, which might be evaluated as sufficiently less intrusive to escape legal regulation. On the other hand, courts will probably limit medications of a more experimental nature, such as lithium used to reduce violence, to competent patients who give informed and voluntary consent.

A number of recent cases, including Rogers v. Okin (1980), Goedecke v. State Department (1979) and In re K.K.B. (1980) appear to require that a patient's objection to medication be respected unless the patient has been determined to be incompetent, i.e., incapable of making a competent or rational decision whether to submit to medication. In Rennie v. Klein (1981), however, the appellate court adopted a somewhat more flexible approach under which a patient's objection could be overriden if medication is a "necessary part" of the treatment plan. If the patient is incapable without medication of participating in any treatment program that provides a realistic opportunity for improvement, the required necessity standard is met. The standard is also met if use of medication would significantly shorten the period necessary to secure improvement or if, without medication, a significant possibility exists that the patient would harm himself or herself or others before improvement took place.

There are similar variations in the procedure for overriding the patient's refusal. Rogers v. Okin (1980), for example, requires that the initial decision concerning a patient's competency be made by a court. Once a court determines that a patient is incompetent for this purpose, however, future specific drug treatment decisions need not be made by the court or even by a court-appointed guardian. Rather, the treatment staff members have primary authority to determine appropriate drug treatment. The court did suggest that it would be necessary to have a periodic review of the propriety of involuntary treatment with medications, with such review being made by a physician who is not part of the treatment staff. The District Court in Rennie v. Klein (1979) permitted the necessary determination to be made by an "independent" psychiatrist after an informal hearing. On appeal, the standard was modified to require only that the attending physician, after a meeting and discussion with the treatment team, conclude that medication is a necessary part of the treatment plan. The institution's medical director or a designee must personally examine the record and agree. Some courts may be receptive to a procedure that would give the treatment team or some similar group, rather than the attending physician, primary responsibility for making at least the initial decision to override a patient's objections.

Courts' willingness to impose limits on the nonconsensual administration of a generally accepted treatment modality, such as the major antipsychotics, suggests caution on the part of practitioners. If a program involves use of medications that are less generally accepted and have higher risk of undesirable side effects, both ethical standards and reasonable anticipation of legal requirements suggest application of consent requirements similar to those discussed above for aversive conditioning programs. On the other hand, programs involving generally accepted and less intrusive medications than the major antipsychotics could reasonably proceed on the basis of a structured staff determination of either incompetency or of a Rennie-like determination that medication is appropriate. However, given the flux in the law as well as the ambiguity of the precise meaning of "competency" as used in the Rogers v. Okin approach and the Rennie analysis, it would be a sound exercise of judgment to override consent only in conjunction with a judicial determination of incompetency.

Medication of Prisoners

The correctional context poses even more complex questions. When nonpsychotic inmates are concerned, it is quite likely that—in the absence of very persuasive evidence to the contrary—courts will regard any medication program designed to reduce violence potential as "experimental." Moreover, it is quite unlikely that nonpsychotic inmates exposed to such a program could reasonably be found incompetent to consent to treatment and therefore in need of a guardian. Any program using medication to reduce violence potential in nonpsychotic patients in the correctional context should therefore require documentation of competency and informed and voluntary consent. The approach suggested above for aversive conditioning programs should probably be used in this case as well.

It is possible that at least some courts would attach less weight to the privacy interests of mentally ill inmates than to those of civilly committed patients. This tendency may apply particularly when the issue is one of using "traditional" medications, such as antipsychotics, for nonconsensual treatment of inmates who suffer from a "traditional" mental illness. It is far from clear, however, whether courts will adopt this position, and there appears to be no persuasive reason why in the nonemergency context the autonomy of a mentally ill prisoner would be more limited than that of a committed patient. Sound policy suggests that mentally ill prisoners' objections to antipsychotic medications should be given the same respect accorded to objections voiced by committed patients. This policy implies that the same procedures required in the mental health context to override a patient's objection should apply in the correctional context when determining whether to override a mentally ill prisoner's objections to medication.

PERSONAL LIABILITY

Increasing "legalization" of the delivery of mental health care has resulted in a corresponding and understandable increase in mental health professionals' concern regarding their personal legal liability. To some extent, the concern with ultimate liability probably reflects a misconstruction of the case law. The Tarasoff cases frequently discussed by therapists did not, for example, hold that the defendant therapists were in fact liable for damages. They merely held that the plaintiff's pleadings were adequate and that the defendants would be liable for damages if the allegations that their conduct did not meet the standard of reasonable professional care had been proven at trial. In a recent New Jersey appellate case in which the court accepted the Tarasoff approach the defendant was found, at trial, non-negligent and thus not liable for damages. Even if ultimate liability is of no concern, however, most professionals will want to avoid the financial, emotional, and professional trauma of being the defendant in litigation.

Plaintiffs may sue in Federal court on the basis that the defendant mental health professionals have violated the plaintiffs' federally protected civil rights. In such cases the law appears to provide a defense that proves that the defendants, even if their actions violated the plaintiff's civil rights, did not know or could not have ascertained with reasonable care that the actions would violate the plaintiff's legal rights (O'Connor v. Donaldson 1975). This defense of "good faith" may not, however, be available if the patient sues in State court on the basis that the defendant's actions came under no legal authorization and thus constituted a tort, such as battery.

Some States do have provisions granting limited immunity to mental health professionals. A Texas statute, for example, provides that any action taken "in good faith, reasonably and without negligence" pursuant to the examination, detention, treatment, or discharge of a person under the State's Mental Health Code is free from all civil or criminal liability (Texas Revised Statutes). Under such provisions, a suit would be permissible on the basis that a clinician was negligent in failing to ascertain that a certain treatment modality could not be used over a patient's objection. Given the uncertain state of the law in many areas, however, a court would undoubtedly find it difficult to conclude that a mental health professional, merely by exercising "reasonable care," could accurately ascertain what would and would not be permissible under yet-to-be developed law.

Moreover, without regard to the formal law, various circumstances may minimize the attractiveness of litigation to a potential plaintiff, thus providing de facto immunity. Most litigation to date has been concerned either with gross violations of law and of what might be termed "human decency" or with administration of care in institutional contexts that, as a whole, were grossly inadequate. A mental health professional is not apt to be thought of as an attractive defendant if, while functioning in a program providing care under reasonable circumstances, that professional misjudged a patient's legal rights after trying to exercise reasonable concern and consideration. Such a person is quite unlikely to find that he or she is the subject of a suit for damages.

As a practical matter, the danger of becoming a defendant in a lawsuit seeking personal liability can be minimized by adhering to the following suggestions:

1. Treatment records should be carefully and comprehensively maintained. The records can demonstrate that the therapist has nothing to hide and help the therapist document his or her actions should this become necessary (see editor's Postscript).

2. Consultation and joint decisionmaking should be pursued in those cases in which it appears necessary to make decisions about matters that might later be found to violate legal standards. Insofar as

possible, the critical decisions should be made by a treatment team or staff rather than by a single therapist. This procedure will document the therapist's concern that a "correct" decision was made in a sensitive area and that the therapist sought other views and input.

3. The therapist may wish to seek legal evaluations of especially critical matters. Public agencies often have access to an agency's legal staff members and can request an evaluation of a proposed program or course of action. If no such access exists, superiors can be asked to provide access to legal advice. Although a lawyer's assertion that an improper course of conduct is "legal" does not make that course of conduct legally permissible, such consultation decreases the therapist's attractiveness as a defendant, especially in litigation seeking personal liability. The record, of course, should document the advice received or the request for access to legal advice.

CONCLUSION

Halleck (1981) has warned that those who develop treatments for deviant behavior have an ethical responsibility to take into account a specific danger: the availability of apparently effective treatment may encourage undue expansion of the definition of "deviance" and inappropriate placement of persons in compulsory treatment. The same general caution undoubtedly applies to those who develop and administer programs that treat violent patients. In addition, as illustrated by the hypothetical case that introduced this chapter, the treatment and handling of violent behavior raises additional legal and ethical issues. This chapter's discussion of these issues has led to a number of conclusions with implications for policy and practice.

Clinicians have an ethical and probably a legal duty to protect potential victims from possible violence at the hands of the clinician's patients. Prior to treatment, patients being treated for violent propensities should be informed that the therapist's first loyalty is to the patient but that, in addition, legal and ethical mandates require that the therapist consider the safety of third persons. When called upon to participate in an evaluation of a subject's "dangerousness," therapists have at least an ethical responsibility to remain within the limits of demonstrated predictive accuracy. While treatment of violent persons without their consent is permitted and probably required in some situations, the legal criteria and procedures for overriding a subject's objection to such treatment are unsettled. The criteria seem to be moving in the direction of increasing complexity.

"Legalization" of the delivery of mental health treatment services in general, and of nonconsensual treatment of the violent person in particular, has created understandable concern on the part of clinicians concerning personal legal liability. While there is no guarantee that a reasonable and good-faith belief in the legal (and ethical) propriety of one's actions will constitute a defense to a lawsuit, careful documentation of the care taken in making difficult decisions can minimize the clinician's vulnerability to suit.

EDITOR'S POSTSCRIPT

There have been three especially noteworthy developments relevant to legal and ethical issues in the treatment and handling of violent behavior. All relate to actions taken by the United States Supreme Court in June and July 1982.

The Supreme Court failed to provide definitive guidance for the law or mental health clinicians in <u>Rogers</u> v. <u>Okin</u>, by then renamed <u>Mills</u> v. <u>Rogers</u> (1982). Instead, the Supreme Court instructed the lower Federal court, the Court of Appeals for the First Circuit, to reconsider its holding in <u>Rogers</u>, taking into account recent developments in Massachusetts law. The Court of Appeals, in turn, certified several issues to the Massachusetts Supreme Court. In <u>Rogers</u> v. <u>Commissioner</u> (1983) the State tribunal held that, under Massachusetts law, a civilly committed patient could be required over objection to submit to treatment by antipsychotic medication only if a court determined that the patient was incompetent and approved a treatment plan including medication. Nevertheless, the earlier opinion of the Court of Appeals in <u>Rogers</u> discussed by Dix continues to represent one possible resolution of the controversy concerning patients' right to refuse medication.

<u>Youngberg</u> v. <u>Romeo</u> (1982), the Supreme Court's second June 1982 decision, is very consistent with the trends, recommendations, and general approach discussed in chapter 9 of this volume. The Federal Constitution, the Court held in <u>Youngberg</u>, mandates that a safe environment must be provided for institutionalized persons and that any decisions to restrain (seclude) a patient must be made in accordance with a professional judgment and not in a cavalier manner. In <u>Youngberg</u>, a case involving a profoundly retarded man who had been both

repetitively injured and restrained in the Pennhurst Institution, the Supreme Court ruled that "If it is cruel and unusual punishment to hold convicted criminals in unsafe conditions, it must be unconstitutional to confine the involuntarily committed—who may not be punished at all—in unsafe conditions" (Youngberg 1982). "The State . . . has the unquestioned duty to provide reasonable safety for all residents and personnel within the institution" (Youngberg 1982). The Supreme Court went on to rule that, for institutionalized persons such as Mr. Romeo, not only are there constitutionally protected interests in safety but also constitutionally protected interests in "freedom from bodily restraint." The patient's liberty interests also "require the State to provide minimally adequate or reasonable training to ensure safety and freedom from undue restraint." The Youngberg case thus affords mentally retarded persons (and most likely mentally ill persons) some minimal constitutional right to treatment in the institution.

The Supreme Court's ruling in Youngberg also touches upon the scope of mental health professionals' liability for failing to assure these constitutionally guaranteed patients' rights. Concerning the decision to restrain residents, the Court ruled that such a decision, if made by a professional, is presumptively valid; liability "may be imposed only when the decision by the professional is such a substantial departure from accepted professional judgment, practice or standards as to demonstrate that the person responsible actually did not base the decision on such a judgment" (Youngberg 1982). The Youngberg case thus affords mental health staff members considerable professional leeway in making decisions to restrain a patient. However, to avoid legal liability, such decisions must represent at least a "professional judgment."

Based on ethical and professional considerations, mental health professionals should, of course, avoid restraining or secluding a patient unless such a decision is clearly justified in terms of the harm to be avoided for the patient or others and the good that will result. The Supreme Court's decision in Youngberg, however, strengthens Dix's recommendation that restraint decisions must be made in a deliberate and professional manner. When the propriety of such decisions is confirmed through consultation or the second opinion approach, Youngberg suggests that mental health professionals will not be liable for violating the patient's constitutional rights.

Finally, in Rennie v. Klein (1982), the United States Supreme Court returned the Rennie case to the United States Court of Appeals for the Third Circuit, directing the lower Federal court to reconsider its earlier opinion in light of Youngberg v. Romeo. Youngberg emphasized that mental health clinicians can be entrusted with substantial discretion in implementing residents' rights to safety and freedom from restraint. The Supreme Court's action in Rennie may reflect a view that clinicians may be given similar discretion to determine when patients' objections to medication should be overridden.

These developments and others that will undoubtedly occur make it clear that continued case law developments in this area need to be monitored by mental health clinicians and by State mental health departments responsible for implementing rules and regulations of the sort discussed by Dix.

LEGAL CASES

Bills v. Henderson, 631 F.2d 1287 (6th Cir. 1980).
Clonce v. Richardson, 379 F.Supp. 338 (W.D. Mo. 1974).
Commissioner v. Myers 399 N.E.2d 452 (Mass. 1979).
Goedecke v. State Department of Institutions, 603 P.2d 123 (Colo. 1979).
In re K.K.B., 609 P.2d 747 (Okla. 1980).
Kaimowitz v. Department of Mental Health (Wayne County, Mich. Cir. Ct., 1973). The unreported opinion is reprinted in part in Miller, F.W.; Dawson, R.O.; Dix, G.E.; and Parnas, R.I. The Mental Health Process. Mineola (N.Y.): The Foundation Press, 1976, at pp. 567–78.
Knecht v. Gillman, 488 F.2d 1136 (8th Cir. 1973).
Lipari v. Sears Roebuck & Co., 497 F.Supp. 185 (D. Neb. 1980).
Mackey v. Procunier, 477 F.2d 877 (9th Cir. 1973).
McIntosh v. Milano, 168 N.J.Super. 466, 403 A.2d 500 (1979).
Mills v. Rogers, 457 U.S. 291 (1982).
O'Connor v. Donaldson, 422 U.S. 563 (1975).
Rennie v. Klein, 476 F. Supp. 1294 (D.N.J. 1979), aff'd in part and rev'd in part, 653 F.2d 836 (3rd Cir. 1981). Remanded 458 U.S. 1119 (1982).
Rogers v. Commissioner, 390 Mass. 489, 458 N.E.2d 308 (1983).
Rogers v. Okin, 634 F.2d 650 (1st Cir. 1980), cert. granted, 101 S.Ct. 1972 (1981).
Romeo v. Youngberg, 664 F.2d 147 (3rd Cir. 1980), cert. granted, 101 S.Ct. 2313 (1981).
Shaw v. Glickman 45 Md.App. 718, 415 A.2d 625 (1980).
Tarasoff v. Board of Regents, 17 Cal.3d 425, 131 Cal.Reptr. 14, 551 P.2d 334 (1976).
Texas Revised Statutes, art. 5547–18.
Vitek v. Jones, 445 U.S. 480 (1980).
Wyatt v. Hardin, 344 F.2d 373 (M.D. Ala. 1972), aff'd, 503 F.2d 1305 (5th Cir. 1976).
Youngberg v. Romeo, 457 U.S. 307, 315, 316, 319, 323, 324, (1982).

REFERENCES AND BIBLIOGRAPHY

American Psychiatric Association. Task Force on Clinical Aspects of the Violent Individual. Washington, D.C.: The Association, 1974.

Ayllon, T. Behavior Modification in Institutional Settings. Arizona Law Review 17(1):3–19, 1975.

Ayllon, T. and Milan, M.A. Correctional Rehabilitation and Management: A Psychological Approach. New York: John Wiley & Sons, 1979.

Blackman, D.E. Ethical issues for psychologists in corrections. In: Monahan, J. ed. Who is the Client? Washington, D.C.: American Psychological Association, 1975. pp. 63–92.

Burns, R. P. Behavior Modification as a Punishment. American Journal of Jurisprudence 22:19–54, 1977.

Clingempeel, W.G.; Mulvey, E.; and Reppucci, N.D. A national study of ethical dilemmas of psychologists in the criminal justice system. In: Monahan, J., ed. Who is the Client? Washington, D.C.: American Psychological Association, 1980. pp. 126–153.

Dix, G.E. "Civil" commitment of the mentally ill and the need for data on the prediction of dangerousness. American Behavioral Scientist 19(3):318–334, 1976a.

Dix, G.E. The death penalty, "dangerousness," psychiatric testimony, and professional ethics. American Journal of Criminal Law 5(2):151–214, 1976b.

Dix, G.E. Administration of the Texas death penalty statutes: Constitutional infirmities related to the prediction of dangerousness. Texas Law Review 55:1377–1384, 1977.

Dix, G.E. Clinical evaluation of the "dangerousness" of "normal" criminal defendants. Virginia Law Review 66(3):523–581, 1980.

Dix, G.E. Tarasoff and the duty to warn potential victims. In: Hofling C.K., ed. Law and Ethics in the Practice of Psychiatry. New York: Brunner/Mazel, 1981a, pp. 118–148.

Dix, G.E. Realism and drug refusal: A reply to Appelbaum and Gutheil. Bulletin of the American Academy of Psychiatry and Law, 9(3):180–189, 1981b.

Friedman, P.R. Legal regulation of applied behavior analysis in mental institutions and prisons. Arizona Law Review 17(1):39–104, 1975.

Ginsberg, M.D. A new perspective in prisoners' rights: The right to refuse treatment and rehabilitation. John Marshall Journal of Practice and Procedure 10(1):173–195, 1976.

Halleck, S.L. Legal and ethical aspects of behavior control. American Journal of Psychiatry 131(4):381–385, 1974.

Halleck, S.L. The ethics of antiandrogen therapy. American Journal of Psychiatry 138(5):642–43, 1981.

Michaels, R. The right to refuse treatment: Ethical issues. Hospital & Community Psychiatry 32(4):251–258, 1981.

Monahan, J. Prediction research and the emergency commitment of dangerous mentally ill persons: A reconsideration. American Journal of Psychiatry 135(2):198–201, 1978.

National Academy of Sciences. The prediction of violent behavior: A methodological critique and prospectus, by Monahan, J. In: Deterrence and Incapacitation: Estimating the Effects of Criminal Sanctions on Crime Rates. Washington, D.C.: Supt. of Docs., U.S. Govt. Print. Off., 1978. pp. 244–269.

O'Brien, K.E. Tokens and tiers in corrections: An analysis of legal issues in behavior modification. New England Journal on Prison Law 3(1):15–46, 1976.

Redlich, F., and Mollica, R.F. Overview: Ethical issues in contemporary psychiatry. American Journal of Psychiatry 133(2):125–136, 1976.

Reiser, S.J. Refusing treatment for mental illness: Historical and ethical dimensions. American Journal of Psychiatry 137(3):329–331, 1980.

Remington, R.E. Behavior modification in American penal institutions. British Journal of Criminology 19(4):333–352, 1979.

Rofman, E.S.; Askinazi, C.; and Fant, E. The prediction of dangerous behavior in emergency civil commitment. American Journal of Psychiatry 137(9):1061–1064, 1980.

Rogers v. Commissioner, 390 Mass. 489, 458 N.E.2d 308, 1983.

Roth, L.H., and Meisel, A. Dangerousness, confidentiality, and the duty to warn. American Journal of Psychiatry 134(5):508–511, 1977.

Roth, L.H. To·respect persons, families, and communities: Some problems in the ethics of mental health care. Psychiatric Digest 40(10):17−26, 1979.

Wexler, D.B. Token and taboo: Behavior modification, token economies, and the law. California Law Review 61(1): 81−109, 1973.

Wexler, D.B. Reflections on the legal regulation of behavior modification in institutional settings. Arizona Law Review 17(1):132−43, 1975.

Winick, B.J. Legal limitations on correctional therapy and research. Minnesota Law Review 65(3):331−442, 1981.

10

TREATING VIOLENT PERSONS IN PRISONS, JAILS, AND SECURITY HOSPITALS

Loren H. Roth, M.D., M.P.H.

In many respects, treating violent persons in prisons, jails, and security hospitals poses problems and opportunities similar to those encountered in other treatment settings. Information provided elsewhere in this volume about treating violence is thus broadly relevant to the concerns of correctional and security mental health personnel. Like violence committed elsewhere, much of the violence committed by inmates of prisons, jails, and security hospitals neither stems from a single cause nor is likely to be corrected by any single intervention. Rather, as in other settings, individual assessment of the violent person and situation, as well as assessment of the social milieu in which violence has occurred, should take place before interventions are designated and treatment outcomes evaluated (see chapter 1).

Treating and managing violent persons, of course, is not the sole concern of jail and prison personnel or of mental health clinicians who work in these settings. Such persons must also provide medical services to all inmates and mental health services to disturbed and other inmates experiencing the varieties of stress that are often features of correctional environments (see generally Toch 1975; Roth 1980; National Institute of Mental Health 1982b).

Compounding the problem of treating persons in correctional and security hospital settings is the fact that such institutions serve disparate functions beyond rehabilitative treatment; they are required to provide custody (in effect, incapacitation) for inmates who have harmed others in the past and who typically are viewed by society as likely to do so again. The clash between corrections' conflicting organizational goals has, for many years, been the bane of correctional workers, planners, and theorists (see, for example, Hepburn and Albonetti 1980). Despite the movement in corrections over the last decade toward punishment and custody and away from rehabilitation, not all workers in this field have abandoned the rehabilitative approach (see, for example, Halleck and Witte 1977). Neither has academic thinking yet given up on future possibilities for a more therapeutic approach to inmates (see generally Martin et al. 1981). The concerns of correctional workers and mental health clinicians in prisons, jails, and other such institutions thus encompass not only preventing violence within the institution, but also such goals as custody, incapacitation, reeducation, and rehabilitation.

Compounding the challenge for correctional workers, particularly those working in overcrowded prisons and jails (Gardner 1982; Allinson 1982), is the pessimism voiced from many quarters whether the prevention of inmate violence is really possible in such pernicious environments, especially without fundamental changes in inmate–inmate and staff–inmate relationships, and, just as important, in the overall structure, organization, and management of the institution. Thus, in discussing basic changes needed in prison organization to combat inmate violence, Cohen (1976, p. 20) recommends grievance procedures, ombudsmen, staff–inmate councils and tribunals, and many other actions that he considers are needed to bring about "fundamental changes in the general spirit or climate of the institution" (see also National Institute of Mental Health 1977).

Bowker (1982), discussing prison victimization (including physical victimization), suggests the following solutions for prevention: modification of the correctional environment to allow better scrutiny of inmate behavior, a correctional ombudsman program, classification by victimization potential, increased institutional security with more attention given to preventing the possession of contraband, visits from loved ones (conjugal visits), normalization of prison industries, increased therapeutic roles for correctional officers, improved staffing, implementation of co-corrections (mixing of sexes), unit management, and lowered incarceration rates. Bowker's recommendations are representative of those who believe violence stems from institutional aspects of prison life. From this perspective, inmate violence is but another manifestation of prisons' general problem in establishing safe living conditions for inmates while providing opportunity structures and other personal motivators likely to inhibit and discourage violence (see generally Johnson and Toch 1982; Cohen et al. 1976).

Investigative reports on outbreaks of extreme violence (both group and individual) at American penitentiaries have resulted in similar recommendations to prevent inmate violence. After inmates overran a New Mexico State prison in 1980 and murdered 33 fellow inmates (some quite sadistically), a subsequent report of the State Attorney General made two major recommendations for change: (1) that New Mexico "establish and fund an incentive-based inmate corrections policy" that would include "a range of programs, housing and job assignments, and other formal incentives [which] are the tools of control"; and (2) that the State "hire and hold accountable stable, professional management to implement that policy" (Attorney General, State of New Mexico 1980, pp. 31-36). Similarly, when eight murders occurred over slightly more than a 2-year period at the Federal Penitentiary at Lewisburg, Pennsylvania, a Board of Inquiry issued a report that contained a list of familiar recommendations: better management at the penitentiary, including management by unit; improved management–staff communications; improved supervision; dispersal of troublesome inmates to other prisons; and other related ideas (Board of Inquiry 1976).

While these approaches to reduce inmate violence make considerable sense and undoubtedly were advisable from a managerial perspective, front-line and even middle-management personnel in correctional institutions note that decisions to implement such recommendations are often beyond their control. Other actions, however, can be taken at the prison and individual inmate levels to reduce inmate violence and support more effective staff functioning. The remainder of this chapter will attempt to identify some types of remedial and preventive actions that are both realistic and achievable.

VIOLENCE AND THE CORRECTIONAL ENVIRONMENT

As Toch and others note, the correctional environment has a differential impact on inmates depending on their backgrounds, personalities, and previous experiences (Toch 1975; Toch 1981; Bukstel and Kilmann 1980; Wiehn 1982). Few believe, however, that the overall impact of current correctional environments in the United States is salutary for the mental health and psychological adjustment of inmates (for example, DeWolfe and DeWolfe 1979). In 1982, 29 States were operating their corrections systems under Federal court order or other instruction to correct conditions such as prison overcrowding; poor medical care; filth; bad food; inadequate plumbing; and lack of counseling, vocational programs, and rehabilitative services (Rawls 1982; see also National Institute of Justice 1980a).

Conditions in correctional institutions that have serious mental health consequences and fall within the scope of "cruel and unusual punishment" include (1) negligent protection or abuse of inmates' personal safety, (2) dangerous and debilitating overall conditions of confinement, and (3) denial of access to medical or mental health care (Dunn 1982). While such institutional conditions do not necessarily cause inmates to become violent, there is general agreement that they do increase the probability of violence among inmates. The base rate of violence perpetrated by inmates living under such adverse environmental circumstances will be higher, as will the numbers of persons suffering injury (victims).

The negative impact of poor institutional conditions is further compounded by trends and patterns that have resulted in the incarceration of an increasing proportion of prison inmates with histories of violent behavior. The proportion of prison inmates who are violent offenders increased from 52 percent to 57 percent from 1974 to 1979. In jails, the proportion of inmates who were violent offenders increased from 26 percent to 30 percent between 1972 and 1978 (Bureau of Justice Statistics 1982b, p. 35).

Increasing prison overcrowding is even more important. The total prison population in the United States in mid-1982 reached 394,380, representing an increase of 6.9 percent in only 6 months. Should current rates of growth continue, the United States prison population would be expected to exceed a half million before the end of 1984 (Bureau of Justice Statistics 1982a). While jails historically have not experienced the same degree of overcrowding, a survey conducted in mid-1982 found that 210,000 persons were confined in local jails, a population that was one-third higher than in 1978 (Bureau of Justice Statistics 1983a). Overcrowding in jails has become a problem, particularly in larger jails in urban areas (Allinson 1982).

For a number of reasons, the jail environment is particularly stressful to inmates. The jail term is a period of rapid change in which the inmate must adjust to sudden loss of freedom, sometimes experiencing drug withdrawal. Although suicide and other severe manifestations of inmate stress are more frequent in jails than in other correctional institutions, jail personnel must also focus on the prevention of inmate violence toward others (see generally Roth 1980; National Institute of Mental Health 1982b; Gibbs 1982). Overcrowding in jails and prisons occurs because of the public's generally tough "lock them up" mentality, because of changes in correctional philosophy about parole, and because of the increased use of determinate sentences (Gardner 1982). Assuming continuing overcrowded conditions, correctional workers face a major challenge in trying to develop interventions that can reduce inmate violence in such environments.

Problems of inmate violence have been noted in wellknown court cases relating to deplorable conditions in both prisons and jails. Pugh v. Locke, a 1976 Alabama case, is such an example. Concerning conditions in Alabama's penal institutions, Judge Johnson noted:

> Violent inmates are not isolated from those who are young, passive or weak. Consequently, the latter inmates are repeatedly victimized by those who are stronger and more aggressive. Testimony shows that robbery, rape, extortion, theft and assault are everyday occurrences among the general inmate population. Rather than face this constant danger, some inmates voluntarily subject themselves to the inhuman conditions of prison isolation cells (Pugh v. Lock 1976, p. 324).

Similar problems have recently been described in the Texas prison system, where the trial court found Texas institutions to be "violence ridden and operated in a manner which placed inmates in a position of authority over other inmates, an authority enforced by violence" (Merritt 1983, p. 158; Ruiz v. Estelle 1980). In 1981, in Texas 11 inmates were killed by other inmates, more than double the number of inmates slain in either of the previous 2 years.

Various jail lawsuits have also featured problems in treating, isolating, or otherwise humanely managing violent inmates who act out. For example, in Owens-EL v. Robinson (1978), a lawsuit dealing with conditions at the Allegheny County Jail in Pittsburgh, Pennsylvania, the court noted that acting-out inmates were placed in restraint rooms, either in a hospital gown or "naked on a canvas cot with a hole cut in the middle. Their body wastes drop through the hole into a tub on the floor underneath the cot." Some inmates were held this way for as long as 29 days. This method was used to handle inmates who exhibited antisocial behavior as well as those who had severe mental disorders; neither group of inmates received adequate medical or psychiatric supervision. There were no psychiatrists or psychologists on the jail staff.

Eventually, as a result of these conditions and later litigation, the court mandated a jail mental health unit with increased medical and psychiatric coverage (Inmates of Allegheny County Jail v. Pierce 1979).

Overcrowding in correctional institutions is of particular concern in preventing violence, whether overcrowding is measured by spatial considerations or by social density (the number and interactional patterns of inmates). In his review of the subject, Clements (1979, pp. 220–222) noted that

> When physical density and spatial configurations prevent privacy or adequate personal space, males are particularly stressed. In a crowded prison setting, allowing for the likelihood that hostile responding is seen as one way of handling problems, aggression, both verbal and physical, will increase. . . . Crowding and idleness are intertwined in a circular cause–effect relationship. Overcrowding means more prisoners without constructive jobs or programs.

Epidemiological studies of inmates' misconduct rates and assaults in correctional institutions have tended to confirm these ideas. For example, McGuire's study of seven Federal correctional institutions showed that higher levels of crowding, greater percentages of new inmates in the confined population, larger institutional scale, and larger percentages of the confined population with a personal offense as the basis for the current incarceration were all linked to higher levels of correctional violence (Federal Prison System 1981). Nacci et al. (1977) found that high population density (low amount of space for inmates) was associated with increased reports by Institution Disciplinary Committees, total assault rates, and assault on inmate rates. The relationship was strongest in juvenile and young adult institutions; and inmates of intermediate adult institutions reacted least violently to overpopulation. In long-term adult institutions, rates of assault on other inmates and high density were related, but Institution Disciplinary Committee reports remained relatively unaffected.

Efforts to reduce stressful effects of overcrowding should consider increasing an inmate's sense of privacy or available "personal space" as well as an inmate's sense of control over other facets of institutional life. A recent study in six Federal prisons investigated the impact of spacial density (square feet per individual) and social density (number of occupants per living unit) on such indexes as inmates' perceptions of the quality of prison housing, illness complaints, and disciplinary records. One finding was that inmates "prefer privacy and a clearly demarcated boundary of 'my space' . . . even if square footage must be reduced in order to achieve such privacy." While inmates preferred single cells to dormitories, "single bunking, spaciousness, and segmenting the dormitories into small bays (partitions) were all associated with reductions in the negative reactions typically associated with open dormitories." The study thus suggests that some negative effects of jail and prison housing and prison overcrowding can be reduced by searching for feasible ways to provide inmates with some sort of "private space" which they can call "their own" (National Institute of Justice 1980b, pp. v, 131; see also Clements 1979).

Smith (1982) suggests a number of other related strategies. It may be possible to implement those strategies in whole or in part in particular jails and prisons: allowing a prisoner to have access to personal living quarters by means of a key; allowing inmates to regulate temperature, ventilation, and lighting within their housing areas; increasing the inmate's opportunity to make personal choices among services, programs, and other activities available in the institution.

Other recent studies provide additional ways to reduce the potential for inmate violence through analysis and manipulation of environmental variables. In a study of battery incidents and batterers in a maximum security hospital, Dietz and Rada (1982) found an association between occurrence of violence and time of day: the frequency of violence peaked when patients went to the dining room for meals. The study also found an association between the occurrence of violence and the social density of various hospital locations: the greater the patient density, the greater the proportion of violent incidents (see also Rogers et al. 1980 for somewhat similar findings).

Another example of environmental influence on violence potential comes from the oldest jail that serves New York City. Correctional workers at the House of Detention on Riker's Island found that most fights and stabbings occurred around the telephones in the facility as large groups of inmates waited to make the single 6-minute daily call that each inmate is allowed. A simple measure, such as installing more telephones, could reduce inmate violence in accordance with some of the social-psychological notions that have been discussed in this chapter, i.e., to identify and reduce situational stresses that appear to affect most deeply inmates in general and some in particular because of their individual psychology, predispositions, or expectations (McGill 1983, p. 38).

Depp (1976), Phillips and Nasr (1983), and others have studied the effect of situational variables on violence in psychiatric wards. In addition to finding, with Dietz and Rada (1982), significant variation in the temporal distribution of patient violence, Depp found that assaultive incidents were not readily explained or predicted by the personal characteristics of the assaultive patient or victim. Instead, factors such as the nature of patient–victim interactions needed to be considered. For example, Depp's study indicated potential for violence was associated with a patient's being "newly admitted" to a unit because of the imposition of controls on the patient by staff members who were less willing to tolerate inappropriate behavior by a patient who basically was a stranger. Phillips and Nasr found that psychotic patients were not necessarily more prone to violence than nonpsychotics, and that the frequency of patient behavior leading to seclusion or restraint appeared to be directly related to stimulation caused by the physical presence of numerous staff or other patients.

Correctional workers, managers, and others responsible for organizing the inmate environment should carefully study patterns of inmate violence as well as catalog and study interactions between inmates and staff (locations, timing, involvement of staff and other inmates) so they will have a sound basis for planning and taking remedial action. The strategies that can be considered include decreasing the numbers of inmates having meals together, increasing or even decreasing the number of staff members at a given location at a given time, and working with staff members to decrease or alter demands placed on inmates (see also Quinsey 1977).

On a broader organizational level, management reports concerning prison inmate violence frequently stress the value of management by unit over centralized management. Levinson recently described unit management in the Federal Prison System, particularly the use of unit management at the new Federal Prison in Butner, North Carolina (Levinson 1982). The concept of a functional unit includes a relatively small number of offenders (approximately 100) who are housed together and work together in close relationships with a multidisciplinary staff that is permanently assigned to the unit. Correctional personnel have decisionmaking authority for discipline and for various aspects of programming within their unit. An offender's placement in a particular living unit is determined by the type of program the offender needs. A prison attempting to incorporate these ideas into its management is, in Levinson's terms, "trying softer."

Linked to the unit management approach is the development of systematic policies and procedures for dealing with particular types of inmates and problems. An example of such a policy is that formulated by the Federal Prison System for its control unit program (Federal Prison System 1979). The policy describes specific rules relating to isolating inmates who are dangerous to others in special control units within the prison. The policy not only mandates that inmates receive hearings prior to such placement (see also chapter 9), but also that, once placed in such units, inmates must be offered various programs and services, including education, work assignments, recreation, case management, and medical and mental health services. Von Holden (1980) has recently described a systematic organizational approach using interdisciplinary teams to treat mentally ill violent offenders in treatment units. The unit attempts to conform its policies and procedures to the usual civil hospital standards (Von Holden 1980).

Other examples of specific types of hospital policies and procedures that can be adapted to prevent and control violence in correctional environments are described in chapter 11 of this volume.

MEDICAL CAUSES OF INMATE VIOLENCE

While there has been much debate about the extent and nature of psychiatric disorders manifested by inmates in prisons and jails, most surveys have concluded that the extent of psychiatric pathology exhibited by inmates in prisons is in the range of 15 to 20 percent (Roth 1980; Monahan and Steadman 1983). Severe psychiatric disorders such as psychoses are experienced by probably fewer than 5 percent of inmates, perhaps as few as 1 to 2 percent (Roth and Ervin 1971; Gunn et al. 1978; Guze 1976; National Institute of Mental Health 1982a). Even Uhlig's study (1976) of 365 disruptive inmates in New England maximum security institutions (58 percent of whom had been previously treated at State mental hospitals) found that only 11.5 percent were presently identified as having a functional psychosis. A recent survey in Pennsylvania found 6 percent of the State and county correctional population to be in need of mental health care and unable to function (Correction-Mental Health Task Force 1981).

In selected jurisdictions, in some jails, and, of course, in special units for mentally disordered offenders, the level of well-defined psychiatric pathology may be far higher, especially in referral populations (see, e.g., Lamb and Grant 1982; Swank and Winer 1976; Petrich 1976). There is no evidence, however, to suggest that most jail inmates are psychiatric cases or should be so treated (Monahan and Steadman 1983).

The implication of these epidemiologic findings is that traditional psychiatric treatment, especially the use of psychotropic medications, is not appropriate for most prison and jail inmates. When problems of violence posed by these inmates can be characterized as being of psychiatric origin, the problems more typically stem from antisocial personality disorders, drug abuse, and alcoholism, and other kinds of interventions are needed (Guze 1976).

Many persons, including mental health as well as correctional workers, nonetheless seem convinced that much of the violent behavior that occurs in prisons and jails is a direct manifestation of mental disorder. They seem to expect the violence will abate, if the prevailing mental disorder is treated. It must be pointed out to these persons that the epidemiologic links between even well-defined psychiatric disorders and the commission of violence are not well understood (see, generally, National Institute of Mental Health 1982a; Monahan and Steadman 1983; Rabkin 1979; Mesnikoff and Lauterbach 1975). Much more needs to be known about relationships between mental disorders and violence, even among identified psychiatrically ill offenders, before general treatment strategies can be applied (see for example Huber et al. 1982). As Taylor notes in her excellent discussion of the literature concerning the relationship between schizophrenia and violence, it is not even currently known "whether violence committed by schizophrenics is any more amenable to psychiatric treatment than other forms of violence for which, by and large, social controls only are applied and considered appropriate" (Taylor 1982, p. 280).

The individual or clinical case level presents a different picture. At that level, one does encounter individual prison and jail inmates who are psychiatrically disturbed, who engage in violent behavior, and whose violence appears to stem directly from their psychiatric disorder (Huber et al. 1982; see also chapter 4 of this volume). While such clinical observations justify the use of medical treatment to reduce some inmate violence, a major point of this chapter is to emphasize that medication to reduce violent behavior in prisons and jails is appropriate only when a genuine psychiatric disorder has been demonstrated.

OTHER CAUSES OF VIOLENCE

It is often difficult for correctional workers to learn precisely why an inmate has been violent or why another has been hurt. Interviews with inmates can, however, provide important clues. Such interviews suggest the presence of treatable mental illness (see generally Roth 1980), point to particular types of stress that an inmate has experienced, and obtain a useful explanation from the inmate as to why the inmate believes he or she was violent. For example, inmates may feel stressed, angry, or resentful because their parole hopes have been dashed, expected visits have not materialized, or for other reasons. Some inmates may view themselves as having a "short fuse." Others, believing themselves to be "under pressure," may feel the need to strike out. While some "pressures" that violent inmates perceive are realistic, others can be a psychological distortion of inmates' views of their surroundings. The feeling of "pressure" can also represent a more general sense of unease, even a chronic "expectational set" on the part of the inmate.

Studies conducted in prison settings suggest that violent inmates are particularly sensitive to encroachment upon their territory or body space (for example, Kinzel 1970). These concerns may represent homosexual fears that the inmate will be either victimized or, alternatively, that he himself will be the aggressor if provoked. Sexual assaults in prison represent far more than an inmate's desire for sexual contact; instead, they are displays of power and aggression to impress or control others in the prison environment (Roth 1972).

In many instances, silence and/or noncooperation on the part of both aggressor and victim prevent the correctional worker or mental health clinician from learning exactly why violence has occurred. The opinion of most prison workers and students of the prison environment, however, is that much violence takes place because of (1) sexual entanglements, (2) the inmate reward and punishment system accompanying illicit prison transactions (e.g., exchange of contraband), and (3) inmate rackets or debts owed by one inmate to another. Some inmates are punished because they have "snitched" (see generally National Institute of Mental Health 1977). Still other violence occurs as a result of gang activities and identifications; gang activities have been a chronic problem in some prison systems, such as California's (Porter 1982). Ziegler's observation seems as true today as it was in 1974: The same old rules still apply in (Folsom) prison: don't gamble, or snitch, or mess around with narcotics or sissies, don't go to the hospital and you will live to a ripe old age. (Ziegler 1974, cited in National Institute of Mental Health 1977, p. 61). Correctional staff members may profess not to know why violence has occurred, advancing "no apparent reason" as the explanation (Quinsey 1977), while, when asked, inmates may cite staff teasing or even staff provocation as the reason for violence.

Learning the causes of inmate violence can be difficult when the violence occurs at night in unsupervised dormitories that staff members are unwilling or unable to monitor closely. An investigation of eight homicides at the Lewisburg Penitentiary in the mid-1970's, however, found that most victims were

> Assaulted for some specific reason. They apparently were not killed indiscriminately but in retaliation for something they had done. . . . The majority of inmates stated that when someone is killed, it is usually because he did something or was involved in some illicit activity. Inmates indicated that they were not in fear of being killed by merely walking around the institution.

Several of the killings at Lewisburg related to some type of homosexual involvement (Board of Inquiry 1976; see also National Institute of Mental Health 1977; Roth 1980).

While this discussion indicates that, in the language of social science, much prison violence is "instrumental in type," that is, planned and performed for a particular purpose or for a particular result, a recent study of street violence committed by British offenders has suggested that what may initially appear to be "instrumental violence" (violence done for a purpose), often overlaps instead with "angry aggression" on the part of the individual (Berkowitz 1980). Thus, before a violent act is defined as having been instrumental—and therefore as having been beyond the control of the correctional worker, other than generally improving the environment—the possible role of poorly controlled anger manifested by a predisposed individual should also be considered.

Attempts have been made over many decades to use profiles or psychological tests to identify violence-prone inmates and isolate them from others. The results have not been too helpful. A recent report from the Federal Prison System (1982) reviews prediction. Three empirical investigations performed at the Federal Penitentiary in Lompoc, California, suggest that, rather than a psychometric (psychological testing) approach, a "custody classification system" based on the inmate's known past institutional behavior is a better predictor of overall inmate adjustment in the prison setting. These findings are not surprising. Most other attempts have been unable to predict a person's future violent behavior on the basis of variables other than the person's known previous behavior in a given setting (see, generally, National Institute of Mental Health 1981; American Psychiatric Association 1974).

The California Department of Corrections' findings about prison violence in San Quentin Prison in 1960 are still representative of those from many other subsequent attempts to differentiate violence-prone inmates on the basis of personal histories prior to imprisonment (Bennett 1976). The study defined violent action in prison as any physical act of harm to another such as stabbing, choking, or beating—with or without a weapon—plus threats and intent to harm. Inmates who exhibited such behavior were compared with others who had no disciplines in their records. Several variables differentiated the two groups of prisoners; the violent prisoners

(1) were younger;
(2) more frequently came from a nonwhite ethnic background;
(3) more frequently had broken homes before age 16;
(4) had missing, alcoholic, criminal, or abusive fathers;
(5) had low educational achievement;
(6) had a prior history of institutional violence;
(7) had four or more institutional disciplinary infractions;
(8) had a prior institutional history of one prison commitment or two jail or juvenile commitments;
(9) were age 12 or under at first arrest;
(10) had a first arrest for robbery or burglary;
(11) had a history of epilepsy; and
(12) had attempted suicide or self-mutilation.

Profiles that emerged for violent inmates in the California study were similar to those of persons who are violent outside of prison. Neither the offender's most serious offense in prison nor prior violent behavior outside prison, however, was found to be related to violent or aggressive behavior within the institution. It is thus often important to relate personal background variables to variables within the institution to explain inmate violence adequately.

PSYCHIATRIC TREATMENT

When an inmate's violence is shown to be associated with medical or mental pathology that requires psychiatric treatment, this author's opinion is that such individuals should initially be treated in special mental health units located within prisons or jails. The traditional approach toward treating mentally ill, violent inmates has been either to not treat them at all or to transfer them to mental hospitals. Most mental hospitals lack the security necessary to control patients who are both mentally ill and criminal. Historically, there have also been many problems in the expeditious transfer of mentally ill prisoners to hospitals. A task force in Pennsylvania recently recommended the creation of special emergency mental health units in some State correctional institutions where mentally ill inmates can be treated for at least short periods of time prior to transfer (Correction-Mental Health Task Force 1981). Under this model, prisoners should also be entitled to due process, i.e., have hearings before being treated without consent in such prison units (see chapter 9 of this volume).

When psychiatric disorder and inmate violence are clearly linked, it is imperative not only that treatment be provided, but that the treatment be appropriate. The treatment must be structured to include a comprehensive approach, and should not be provided only for social control of violent behavior. This principle cannot be emphasized enough. Institutional surveys and more informal investigations by the lay press emphasize problems in the overuse and unsupervised use of psychotropic medications in prisons, jails, juvenile institutions, institutions for the mentally retarded, and elsewhere (see for example Committee on the Judiciary, United States Senate 1977, volumes 1-3). Well-known legal cases, such as Nelson v. Heyne (1974), have found that medication to control behavior has been misused.

There have traditionally been many problems in delivering medical care in correctional institutions (see, for example, Goldsmith 1975), and medical and mental health standards are only now beginning to be implemented in prisons and jails (American Correctional Association 1981; American Medical Association 1979a, 1979b; American Public Health Association 1976; Anno 1982). It is therefore critical that the techniques be adequately monitored when medical techniques are used to treat violent behavior in institutions. The author further believes that the use of atypical, nontraditional medical technologies (such as using drugs for punishment under aversive paradigms) should not be permitted in correctional institutions. Several court decisions during the 1970's condemned the use of nontraditional medical technologies such as breath-stopping drugs to modify inmate behavior in institutions (Winick 1981).

Even the use of standard psychotropic (antipsychotic) medication in correctional settings requires careful scrutiny. A recent General Accounting Office report called attention to problems with the use of multiple drugs (polypharmacy) in treating disturbed prisoners and noted the absence of consistent policies and procedures regarding such use (General Accounting Office 1979, p. 17). The sum of $518,000 was recently awarded to a prisoner who suffered bodily harm when he was administered excessive amounts of an antipsychotic drug (Prolixin Decanoate®) in prison under inadequate medical supervision (McDonald 1979).

Prison physicians and correctional administrators should be aware that Psychotropic Drug Screening Criteria (i.e., standards for the use of antipsychotic medication) are now available (Dorsey et al. 1979; see also chapters 1 and 4 of this volume). The use of both antipsychotic drugs and antianxiety drugs (e.g., the benzodiazepines—Librium®, Valium®) in the correctional setting should be carefully considered. There are data suggesting that antianxiety drugs may, at times, increase rather than decrease human aggression (Tranquillizers causing aggression 1975).

"Geographic cures" are a problem noted in surveys relating to psychiatric care in prisons and jails. Such cases take place when mentally ill inmates are transferred from the corrections system to the mental health system and back again without definitive care being provided for inmates in any setting (General Accounting Office 1979, p. 15). If care is provided, continuity of care may become a problem. For example, once inmates return to prison from a hospital setting, they typically receive poor medical supervision and usually discontinue medication.

As indicated earlier, this author believes that mentally ill inmates should initially receive treatment whenever possible from special mental health units located in prisons or jails. When it is necessary to transfer inmates to treatment facilities outside the correctional institution, arrangement should be made to provide adequate "outpatient" care to the inmates after they return to the correctional settings. At a minimum, therefore, prisons and jails need to develop capabilities to provide adequate mental health care to inmates both on a short-term emergency basis and after their return from a treatment facility (see generally Roth 1980; National Institute of Mental Health 1982b).

The most thorny aspect of establishing mental health treatment units in correctional settings is operational control. Who should have authority—Corrections? Mental Health? Also, assuming such units exist, how are adequate mental health care standards to be maintained?

Unfortunately, there are no easy answers to these questions. Adequate solutions will require much greater cooperation between mental health authorities and correctional authorities than has traditionally existed. There is no inherent reason why concern for proper mental health care within correctional settings cannot be harmonized with the understandable concern of correctional administrators to maintain security in their institutions.

A MODEL FOR TREATING VIOLENT BEHAVIOR

Monahan and Klassen (1982), modifying Novaco (1979), have recently proposed a model of violent behavior that is useful for the correctional setting, both in terms of preventing violence and in planning longer term treatment approaches for violent offenders and patients. This model does not overly rely on the individual pathology or psychopathology model. It instead incorporates recent developments in the area of cognitive psychology and cognitive treatment, while turning attention to situational variables—How do offenders appraise their situation? How do they subsequently feel and act?

According to the model, attention is first given to the environmental events that can affect a person, such as frustrations, annoyances, insults, and assaults by another (Monahan and Klassen 1982, p. 311). How does the potentially violent person evaluate these events? Are these events interpreted by the person as provocation? What are the person's fantasies and/or expectations about what will occur next? Are these expectations realistic or a misinterpretation of the event? How do the person's cognitive processes then affect his or her mood? Does the person become angry or, alternatively, is anger inhibited because the person feels anxious, fearful, or even empathic toward another? What does the person do? Does the person show a behavioral coping response of violence (assault) or of nonviolence (withdrawal or avoidance)?

This model of violent behavior and longer term treatment intervention has potential value for corrections. First, it points to different loci for intervention. Can, for example, the correctional environment be restructured to reduce stresses and provocations for predisposed individuals? Next, can the individual be helped, taught to correctly interpret the environment or develop alternate coping responses? Individuals can be taught to recognize their danger signals (such as rising anger), to monitor their thoughts, moods, and expectations, and to act differently.

The Monahan and Klassen approach integrates others' previous observations that violence should be considered from an interactional perspective. In analyzing recurrent violent behavior committed by police officers, by persons who assault police, and by prison inmates and parolees, Toch found that "to understand violence it is necessary to focus on the chain of interactions between aggressor and victim, on the sequence that begins when two people encounter each other—and which ends when one harms or even destroys the other" (Toch 1969, p. 6). Reviewing and attempting to understand interactions between violent inmates and others may reveal the psychology of the violent inmate. Did the violent inmate's response to the victim's actions serve to compound the injury that was eventually inflicted?

In working with persons who become chronically angry, Novaco developed a model for therapy that incorporates three treatment phases: cognitive preparation, skill acquisition, and application training (Novaco 1979). The cognitive phase involves helping the person to identity circumstances that trigger anger so the person learns what arouses his or her anger. Anger management techniques are then designed to help the person cope better and handle conflict and stress. The skill acquisition phase involves learning new cognitive and behavioral coping skills. The therapist suggests alternative coping activities, models or demonstrates these techniques, and has the client rehearse the behavior. Finally, the phase of application training allows the person to test his or her new proficiency by applying anger control methods to provocations that are regulated by the therapist. This overall technique is described as "stress inoculation" (see also Meichenbaum 1977; Frederiksen and Rainwater 1981).

While these newer cognitive psychology and social-psychological techniques for altering violent or angry behavior have not generally been part of forensic psychiatry, some traditional programs and approaches for evaluating and treating mentally disordered violent offenders have come to recognize the importance of this way of thinking about violence. Thus, in working with and evaluating dangerous persons at the Bridgewater, Massachusetts, institution, Kozol et al. (1972) stress the importance of reviewing with the offender the exact circumstances of the offense and how he or she regarded and treated the victim. The therapist then compares the offender's account of the crime with the victim's to better understand and help modify the offender's psychology. Step-by-step analysis of the offense and how the offender viewed the victim helps to explain how the victim might have rewarded or otherwise reinforced the offender's actions.

Wiest (1981) has described a similar approach toward treating offenders at the Atascadero State Hospital in California (the State's primary institution for sex offenders and the criminally insane). Wiest notes that a "first step should be a detailed history of the criminal act, in a process requiring the client 'to walk the therapist through the crime.' This procedure provides invaluable information both for assessing treatability and for evaluating change" (see also Groth et al. 1977). Strup's work is also relevant (Strup 1968). He describes an "amnestic analysis": Offenders at the Herstedvester Institution review their experiences with the therapist in order "to recognize unsatisfactory personality patterns and notice how these reoccur in a peculiarly stereotyped way in many interpersonal situations." One conclusion from this work "has been the clear recognition that the majority of our people are handicapped and hurt primarily by their special way of perceiving and reacting to external situations" (pp. 83–84).

These observations, coupled with the ideas of Monahan and Klassen (1982), Toch (1969), and others, suggest certain therapeutic approaches that may be pursued when working with violent inmates in institutional settings. Therapists should attempt to take advantage of naturally occurring incidents in the institution (and later in the community) to help inmates understand how and why they act as they do, how their appraisal of their environment and their interactions with others culminate in violence, and what could be done instead. These approaches go beyond those usually employed in traditional group therapy with violent persons (see for example Carney 1978, chapter 3). Interactional approaches can also be integrated into groups. Monitored group interactions can offer the opportunity for violent persons to become provoked, experience pressures, and learn more about their social interactions with others that may stimulate violence (Toch 1969, p. 232–233).

A case example involving an interactional approach treatment of a violent inmate follows:

Case Example. A 28-year-old man was incarcerated for assault with a deadly weapon. While he suffered from temporal lobe epilepsy (he had epileptic fits in which he would silently mutter to himself and seemingly be out of contact with others), the patient's history also revealed that he became periodically angry and quarrelsome. These episodes occurred even when he was not having seizures. When he believed he was being teased or laughed at, the patient struck out at others. Thus, he became involved in frequent fights in which he was often the loser, even taking on the prison guards at times. Eventually, while being treated for his medical problems, the inmate was befriended by the prison medical doctor. The inmate explained that he hated to be ridiculed and that he believed others thought badly of him because he had epilepsy. Therefore, he was continually monitoring his environment to check on the reactions of others.

To help him control and better understand his behavior, the inmate was asked to complete a diary of his activities in which he would note his moods and describe his interactions with others. The therapist reviewed this diary with the inmate. First-hand observation of the inmate's behavior was also deemed necessary. For a period of time, therefore, the inmate worked in the prison hospital, where his behavioral interactions could be observed. This enabled the therapist to compare his (the therapist's) observations of the inmate's behavior with the inmate's own evaluation of his situation. The inmate did a very good job in working in the hospital environment. He worked well with others, and with instructions was eventually able to recognize that some of his interactions with others (which he had interpreted as "making fun of him") were not really that. As these episodes were discussed, the inmate learned to "walk away" when he was upset and to review whether his appraisal of the situation was correct. Even though the number and severity of the inmate's seizure episodes continued to be the same, the inmate became involved in far fewer fights.

COMMUNITY AFTERCARE

All of the described approaches to treating violent behavior also point to the importance of aftercare following discharge from an institution. The former inmate must, when discharged, learn to cope with new environmental stresses and pressures. As suggested by Gunn and Robertson (1982), treatment in the institution cannot change what will later occur in the community. The prisoner must relearn in the community what has been learned in the institution as other opportunities for, and provocations toward, violence occur. Followup studies of former mental patients and offenders have recently demonstrated an association between situational events and the reemergence of disputes.

> Violence is greatest when the dispute is outside of the home, late at night, when alcohol or drugs have been used by either party involved, in the presence of third parties, where strangers are involved, and where the antagonist is larger and stronger than the respondent. . . . (M)ental patients are much more apt than either offenders or the general population to involve family members in their more violent disputes. . . . (A)lcohol and drugs are especially involved in offender violence (Steadman 1982, p. 182; see also Bureau of Justice Statistics 1983b).

Provocations toward violence in the community are different from those that the inmate has encountered in the institution. Treatment in a well-structured outpatient clinic or setting can provide needed assistance and supervision for the former inmate as well as facilitate preventive return to prison or to a mental institution should this be indicated.

Some aftercare program models have recently been developed. For example, Goldmeier has provided information on Hamilton House, a halfway house attached to a Maryland institution for mentally disordered offenders (Clifton T. Perkins State Hospital). The patient's behavior is tested and observed in a less structured setting than the institution, and new learning takes place: "staff view . . . common crises such as the loss of a job or rebuff in a relationship as not necessarily negative in that with timely help, the resident . . . (can) often develop new ways of coping" (Goldmeier et al. 1980, p. 77).

Rogers and Cavanaugh (1981) have recently described a community (outpatient) treatment program for potentially violent offender patients:

> The center makes a long-term commitment to the individual to follow his treatment and, in situations of decompensation, to facilitate immediate rehospitalization. . . . The treatment staff is sensitized to subtle changes in patients' ability to respond appropriately to stress and modulate their own aggressive behavior and impulses (p. 55).

While some patients must be rehospitalized, both Goldmeier et al. and Rogers and Cavanaugh present favorable statistics concerning reduction of violence. Outpatient treatment of violent offenders (or offender-patients) with underlying characterological problems is especially important. These persons need to be given an opportunity in the community to make new kinds of friendships and form group affiliations that can serve as alternatives to antisocial behaviors (Vaillant 1975).

The importance of a community follow-through phase of treatment is further highlighted by data from the Patuxent institution, which is devoted to the treatment of recurrent criminality, treating so-called "defective delinquents." The recidivism rate for a fully treated group of patients (persons going through the institutional program who were on parole/outpatient status for 3 years) was only 7 percent. This compares with a recidivism rate of 46 percent among men who received only inhouse treatment and never made parole status (Carney 1974; Carney 1978).

STAFFING PROBLEMS

It has always been difficult to maintain an adequate cadre of persons with therapeutic interests in prisons, jails, and security hospitals (Roth

1980). In 1979, the Federal Bureau of Prisons had 20 full-time psychiatrists and about 100 full-time psychologists serving about 28,000 prisoners. One Federal institution had no psychiatrist at all, even on a part-time basis. Shortages of mental health personnel were even greater in State prisons (General Accounting Office 1979, p. 47), most of which did not have an adequate mental health component (Smith 1974; see also Clements 1982).

The traditional custodial orientation of correctional institutions is also difficult to overcome or even to modify. Even when authorized attempts are made to develop more adequate and comprehensive treatment orientations, numerous organizational factors make it difficult to move "from maximum security to secure treatment" (Steadman et al. 1978). Faced with these obstacles as well as the paucity of treatment resources, many veteran mental health workers eventually feel the need to move out. The novice worker is apt to be quickly bewildered, overwhelmed, and then leave (Roth 1980).

Self-scrutiny and peer support are essential for treatment staff who are willing to work with violent inmates and mentally ill offenders. It is essential to understand one's own reactions to working with such persons in closed settings to maintain morale and good functioning. Stress is inevitable in environments with a high potential for violence. "Attitudes" that staff members may unconsciously develop (including existing "attitudes" the worker brings to the job) can sometimes play a role in provoking inmate violence and/or in mishandling violent encounters (Madden et al. 1976). Inmate violence can cause problems in interstaff communications and in staff-inmate communication (Cornfield and Fielding 1980). Staff easily develop feelings of fearfulness and anxiety; unless properly attended to, these feelings can result in either inappropriate denial or the development of punitive attitudes (Lion and Pasternak 1973). Withdrawal and apathy may result, even among mental health professionals whose business it is to be aware of and attend to such feelings (Cumming and Solway 1973). Burnout is frequent.

Peer review of behavior and feelings is essential to combat such problems. Staff members, who vary in their degree of expertise in coping with violence, must be given regular opportunities to compare notes and share their own feelings and reactions to working with violent inmates. Group analysis and recapitulation of violent incidents, including how these incidents were handled or might have been handled, is vital to preventing burnout. Group interaction also serves as a highly important means to provide continuing education to staff members (see generally Toch 1969; National Institute of Mental Health 1977, chapter 3).

This author's experience has been that working only with violent persons in closed settings for sustained periods of time is too great a stress for staff members who seek to preserve a therapeutic orientation. To function effectively over time, these staff members require some time away from the prison, jail, or security hospital, not only for respite but also as a reminder that most persons are not violent and that dealing effectively with the treatment needs of violent persons is one of the most challenging—and potentially professionally rewarding—of all the tasks that can confront a mental health practitioner. Staff members should also be encouraged to visit other institutions that cope with violent people, including settings that may have more treatment resources than their own. Such visits provide another opportunity for staff members to share experiences—including "war stories"—that can help identify better ways to meet the problems back home.

REFERENCES

Allinson, R. Overcrowding is now a national epidemic. Corrections Magazine 8(2):18–24, 1982.

American Correctional Association. Standards for Adult Correctional Institutions, 2d Edition. College Park, Md.: the Association, 1981.

American Medical Association. Standards for Health Services in Jails. Chicago: the Association, 1979a.

American Medical Association. Standards for Health Services in Prisons. Chicago: the Association, 1979b.

American Psychiatric Association. Clinical Aspects of the Violent Individual. Task Force Report 8. Washington, D.C.: the Association, 1974.

American Public Health Association. Standards for Health Services in Correctional Institutions. Washington, D.C.: the Association, 1976.

Anno, J. The role of organized medicine in correctional health care. Journal of the American Medical Association 247(21):2923–2925, 1982.

Attorney General, State of New Mexico. Part II. The last ten years. Conditions leading to the riot. Conclusions and recommendations. In: Report of the Attorney General on the February 2 and 3, 1980 Riot at the Penitentiary of New Mexico. Santa Fe, N. Mex., 1980.

Bennett, L.A. The study of violence in California prisons: A review with policy implications. In: Cohen, A.K.; Cole, G.F.; and Bailey, R.G. Prison Violence. Lexington, Mass.: D.C. Heath, 1976. pp. 149–168.

Berkowitz, L. Is criminal violence normative behavior? Hostile and instrumental aggression in violent incidents. In: Bittner, E., and Messinger, S.L., eds. Criminology Review Yearbook. Vol. 2. Beverly Hills: Sage, 1980. pp. 387–400.

Board of Inquiry. United States Penitentiary, Lewisburg, Pennsylvania. Washington, D.C.: Federal Bureau of Prisons, 1976.

Bowker, L.H. Victimizers and victims in American correctional institutions. In: Johnson, R., and Toch, H., eds. The Pains of Imprisonment. Beverly Hills: Sage, 1982. pp. 63–76.

Bukstel, L.H., and Kilmann, P.R. Psychological effects of imprisonment on confined individuals. Psychological Bulletin 2:469–493, 1980.

Bureau of Justice Statistics. Prisoners at midyear 1982. Bureau of Justice Statistics Bulletin, Oct./Nov. 1982a.

Bureau of Justice Statistics. Violent Crime in the United States. National Indicators System, Report Number 4. Briefing Book NCJ-79741. Washington, D.C.: U.S. Dept. of Justice, Sept. 1981, Revised Feb. 1982b.

Bureau of Justice Statistics. Jail inmates 1982. Bureau of Justice Statistics Bulletin, Feb. 1983a.

Bureau of Justice Statistics. Prisoners and drugs. Bureau of Justice Statistics Bulletin, Mar. 1983b.

Carney, F.L. The indeterminate sentence at Patuxent. Crime and Delinquency 20(2):135–143, 1974.

Carney, F.L. Inpatient treatment programs. In: Reid, W.H., ed. The Psychopath. A Comprehensive Study of Antisocial Disorders and Behaviors. New York: Brunner/Mazel, 1978. pp. 261–285.

Clements, C.B. Crowded prisons. A review of psychological and environmental effects. Law and Human Behavior 3(3):217–225, 1979.

Clements, C.B. Psychological roles and issues in recent prison litigation. In: Gunn, J., and Farrington, D.P., eds. Abnormal Offenders, Delinquency, and the Criminal Justice System. Vol. I. New York: John Wiley, 1982. pp. 37–59.

Cohen, A.K. Prison violence: A sociological perspective. In: Cohen, A.K.; Cole, G.F.; and Bailey, R.G. Prison Violence. Lexington, Mass.: D.C. Heath, 1976. pp. 3–22.

Cohen, A.K.; Cole, G.F.; and Bailey, R.G. Prison Violence. Lexington, Mass.: D.C. Heath, 1976.

Committee on the Judiciary, United States Senate. The Abuse and Misuse of Controlled Drugs in Institutions. Vols. I, II, and III. Hearings before the Subcommittee to Investigate Juvenile Delinquency. 94th Congress, 1st Session, July-Aug. 1975. Washington, D.C.: U.S. Govt. Print. Off., 1977.

Cornfield, R.B., and Fielding, S.D. Impact of the threatening patient on ward communications. American Journal of Psychiatry 137(5):616–619, 1980.

Corrections/Mental Health Task Force. The Care and Treatment of Mentally Ill Inmates. Report of the Task Force. Harrisburg, Pa.: Commonwealth of Pennsylvania, 1981.

Cumming, R.G., and Soloway, H.J. The incarcerated psychiatrists. Hospital & Community Psychiatry 24(9):631633, 1973.

Depp, F.C. Violent behavior patterns on psychiatric wards. Aggressive Behavior 2:295–306, 1976.

DeWolfe, R., and DeWolfe, A.S. Impact of prison conditions on the mental health of inmates. Southern Illinois University Law Journal 1979(4):497–533, 1979.

Dietz, P.E., and Rada, R.T. Battery incidents and batterers in a maximum security hospital. Archives of General Psychiatry 39(1):31–34, 1982.

Dorsey, R.; Ayd, F.J.; Cole, J.; Klein, D.; Simpson, G.; Tupin, J.; and DiMascio, A. Psychopharmacological screening criteria development project. Journal of the American Medical Association 241(10):1021–1031, 1979.

Dunn, C.S. Foreword. In: Johnson, R., and Toch, H., eds. The Pains of Imprisonment. Beverly Hills: Sage, 1982. pp. 9–11.

Federal Prison System. Control unit programs. Program Statement, Number 5212.3. Washington, D.C.: U.S. Dept. of Justice, July 16, 1979.

Federal Prison System. Violence in Correctional Institutions: Conceptual and Empirical Analyses, by McGuire, W.J. Abstract of a report completed in March 1981. Washington, D.C.: Federal Prison System Library.

Federal Prison System. Predicting violent behavior in a prison setting, by Moss, C.S., and Hosford, R.E. Progress Reports 1(2):ii–30, 1982.

Frederiksen, L.W., and Rainwater, N. Explosive behavior: A skill development approach to treatment. In: Stuart, R.B., ed. Violent Behavior: Social Learning Approaches to Prediction, Management and Treatment. New York: Brunner/Mazel, 1981.

Gardner, R., Jr. Prison population jumps to 369,725. Corrections Magazine 8(3):6–11, 1982.

General Accounting Office of the United States. Prison Mental Health Care Can Be Improved by Better Management and More Effective Federal Aid. By the Comptroller General of the United States, Report to the Congress. (GGD-80-11) Washington, D.C.: U.S. General Accounting Office, Nov. 23, 1979.

Gibbs, J.J. The first cut is the deepest: Psychological breakdown and survival in the detention setting. In: Johnson, R., and Toch, H., eds. The Pains of Imprisonment. Beverly Hills: Sage, 1982. pp. 97–114.

Goldmeier, J.; White, E.V.; Ulrich, C.; and Klein, G.A. Community intervention with the mentally ill offender: A residential program. Bulletin of the American Academy of Psychiatry and the Law 8(1): 72–82, 1980.

Goldsmith, S.B. Prison Health. Travesty of Justice. New York: Prodist, 1975.

Groth, A.N.; Burgess, A.W.; and Holmstrom, L.L. Rape: Power, anger, and sexuality. American Journal of Psychiatry 134(11):1239–1243, 1977.

Gunn, J., and Robertson, G. An evaluation of Grendon Prison. In: Gunn, J., and Farrington, D.P., eds. Abnormal Offenders, Delinquency, and the Criminal Justice System. Vol. I. New York: John Wiley, 1982. pp. 285–305.

Gunn, J.; Robertson, G.; Dell, S.; and Way, C. Psychiatric Aspects of Imprisonment. New York: Academic Press, 1978.

Guze, S.B. Criminality and Psychiatric Disorders. New York: Oxford University Press, 1976.

Halleck, S.L., and Witte, A.D. Is rehabilitation dead? Crime and Delinquency 23(4):372–382, 1977.

Hepburn, J.R., and Albonetti, C. Role conflict in correctional institutions: An empirical examination of the treatment-custody dilemma among correctional staff. Criminology 17(4):445–459, 1980.

Huber, G.A.; Roth, L.H.; Appelbaum, P.S.; and Ore, T.M. Hospitalization, arrest, or discharge: Important legal and clinical issues in the emergency evaluation of persons believed dangerous to others. Law and Contemporary Problems 45(3):99–123, 1982.

Inmates of Allegheny County Jail v. Pierce, 612 F.2d 754 (3d Cir. 1979); opinion and order of D.J. Cohill, Apr. 17, 1980, on remand (W.D.Pa. 1980).

Johnson, R., and Toch, H., eds. The Pains of Imprisonment. Beverly Hills: Sage, 1982.

Kinzel, A.F. Body-buffer zone in violent prisoners. American Journal of Psychiatry 127(1):59–64, 1970.

Kozol, H.L.; Boucher, R.J.; and Garofalo, R.F. The diagnosis and treatment of dangerousness. Crime and Delinquency 18:371–392, 1972.

Lamb, H.R., and Grant, R.W. The mentally ill in an urban county jail. Archives of General Psychiatry 39(1):17–22, 1982.

Levinson, R.B. Try softer. In: Johnson, R., and Toch, H., eds. The Pains of Imprisonment. Beverly Hills: Sage, 1982. pp. 241–255.

Lion, J.R., and Pasternak, S.A. Countertransference reactions to violent patients. American Journal of Psychiatry 130(2):207-210, 1973.

Madden, D.J.; Lion, J.R.; and Penna, M.W. Assaults on psychiatrists by patients. American Journal of Psychiatry 133(4):422–436, 1976.

Martin, S.E.; Sechrest, L.B.; and Redner, R., eds. New Directions in the Rehabilitation of Criminal Offenders. Washington, D.C.: National Academy Press, 1981.

McDonald, M.C. Damages awarded in drug misuse case. Psychiatric News 24(8):1, Apr. 20, 1979.

McGill, D.C. At shabby jail, controversy on crowding. New York Times, Apr. 2, 1983. pp. 2, 38.

Meichenbaum, D. Cognitive-Behavior Modification. An Integration Approach. New York: Plenum, 1977.

Merritt, F.S. Corrections law developments: Prisoners' rights litigation in the 1980s. Criminal Law Bulletin 19(2):157–161, 1983.

Mesnikoff, A.M., and Lauterbach, C.G. The association of violent dangerous behavior with psychiatric disorders: A review of the research literature. The Journal of Psychiatry and Law 3(4):415–445, 1975.

Monahan, J., and Klassen, D. Situational approaches to understanding and predicting individual violent behavior. In: Wolfgang, M.E., and Weiner, N.A., eds. Criminal Violence. Beverly Hills: Sage, 1982. pp. 292–319.

Monahan, J., and Steadman, H.J. Crime and mental disorder: An epidemiological approach. In: Morris, N., and Tonry, M.H., eds. Crime and Justice: An Annual Review of Research. Chicago: University of Chicago Press, 1983.

Nacci, P.L.; Teitelbaum, H.E.; and Prather, J. Population density and inmate misconduct rates in the federal prison system. Federal Probation 41:26–31, 1977.

National Institute of Justice. American Prisons and Jails. Volume I: Summary and Policy Implications of a National Survey, by Mullen, J. Washington, D.C.: U.S. Govt. Print. Off., 1980a.

National Institute of Justice. The Effect of Prison Crowding on Inmate Behavior, by McCain, G.; Cox, V.C.; and Paulus, P.B. Washington, D.C.: U.S. Dept. of Justice, Dec. 1980b.

National Institute of Mental Health. Police, Prisons, and the Problem of Violence, by Toch, H. Crime and Delinquency Issues: A Monograph Series. DHEW Publ. No. (ADM)76-364. Washington, D.C.: Supt. of Docs., U.S. Govt. Print. Off., 1977.

National Institute of Mental Health. The Clinical Prediction of Violent Behavior, by Monahan, J. Crime and Delinquency Issues: A Monograph Series. DHHS Publ. No. (ADM)81-921. Washington, D.C.: Supt. of Docs., U.S. Govt. Print. Off., 1981.

National Institute of Mental Health. Intervention models for mental health services in jails, by Brodsky, S.L. In: Mental Health Services in Local Jails: Report of a Special National Workshop, by Dunn, C.S., and Steadman, H.J., eds. Crime and Delinquency Issues: A Monograph. DHHS Pub. No. (ADM)82–1181. Washington, D.C.: Supt. of Docs., U.S. Govt. Print. Off., 1982a. pp. 126–148.

National Institute of Mental Health. Mental Health Services in Local Jails: Report of a

Special National Workshop, by Dunn, C.S., and Steadman, H.J., eds. Crime and Delinquency Issues: A Monograph. DHHS Pub. No. (ADM)82–1181. Washington, D.C.: Supt. of Docs., U.S. Govt. Print. Off., 1982b.

Nelson v. Heyne, 491 F.2d 352 (7th Cir. 1974).

Novaco, R. The cognitive regulation of anger and stress. In: Kendall, P., and Hollon, S., eds. Cognitive Behavioral Interventions: Theory, Research, and Procedures. New York: Academic Press, 1979. pp. 241–285.

Owens-EL v. Robinson, 442 F. Supp. 1368 (W.D. Pa. 1978).

Petrich, J. Psychiatric treatment in jail: An experiment in health-care delivery. Hospital & Community Psychiatry 27(6):413–415, June 1976.

Phillips, P., and Nasr, S.J. Seclusion and restraint and prediction of violence. American Journal of Psychiatry 140(2):229–232, 1983.

Porter, B. California prison gangs: The price of control. Corrections Magazine 8(6):6–19, 1982.

Pugh v. Locke, 406 F. Supp. 318 (M.D. Ala. 1976).

Quinsey, V.L. Studies in the reduction of assaults in a maximum security psychiatric institution. Canada's Mental Health 25:21–23, 1977.

Rabkin, J.G. Criminal behavior of discharged mental patients: A critical appraisal of the research. Psychological Bulletin 86(1):1–27, 1979.

Rawls, W., Jr. Crises and cutbacks stir fresh concerns on nation's prisons. New York Times, Jan. 5, 1982. p. A-1.

Rogers, R., and Cavanaugh, J.L. A treatment program for potentially violent offender patients. International Journal of Offender Therapy and Comparative Criminology 25(1):53–59, 1981.

Rogers, R.; Ciula, B.; and Cavanaugh, J.L., Jr. Aggressive and socially disruptive behavior among maximum security psychiatric patients. Psychological Reports 46:291–294, 1980.

Roth, L.H. Foolishness of clustering dangerous individuals. Sexual Behavior 2(1):43, 1972.

Roth, L.H. Correctional psychiatry. In: Curran, W.J.; McGarry, A.L.; and Petty, C.S., eds. Modern Legal Medicine, Psychiatry and Forensic Science. Philadelphia: F.A. Davis, 1980. pp. 677–719.

Roth, L.H., and Ervin, F. Psychiatric care of federal prisoners. American Journal of Psychiatry 128:424–430, 1971.

Ruiz v. Estelle, 503 F. Supp. 1265 (S.D. Tex. 1980).

Smith, C.E. Psychiatry in corrections: A viewpoint. Mississippi Law Journal 45(3):675–683, 1974.

Smith, D.E. Crowding and confinement. In: Johnson, R., and Toch, H., eds. The Pains of Imprisonment. Beverly Hills: Sage, 1982. pp. 45–62.

Steadman, H.J. A situational approach to violence. International Journal of Law and Psychiatry 5(2):155–186, 1982.

Steadman, H.J.; Cocozza, J.J.; and Lee, S. From maximum security to secure treatment: Organizational constraints. Human Organization 3:276–284, 1978.

Strup, G.K. Treating the "Untreatable." Chronic Criminals at Herstedvester. Baltimore: Johns Hopkins Press, 1968.

Swank, G.E., and Winer, D. Occurrence of psychiatric disorder in a county jail population. American Journal of Psychiatry 133(11):1331–1333, 1976.

Taylor, P. Schizophrenia and violence. In: Gunn, J., and Farrington, D.P., eds. Abnormal Offenders, Delinquency, and the Criminal Justice System. Vol. I. New York: John Wiley, 1982. pp. 269–284.

Toch, H. Violent Men. An Inquiry into the Psychology of Violence. Chicago: Aldine, 1969.

Toch, H. Men in Crisis. Human Breakdowns in Prison. Chicago: Aldine, 1975.

Toch, H. A revisionist view of prison reform. Federal Probation 45(2):3–9, 1981.

Tranquillizers causing aggression. British Medical Journal 1(5950):113–114, Jan. 18, 1975.

Uhlig, R.H. Hospitalization experience of mentally disturbed and disruptive, incarcerated offenders. The Journal of Psychiatry and Law 4(1):49–59, 1976.

Vaillant, G.E. Sociopathy as a human process. A viewpoint. Archives of General Psychiatry 32:178–183, Feb. 1975.

Von Holden, M.H. An open-system approach to the mental health treatment of violent offenders. Psychiatric Quarterly 52(2):132–143, 1980.

Wiehn, P.J. Mentally ill offenders: Prison's first casualties. In: Johnson, R., and Toch, H., eds. The Pains of Imprisonment. Beverly Hills: Sage, 1982. pp. 221–237.

Wiest, J. Treatment of violent offenders. Clinical Social Work Journal 9(4):271–281, 1981.

Winick, B.J. Legal limitations on correctional therapy and research. Minnesota Law Review 65:331–422, 1981.

11

Management and Control of Violent Patients at the Western Psychiatric Institute and Clinic

Vivian Romoff, R.N., M.S.N.

Coping with patient violence is an occupational hazard for mental health administrators as well as for mental health treatment staff. This chapter will view the problem from the administrator's perspective, drawing on policies and procedures that have been developed at the Western Psychiatric Institute and Clinic (WPIC) in Pittsburgh. WPIC is a short-stay university hospital that treats a wide range of voluntary and involuntary patients. Some of these patients manifest violent behavior while hospitalized at WPIC for periods ranging from a few weeks to a few months.

A key assumption in this chapter is that all mental health facilities—whether located in State hospitals, community settings, or jails and prisons—have a responsibility to develop clearly written policies and procedures for the treatment and management of violent patients. Guidelines of this type are needed not only to protect such patients, but also to minimize the harm and disruption that violent patients can inflict on other patients and on staff. Selected written WPIC policies and procedures reproduced in this chapter illustrate types of guidelines that are needed to ensure adequate management of violent patients in mental health settings.

ADMISSIONS POLICY

The first order of business for the mental health facility's administrator is to determine the types of violent or potentially violent patients that are acceptable for admission to the facility. The administrator must consider the facility's usual mix of patients, availability of treatment staff, security capabilities, and other related factors. WPIC's approach to admission is described below. While WPIC must accept virtually all acutely disturbed patients from its catchment area (referral to a State hospital is permitted only after a period of community treatment), WPIC does have some leeway in deciding whether to admit mentally retarded persons, mentally ill persons with criminal charges against them, and persons with an outstanding criminal charge who are referred or self-referred for psychiatric hospitalization.

A formal conceptual framework has been developed at WPIC in order to evaluate which violent or potentially violent persons are suitable for admissions. While the five categories are admittedly crude, they serve a highly useful administrative purpose. The categories can provide a basis for developing similar typologies that may be suitable for use by other mental health facilities (for example Huber et al. 1982):

1. Violent behavior as symptom of "core" psychiatric illness with no criminal charge outstanding. Persons in this category are clearly candidates for admission to WPIC. Their history typically indicates that violence occurs only as a symptom or sign of the acute phase of some well-defined clinical syndrome such as a mania, depression, or psychosis that is part of schizophrenia. Their violent behavior usually consists of episodic aggression, fighting, shows of hostility, angry or paranoid behavior, and other types of disruptive, agitated behavior. Such violence is generally not so severe that it would ordinarily be viewed as "criminal." If it does exceed the limits of the law, such persons are usually so obviously psychiatrically ill that criminal charges are deemed inappropriate in all but the most serious cases (Monahan et al. 1979).

Persons who fit this description are highly appropriate for treatment in a short-stay community or university hospital for they clearly are mentally ill. These persons usually respond quickly to medication and to the conventional psychosocial therapies and structured programs provided in a short-stay hospital. Staff members can expect that proclivities to violent behavior will decrease as treatment takes effect. If treatment is maintained after hospitalization, the likelihood of future violence can be decreased.

2. Criminal violence plus "core" psychiatric illness. Some violent persons brought to WPIC have been charged with a crime and are obviously psychiatrically ill. Others are psychiatrically ill, and staff are informed that criminal charges will be pressed if these persons are not

admitted to the hospital. While WPIC has no hard and fast rules governing individual admissions, some of these persons are more suitable for admission to the Pittsburgh jail, which has a mental health facility that can accept and treat violent mentally disordered offenders.

When a patient meeting one of the above descriptions is brought to WPIC, the admissions unit is responsible for obtaining accurate information on the criminal charges that have been or may be brought against the patient, the patient behaviors that are the basis for such charges, and the legal actions that are planned if the patient is or is not admitted to the hospital. Failure to obtain this information prior to admission can create difficulty for the hospital. Other patients and staff can be exposed to undue risk when a patient is admitted without adequate knowledge of the behavior that provoked arrest or the likelihood of arrest.

Admission of a criminally charged patient poses a number of problems for a community or university hospital. A prime issue is whether the hospital can provide sufficient security to ensure that the patient does not abscond or repeat criminal behavior while in the hospital. If a previously unlocked ward has to be locked to accommodate the new arrival, freedom of other patients may be infringed. When possible, mental hospitals should try to establish and maintain collaborative working relationships with nearby jails that have facilities to receive and treat mentally disordered offenders. These relationships will facilitate transfers to the jail when indicated (Huber et al. 1982).

Some criminally charged patients can gain admission to the hospital on the basis of incomplete information provided to the staff. Then, after some period of hospitalization, staff may learn through other sources that the case is more complicated than it first appeared, e.g., the patient has absconded from somewhere else, the patient has serious charges pending in another jurisdiction, or the police wish to interview the patient on the ward or detain the patient upon release. Depending on the patient's ward behavior, the seriousness of the newly discovered charges, or the increased level of security that may now be required, it may be advisable to transfer the patient to a jail mental health unit.

Because all of the patients in this category are psychiatrically disordered, they should continue to receive mental health treatment. When excluding such a patient from admission or later transferring the patient to the criminal justice system, the psychiatric hospital has a fundamental duty to provide accurate and timely information on the patient's psychiatric status to those who will be responsible for treatment (Huber et al. 1982). State mental health statutes or regulations concerning preservation of patient confidentiality may specifically authorize sharing such information; if not, it would be entirely appropriate and, indeed, desirable to effect changes that will permit such sharing of information in future. The patient can facilitate matters by consenting to the sharing of such information. If the information suggests to the jail mental health unit that the patient cannot receive proper treatment in the jail, this unit can then take action to have the patient transferred to a special forensic mental health facility.

3. Characterologic violence plus "core" psychiatric illness. These patients' behavioral histories suggest propensities to commit violence whether or not they are in the acute phase of well-defined "core" psychiatric illness. They usually have diagnoses on both the Axis I and Axis II portions of the Diagnostic and Statistical Manual (DMS III) classification. In addition to well-defined clinical syndromes, they also have an underlying characterologic or personality disorder. When such persons are violent it is often unclear whether the violence is the result of their Axis I diagnosis (depression, schizophrenia, organic or toxic syndrome), personality disorder, or some other set of factors or circumstances.

In deciding whether to admit such persons, staff must remember that the major benefit of psychiatric hospitalization in such cases is usually treatment of the Axis I disorder (i.e., clinical syndrome), not the underlying personality disorder. Once the clinical syndrome is alleviated, the patient is normally discharged. Hospital staff should recognize that these patients can be violent while in the hospital, even while their Axis I disorder is responding to treatment. Staff should also anticipate that the patient may become violent again after release into the community despite a period of successful hospital treatment. Preventing violent behavior by personality-disordered persons usually requires extended outpatient treatment rather than, or in addition to, shortterm hospitalization.

4. Mental retardation, violent behavior, and "core" psychiatric illness. WPIC occasionally admits mentally retarded persons who are mentally ill. The purpose of admission, however, is only to treat the concurrent psychiatric disorder. Once that illness is treated, WPIC discharges the patient to the community, to a community program, or to some other specialized facility.

WPIC does not consider violence by a mentally retarded person to be sufficient grounds for admission. If psychiatric illness is also present, the mentally retarded person may be admitted, but the proclivity to violence may persist despite successful psychiatric treatment that leads to eventual discharge from WPIC. Continuing proclivity to violence is not a criterion for retention in WPIC after psychiatric treatment is concluded.

5. Criminal violence and no "core" psychiatric illness. Persons who have been arrested for a violent crime and have no serious mental disorder are sometimes brought to WPIC by police or other persons. Some come to the hospital for court-ordered examinations or as a prelude to a court-mandated period of probation. Some are self-referred.

WPIC's policy is to deny admission to such persons to the maximum extent feasible. Because these persons do not manifest any serious psychiatric disorder, their presence as inpatients is inappropriate and may require the imposition of security measures that could otherwise be avoided. Most court-ordered mental examinations can and should be performed in criminal justice and outpatient settings.

Other Considerations

This typology of violent persons has advantages beyond controlling admissions. The explicit categorization of violent persons into different groups communicates to clinical staff that the hospital administration understands and recognizes that not all violence is a product of psychiatric illness. Categorization also acknowledges that the fact that a person has committed a violent act does not necessarily make that person a suitable candidate for admission to the hospital (Monahan 1973). The typology can help alert staff that some admitted patients are more likely than others to continue to manifest violent behavior while in the hospital.

WPIC has also found it useful to keep in the admissions area a "lethality file." This file lists persons who have previously been hospitalized at WPIC and includes the names and behavior of all patients who have committed violence while under treatment at WPIC. The file entry contains a description of the specific types of violence the patient committed, such as "tried to strangle a nurse." Entries into the lethality file must be submitted for each violent incident in the hospital.

The lethality file is consulted by admissions staff whenever a former WPIC patient is considered for rehospitalization. The file provides quick and specific information on the patient's previous violent behavior that otherwise could not be obtained without retrieving the patient's full hospital record and searching through it for possible indications of violent behavior. With the information already collected in the lethality file, staff can more readily assess the risks for violence if the person is readmitted to the hospital, and can alert treatment staff accordingly.

TREATMENT POLICY

A key issue in managing violent patients is the organization of treatment. Should there be a separate unit for such persons, or should they be incorporated in the overall patient mix?

Most clinicians believe that it is better to "mainstream" violent patients rather than cluster them into a separate violent unit where there is always the danger that one patient's violence will elicit comparable behavior from other violence-prone patients. At WPIC, violent patients are distributed according to their treatment needs into units that are divided along developmental and diagnostic parameters. Violent patients may be found in any of the following types of inpatient units at WPIC: children's units, an adolescent unit, an adult unit for patients with affective (mood) disorders; an adult unit for patients with schizophrenia; an adult unit for patients with anxiety disorders, substance abuse, and obsessional disorders; a unit for acutely psychotic patients who are first admissions; and a geriatric unit.

Violent patients are expected to participate fully in the treatment programs of the units to which they are admitted and to make use of the variety of available socialpsychological therapies to learn how to talk out rather than physically act out their problems. Staff energy is focused on engaging patients with an intensive, verbally oriented treatment milieu that employs exploration of feelings and cognitive restructuring techniques as well as medication for those patients who require it. Although some assaultive patient behavior does occur, the frequency of these incidents has been observed to decline at WPIC as treatment units successfully structure and occupy the violent patient's day. The highest incidence of assaultive patient behavior at WPIC tends to occur in the children's and adolescent units, adult schizophrenia unit, and the unit that admits acute first-admission psychotic patients.

CLINICAL STAFF COMPOSITION

The composition of nursing and other clinical and support staff is critical to the effective management and treatment of violent patients. Although the ultimate responsibility for patient care rests with the physicians, patients spend the vast majority of their time with and under the supervision of psychiatric nurses and other nonphysician staff.

Traditionally, the fear of patient violence has resulted in placing more male staff on psychiatric inpatient wards, with the males functioning primarily as nonprofessional aides to female psychiatric nurses. In some facilities, the perceived need for protection is so great that male aides exert excessive control over the professional staff and over decisions regarding patient management and care.

In an important study, Levy and Hartocollis (1976) compared two psychiatric inpatient units, one with the traditional female nurse-male aide staffing pattern, the other staffed entirely by female nurses and aides. The two units were similar in all other respects. The researchers hypothesized that "violence-prone patients may find female nurses and aides less provocative than male staff and that, conversely, when confronted with threatening patients in the absence of male aides, female staff may be more apt to rely on nonaggressive manners and feminine intuition rather than resort to reactive, policelike methods, which are typical of masculine behavior and values in our culture" (p. 429).

During the 1-year period of the study, 13 instances of assaultive behavior initiated by 5 patients occurred on the traditionally staffed unit. No acts of physical violence occurred on the unit with the all-female staff, even though there were several crises and episodes of disorganization that involved threatening patient behavior and abusive language. During such episodes, it was observed that male patients helped the all-female staff contain the aggression of their fellow patients.

Levy and Hartocollis (1976) concluded from their research that the exclusive use of female staff could help keep the incidence of other-directed patient violence in a psychiatric hospital to a minimum, and that the absence of male aides could assist rather than hamper the treatment process. The researchers also noted that psychiatric hospitals' traditionally heavy reliance on male aides could be a self-fulfilling prophecy. "When a male aide is used as an instrument of confrontation, the probability of violence becomes greatly enhanced because the male aide's formal or informal role as masculine authority is based on the intent to do violence. This intent is potentiated by female nursing personnel who expect the male aide to confront troublesome patients for them" (p. 431).

WPIC relies heavily on female staff in all its inpatient psychiatric units. Male aides are used only on the night shift in a few wards. Almost all other nonphysician staff—nurses, social workers, etc.—are female. There are no empirical data regarding the impact of the predominantly female staff on patient violence, as compared to the female nurse–male aide staffing pattern that prevailed at WPIC a decade ago. The hospital staff's experience, however, has been that female staff are often more effective in preventing and managing patient violence than are male staff simply because violence-prone mental patients tend to perceive females as less physically threatening and as less suitable targets for assault. On those occasions when female staff do need male assistance in controlling a violent patient, they typically receive help from the WPIC security staff.

CLINICAL STAFF TRAINING

Staff training is central to the implementation of effective hospital policies and procedures for the clinical management of violent patients (see, e.g., Gertz 1980; "Staff said to need training in managing violent patients," 1981; Hackett 1981; Nigrosh 1981; Lehmann 1982). When first employed in inpatient psychiatric settings, clinical staff generally have only a very limited knowledge of the special issues and problems posed by violent patients. New psychiatric residents at WPIC are given special training in the prevention and management of patient violence before they go on the wards. Nurses, social workers, and other clinical staff receive 2 weeks of initial clinical orientation training. A total of 18 training hours, devoted to the clinical management and prevention of patient violence, cover the following topics: WPIC policies and procedures for the prevention of patient violence and management of violent patients (4 hours), psychiatric diagnosis (2 hours), safety procedures (2 hours), psychopharmacology (4-1/4 hours), mental health law (1-1/2 hours), and cold wet pack (2 hours). These skills are periodically updated, and staff receive annual certification in crisis control.

Senior clinical nurse administrators make daily rounds to identify violent patients, assure the adequacy of provisions for that patient's care and treatment, and assess related staff needs for consultation and training.

SECURITY

WPIC's policy is that clinical staff manage all threatened or actual patient violence. In most instances, clinical staff within the individual treatment units handle such violence unaided, but situations do occasionally arise in which additional help is needed. WPIC has established a program that is staffed by male safety officers who are responsible for environmental and personal safety. These officers receive special training in the management of patient violence and are deployed by the hospital in central locations from which they can move rapidly to a treatment unit as needed.

The procedure by which clinical staff can obtain help from the safety department and other WPIC personnel is described in the WPIC policy manual:

I. Policy

It is the policy of the WPIC to provide a reliable and efficient method by which inpatient units and the entire Institute can obtain assistance from safety personnel and from extra nursing personnel, physicians and/or other staff when needed. Situations wherein extra personnel may be needed immediately include instances of extreme hyperactivity and damage to persons or property.

II. Procedure

A. Levels of assistance are secured as follows:

1. Dial extension 2100 (front desk). If phone is repeatedly busy, dial safety office directly, extension 2199.

2. Identify yourself and your exact unit or department location.

3. State the Security Level of Assistance required:

Security Level 1

This code indicates an IMMINENT DANGER situation, where safety officers are needed immediately. All officers on duty must respond to this code. An example of proper use of this code would be to control an extremely violent and physically abusive patient or visitor who must be secluded or subdued.

Security Level II

This code indicates a situation where safety officers are not needed immediately but should respond as soon as possible. At least two officers should respond to this code. Examples of this code are a wet pack procedure, transfer of a patient to a different seclusion room, medicating a patient, or escorting a patient to a hearing.

Security Level III

This indicates a situation where safety officers are needed only at their earliest convenience. Only one officer needs to respond to this code unless requests for additional officers are stipulated. Examples of this code are a mealtray removal from a seclusion room, an elopement, or a patient who requires observation.

B. If the situation becomes <u>very critical</u> and/or the Security Level I assistance was insufficient, follow points 1 and 2 in the above section and request <u>AN EMERGENCY</u> "TONE ALARM PAGE." State the type and number of personnel needed (e.g., all available men, all available clinical staff, etc.). Tone alarm is an audio page preceeded by an alert alarm tone over the paging system.

1. When an emergency or tone alarm page is announced, <u>ALL</u> personnel requested are expected to respond to the page by going immediately to the area where the emergency exists: the needs of the Institute (as announced by the page operator) supersede the routine clinical activities in any one program for the brief period of time that the emergency exists. One or two experienced representatives from each inpatient unit are expected to respond to an emergency or tone alarm page.

2. All staff should use only the center stairwell so that everyone will be entering the area as quickly as possible from the same direction.

3. One staff member in the area where the emergency exists is in charge and provides the leadership for the situation: this requires giving clear directions and expectations to staff/safety officers from other areas of WPIC responding to the emergency page or the levels of assistance.

4. Patients on special constant observation must not be left alone and staff must secure coverage of them before leaving the unit to respond to a page.

5. Do not unduly deplete your own unit/ department of clinical staff. Desk personnel are equipped with paging, alarms, elevator controls, and "beepers." Be sure to stay in contact with the desk and keep them informed of developments during an emergency and let them know when the situation has been resolved.

6. Isolate and provide support to the group of patients not involved in levels of assistance or emergencies away from the area where the emergency exists.

C. To promote communications and collaboration between the inpatient units and the safety program, a staff member of the inpatient unit will keep safety officers advised of unit/patient status at the beginning of each shift.

D. Conferences should be conducted among and initiated by safety, clinical staff, and any personnel upon completion of an assistance or emergency request to evaluate effectiveness of the process.

The Director of Safety Department, the Director of Nursing, and head nurses at WPIC meet monthly to review any problems or issues that may have developed with respect to effective coordination among their departments. Head nurses and charge nurses are responsible for alerting the Department of Safety to developments within treatment units that may affect security requirements. For example, WPIC may experience an unusually high number of admissions of violence-prone patients within a short period of time, with a corresponding need for a temporary increase in the Safety Department's staff. Temporary shortages of clinical staff due to viral illnesses during the winter may also affect security needs.

PREVENTION OF VIOLENCE

WPIC has developed a written Violence Prevention Policy designed to help clinical and other staff reduce patient violence while maintaining a therapeutic milieu that is constructive to patient dignity and treatment. In addition to providing guidance on issues related to prediction of violent behavior and intrapersonal causes of violence (such as cerebral dysfunction, sleep deprivation, hallucinations, paranoia), the WPIC policy discusses ways to avoid provocative situations on the inpatient unit and clinically help patients talk out feelings rather than act them out physically.

A. Provocative Situations on the Inpatient Unit

    1. The Composition of the Nursing Staff. [The WPIC policy here discusses material already covered in this chapter on how the use of a largely female staff on inpatient units can help reduce violence.]

    2. Racial Issue. Staff members' and patients' racial feelings and opinions can influence behavioral patterns. The literature concerning "self-integration" of racial identity suggests that individuals in the confrontation stage may be more prone to be distrustful of members of the opposite race (Milliones 1980); this in turn may possibly contribute to violence. Also, Leonard and Taylor (1981) experimentally demonstrated that racial prejudice

affects the "target of aggression." It has been proposed that prejudice facilitates "indiscriminate aggression" in the presence of a clear threat and "selective aggression" (i.e., prejudiced subjects choosing members of the opposite race) in the presence of an ambiguous threat. Many times patients will experience ambiguous threats while also coping with cognitive disorganization, confusion, intoxication, and/or other acute mental states. Staff should also try to be continually aware of "outside" social and racial tensions that could influence a biracial therapeutic relationship; these variables should be considered along with racial feelings during analyses of transference and countertransference phenomena.

3. The Use of Punching Bags and Other Physical Activities to Help Patients Express Aggressive Urges. Such cathartic aggressive behavior may seem therapeutic but in a permissive setting may maintain a patient's aggressive behavior at its original level or increase it. The use of physical activities (basketball, etc.) must be subordinate to the therapeutic focus of having patients develop cognitive abilities to understand the causes and events that precede violent behavior. Verbal work takes precedence over physical activities.

4. Patient Experiencing Verbal Insults or Humiliation from Staff in the Form of Verbal Threats or Attempts through Bantering or Ridicule to Disapprove of the Patient's Behavior. Insults or embarrassing situations can provoke aggression in patients who are prone to be aggressive and also in normally non-aggressive patients.

5. Staff Fear of the Patient will Exacerbate the Patient's Potential for Violence. Patients who are frightened of losing control of themselves and who are depending on staff to assist with controls will not be reassured by a frightened staff. If staff become overly anxious while managing a violent patient, the potentiality for that patient's violence increases. Staff need to spend time understanding their own concerns for personal safety and the ways in which their usual defense mechanisms may influence a patient's potential for behaving destructively (DiBella 1979). Staff need to be taught how to monitor their own feelings, when to ask for help, and when to terminate an interaction with a patient—e.g., when they feel that a patient is losing control and that they also are not in control of the situation.

B. Clinical Management of Potential Violence

1. The guiding principle is to assist the patient talk out feelings rather than act them out physically. Helping the patient change from a physical style of responding to his feelings to a more cognitive verbal style should pervade all treatment with potentially violent patients.

2. When the patient is clearly angry or verbally abusive, staff must acknowledge the patient's angry feelings and behavior. Focus on the process of the interaction, rather than only the content, is an important shift of emphasis in such situations.

3. In many instances, the patient's anger can be diluted before physical aggression takes place. At times one-to-one verbal interaction with staff is the intervention of choice; at other times the use of a structured, wellrun patient-staff group meeting can be effective in diluting anger and reassuring the patient that he will not be allowed to lose control. Well-timed use of humor by those staff gifted with a tasteful sense of humor is quite effective in diluting anger. If the patient is prevented from exploding and losing control, his self-respect and dignity will have been maintained.

4. Individual or group work with potentially violent patients acknowledges their feelings and helps them to express anger in socially acceptable and controlled ways. This type of limit setting is experienced as reassuring by most patients.

5. The verbal and cognitive work with potentially violent patients involves helping these patients learn to understand and predict their own violent impulses. Only then does the patient have mastery over when to get help to prevent loss of control.

6. Some patients, though chronically threatening, hostile, and frightening to others, seldom if ever strike out. It is important that such persons not be provoked to violence. Neither, however, can such patients be permitted to intimidate staff or other patients or "have the run of the ward." A firm but empathetic style, with clear-cut limit setting is needed in dealing with these patients. Staff should clearly indicate that violence will not be tolerated on the ward and that the patient will be prevented from becoming violent.

7. Potentially violent patients should be informed by those caring for them that they are "frightening" to other people. The reasons why they are frightening should be explained. Potentially violent patients are not always aware of the extent to which their behavior disturbs others. They should also be informed of

the actions that they can request in order to prevent their becoming violent—e.g., more medication, more interpersonal contact with staff, wet packs, seclusion.

MANAGEMENT OF VIOLENCE

The WPIC policy statement for the management and control of
violent patients recognizes that actual outbreaks of patient violence are
an unpreventable occupational hazard for mental health workers. "Violence" is defined in the policy statement as hitting or striking behavior
by a patient toward another patient or toward staff members or accomplished destruction of property.

WPIC controls actual or imminently threatened violence through
the use of "underwhelming force" when possible and by the use of
"overwhelming" force if necessary. All inpatient nurses, psychiatrists,
and social workers are trained in handling and defusing violent incidents in ways that do not require physically overpowering the patient:
this is what is meant by "underwhelming force." When the situation
requires physical restraint or physically overpowering the patient—
i.e., "overwhelming force"—the clinical staff call for WPIC safety personnel and other outside assistance as needed.

The following instructions regarding the management of violent
incidents are taken from the WPIC policy manual:

F. When the patient is about to be violent or has a violent outburst:
   1. Don't walk away from the patient.
   2. Acknowledge the patient's feelings and attempt to talk the
   patient down. Here the use of "underwhelming force" is useful.
   Talking alone with one woman (mental health professional) about
   what the patient is feeling and about what has happened may
   be calming. The staff member and the patient should be able to
   perceive the safety of the interaction because other staff are available at a distance.
   3. If medication is useful and appropriate for the patient, then
   give the medication with the message that the medication will
   help him control himself. Violent or suspicious patients may be
   fearful that you are trying to "snow" them and may refuse medication. The use of medication is to be carefully explained. If
   the patient refuses medication, give the patient some "elbow
   room." A dignified 10-minute time period for the patient to take
   medication on his own is preferable. If medication must be given
   against the patient's will, then prepare IM medication with staff

prepared to use "overwhelming force," if necessary. In general, if the patient is thought to be violent as a consequence of delusions or hallucinations secondary to a psychosis, an antipsychotic is used.

4. The use of "overwhelming force" may be needed to give medication or to walk a patient to a quiet room or to seclusion. Remember, patients who are violent are often reacting to feelings of helplessness and loss of control. It is provocative rather than reassuring to the patient if, from his perspective, he perceives there is going to be a battle to control his behavior. It is not necessary that the patient be physically restrained or overpowered: sometimes merely approaching the patient with a clear show of force, plus making a statement by one of the group that his behavior must cease, is sufficient to cause the behavior to cease. The patient must not be touched unless there is clearly enough manpower on hand to control the patient.

5. A quiet room or seclusion may be used as a temporary and nonpunitive way of helping the patient calm down and regain control of himself before discussing his violent feelings and behavior. It is important to understand that placing the patient in isolation will not help the patient learn about his experience during the critical time for learning immediately following a violent incident. Isolation should be as brief as possible and followed by the psychological work that is needed by the patient.

6. The staff member most appropriate to be with the patient during this time of fear and violence is the one who has the best rapport with the patient—not necessarily the one with the most authority, rank, etc. Effective interpersonal understanding and intervention with such patients requires rapport.

7. Other patients should be accompanied away from the area where the violent patient is being controlled.

8. Post-violence analysis conference can and should be called by anyone involved in the incident to determine what was well done, what could have been handled better, and how future such incidents might better be predicted and prevented.

SECLUSION

WPIC's policy is to minimize the use of seclusion and restraints—leather, cold wet pack, posey (harness)—to control patient behavior, including violence. Interpersonal and pharmacologic interventions are preferred. In some situations, however, seclusion and restraint become necessary. The following material from the WPIC policy manual describes the procedures that are employed for seclusion. The reader will note that the discussion is quite detailed; it addresses practical issues that can have a very real impact on patient dignity and on the course and success of treatment.

I. POLICY

It is the policy of Western Psychiatric Institute and Clinic to minimize the use of seclusion as a method of restraint. In situations where seclusion is used, WPIC faculty and staff will adhere to Pennsylvania State policy regarding seclusion and its use.

II. DEFINITION

Seclusion is usually defined as "The placement of a patient in a locked room." At WPIC this definition is expanded to include both locked and unlocked seclusion (seclusion room door unlocked). The following criteria and regulations pertain to the use of both types of seclusion.

III. CRITERIA FOR USE OF SECLUSION

Seclusion may be used to protect the patient against himself, to protect others from aggressive acts of the patient, to decrease the level of stimulation when a patient is in a state of hyperactivity, and only when less restrictive measures have proven ineffective. In all cases the reasons for imposing seclusion and the conditions under which it operates or will be lifted must be clearly defined, recorded, and an attempt made to explain the same to the patient. Before secluding any patient, including patients who are assaultive, abusive, or uncontrollably selfdestructive, consideration must be given to using other types of patient management. Other types of patient management include:

1. Physician evaluation of patient
2. Review of psychopharmacological management
3. Interpersonal intervention
4. Use of the patient's hospital room as a "quiet room" (requires constant observation)
5. Assigning staff to spend time individually with patient
6. Use of cold wet packs

Seclusion may not be used for behaviors such as pacing on a ward and where there is otherwise no clear and present danger.

IV. DEFINITION OF SECLUSION CO

Seclusion CO connotes Seclusion "Constant Observation." A staff member is present in the seclusion room hallway, positioned directly outside the seclusion room door, continuously observing the patient through the window (if clinically feasible) as well as vigilantly listening for any unusual noise that would warrant the staff member's immediate investigation.

V. REGULATIONS GOVERNING THE USE OF SECLUSION

A. Patients may be placed in seclusion only on the written order of a physician, except in emergency situations where less restrictive means of control are not feasible and in which it is obvious that patients could harm themselves or others. Such a written order shall be promptly supported by a notation in the patient's record.

B. The written order may be made only after the patient has been seen by a physician who has evaluated the patient's need for seclusion.

C. Emergency use of seclusion shall be for no more than 1 hour and shall employ the above procedure, and staff will enter a written order in the patient's record.

Standing orders for seclusion may not be written routinely upon a patient's entry to WPIC. If there are emergencies, seclusion is always possible, and is both legally and medically proper and possible, without a physician's order. Physicians must subsequently then evaluate the patient and confirm, via written order, the need for seclusion.

D. Any order for seclusion made by a physician shall be effective for no more than 12 hours, and a physician shall maintain a continuing review of the patient's condition and the need for his seclusion. An order must be renewed after each 12-hour period if seclusion is to be continued.

E. WPIC requires that Program Directors, as well as physicians ordering seclusion, evaluate the patient's need for seclusion on at least a twice daily basis. The Program Director as well as the physician should indicate in the record why the patient continues to require seclusion. To use seclusion for a period of time in excess of 96 hours in a patient's total hospital stay requires consultation from the Law and Psychiatry Program, and authorization from the Director of Adult Services, or in case of children, the Director of Children's Services.

F. While in seclusion, the patient must be maintained on the Seclusion CO level, and the clinical ward personnel must chart the physical and mental condition of the patient. The patient shall have the opportunity to use the bathroom as requested. The patient shall be given the opportunity to bathe or shower at least every 24 hours or as necessary in the case of special circumstances such as incontinence.

VI. STAFF PROCEDURE AND TECHNIQUES
  A. Long-Term Preparation
    1. Preparation of Materials for Seclusion
      a. Every seclusion room should be equipped with a mat and patient gown at all times.
      b. Assure that the doors of the seclusion room to be used are unlocked and open.
      c. The nurse should prepare patient medication (oral and IM) so that if the patient needs to be medicated, it can be administered immediately after the patient has been placed in the seclusion room.
    2. Evaluation of Staffing Needs
      Personnel from other units should be summoned to seclude a patient only when absolutely necessary. These personnel should return to their assigned duty areas as soon as possible. A minimum of three people is needed to seclude a patient.
    3. All discussion with the patient in question should take place before a decision to seclude is made. Once the decision to seclude is agreed upon, it must be consistently carried through.
  B. The Call for Assistance
    1. Non-Emergency Situation Requiring Additional Personnel. Situations such as medicating a patient who is already in seclusion, and removing a patient from cold wet pack are not considered emergency situations. Calling for assistance during such occasions should be done via telephone and not by the hospital paging system. Although these are not crisis situations, staff personnel are expected to respond to the call as soon as possible.
    2. Emergency Situations Requiring Immediate Assistance. An emergency is any situation wherein additional staff are needed immediately. Such a situation may be that of extreme hyperactivity or destruction of person or property. The nurse in charge will evaluate the situation and decide whether an emergency tone alarm page is necessary.
  C. Seclusion Preparation

1. Information and Instruction

   When summoned help arrives on the unit, time permitting, the staff member on that unit should inform the off-unit staff of the patient's condition and plans for staff intervention. Proceed to identify the following:

   a. The "charge person." This person will coordinate the staff who are going to participate in escorting the patient to seclusion. The charge person will assign personnel to make physical contact with the patient if he is combative. Ideally, the staff person directing the seclusion should be someone familiar with the patient to be secluded. This staff person should also be the only person to carry on any verbal exchange with the patient.

   b. The name and brief description of the patient. Identify any history or possibility of combative behavior.

   c. State which seclusion room will be used and whether or not medications will be administered to the patient.

2. In preparation for the seclusion, staff personnel should remove all their personal articles such as glasses, pens, pins, watches, neckties, etc. All of these items are potentially dangerous to both staff and patients.

3. The ward area should then be cleared of both patients and any articles which could impede a successful seclusion. Patients, as well as visitors, may be tactfully asked to leave the particular area.

D. Seclusion Procedure

1. Verbalization

   a. The patient should be approached by the "charge nurse" in a calm, reassuring manner. The charge person should stand in front of, or on the side of the patient, with his/her arms casually crossed over the chest area. In this position the patient should be given an opportunity to verbalize his/her difficulties, fears, etc., rather than physically expressing them in a combative style. Avoid a lengthy discussion.

   b. Request the patient to walk to a quiet area or the seclusion room. If this fails, tell the patient he/she must do what you have stated and what you will do if he/she does not. The patient must be given the choice of walking voluntarily to the seclusion room or being taken there. If the patient is physically out of control by the time staff arrive, they will begin to use physical techniques to control the patient.

c. Any hesitation or disorganization on the staff's part will contribute to increasing the patient's anxiety and loss of control. When a patient refuses to cooperate, there is no further discussion. The assignments previously decided upon must be carried out by staff immediately and without disagreement.

2. <u>Physical Control Techniques</u>

The physical techniques taught and used at WPIC are based on a system called "Physical Crisis Intervention" (National Crisis Prevention Institute, 1984). The procedures are taught to clinical staff in a special eighthour Crisis Control Workshop. A brief description of the basic intervention follows:

a. One staff person approaches patient from slightly to the left and one person slightly from the right. The one or two remaining staff form a semi-circle around the patient. This appears as a triangle with the patient at the center point.

b. If the patient strikes out, the staff person targeted grasps the patient's other wrist.

c. The patient's arms are then brought to his side and then back and the elbows are locked. Without using own muscle power, the staff member is controlling the patient by taking advantage of their forward momentum. By pivoting and stepping in front of the patient his forward momentum is then stopped.

d. The third and fourth staff members assist by approaching the patient from behind and help to keep the patient's balance and confine his movements by holding the patient's belt or other article of clothing around his waist.

e. The patient is then lowered to the floor in a "take down" technique. Staff should be as close to the patient's body as possible. Staff hip should be in contact with the patient's hip. Then slide to the side of the patient at a 90-degree angle. The team member in the rear controls the patient's legs. The patient is then held in a "hold" position on the floor. Again 3–4 staff members, male or female, can control most patients.

f. Staff should not be in a hurry to transport the patient. If indicated, medication may be given intramuscular at this time. After the patient has calmed somewhat, he may be turned and carried. Never turn a patient before you are prepared to carry him.

g. The staff member on the right "steps over" the patient while controlling his arm. Staff member on the left "tucks in" the patient's left arm of the turn. Staff member holding legs initiates the turn.

h. Four staff are then needed to carry the patient, one securing each extremity. The patient should also be supported beneath the shoulders and legs while being carried. A fifth staff member may be used to help secure the patient's hips and trunk.

i. Transportation of the patient should be a steady movement—DO NOT RUSH.

j. When the patient is placed in the seclusion room, he should be placed on the mattress facing away from the door.

k. Staff should now proceed to quickly remove all the patient's clothing and personal belongings. This should include all belts, jewelry, watches, and cigarettes. Valuables should be locked in the nursing office. Certain patients may be allowed to wear their own clothing. Others should be put in hospital gowns.

l. If medication injections are to be administered, keep the patient lying face down on the mat while securely bracing the buttocks to prevent difficulty during the injection. Whenever possible IM injections should be given in the anterior thigh.

m. The nurse should be the first person to leave the inner area of the seclusion. Other staff should leave the seclusion room quickly and systematically. The staff person in control of the patient's arms will instruct (quietly or with a nod so that the patient is not aware of exit proceedings) the person in control of the waist-trunk to leave the seclusion first, followed by the person in control of the legs. Finally, the person in control of the arms will leave the room. The patient should be left in a sitting position with his back to the seclusion room door.

n. If the patient continues to be aggressive when the staff is attempting to leave the seclusion room, the patient may further be isolated by turning him/her over on the floor against the north wall of the seclusion room (under the window) and firmly placing the mat on top of the patient. This will significantly retard the patient's attempts at getting up off the floor and to the door before it is closed.

o. The first person out of seclusion (person in control of patient's waist) should stand slightly behind the seclusion room door and be prepared to quickly close the door after the last staff person has left the room. Care should be taken so as not to slam the door on any part of the patient's body.

p. A patient in locked seclusion must be maintained on Seclusion CO status. A registered nurse is responsible for completion of the seclusion record sheet (see inserted example sheet). Patients in seclusion who are observed or thought to be banging their heads or other parts of their body on the seclusion room walls should immediately be removed and put in a cold wet pack unless cold wet pack is contraindicated for that patient. A physician should be called immediately to re-evaluate the patient's condition.

q. The continued need for locked seclusion should be constantly re-evaluated. The patient should be removed from locked seclusion if he/she could be managed in a quiet room and/or on special constant observation. A registered nurse is responsible for finalizing the decision to remove a patient.

E. Care of the Secluded Patient
   1. Toileting the Secluded Patient
      a. When it is necessary to take the secluded patient to the bathroom, floor personnel should first carefully evaluate assistance needed. Before entering the seclusion room, ask the patient to step back and away from the door and up against the far wall. This will prevent the patient from rushing the staff at the doorway. The patient is then taken out of seclusion and escorted to the seclusion room bathroom. Monitoring the patient while in the bathroom can be left up to the discretion of the staff. High-risk patients should be monitored while using either the toilet facilities or shower in the seclusion room. Care should be taken not to leave glass or other potentially dangerous items in the seclusion room bathroom.

WESTERN PSYCHIATRIC INSTITUTE AND CLINIC
UNIVERSITY OF PITTSBURGH

SECLUSION RECORD

IMPRINT PLATE

The initiation or discontinue of seclusion must have a corresponding note in the progress. notes which reflects the the clinical rationale for the change. A new record sheet is to be initiated each time the patient is placed in seclusion.

Date of Seclusion: _____   Date of Removal: _____
Time of Seclusion: _____   Time of Removal: _____
Secluded by: _____   Removed by: _____

Total Time in Seclusion: _____ Hrs. _____ Min.

Date	Time SCO Started	Time SCO Ended	Total Hr.	Time Min.	Observed by Name and Discipline	Behavioral Observation of Patient

PITT 1309 (681)

Figure 1. Example of a Seclusion Record Form

2. Feeding the Secluded Patient

a. When the patient is in locked seclusion during meal time, a special dietary tray is ordered. This type of food order comes on a cardboard tray with paper dishes. Food items on the finger food tray are those kinds which can be easily consumed without the use of silverware. Included are such things as sandwiches, fresh fruit, cookies, etc. Giving the secluded patient hot coffee with the meal should be left up to the discretion of the unit staff. Care should be taken to prevent the patient from throwing any hot beverage at staff. The coffee should be supplied in a paper cup and always have a plastic lid on it.

When removing a food tray from the seclusion room, be certain to check to see that all eating utensils that went in with the tray are being returned by the patient.

NOTE:

When taking a tray into seclusion never hand the tray to the patient. Have the patient step back and then place the tray on the floor. Do not bend over in front of or below the secluded patient when handling food trays or other procedures inside the seclusion room. Face toward and keep your eye on the secluded patient at all times while inside the seclusion room.

3. Charting

The need for seclusion and the patient's behavior during seclusion must be documented in detail in the Patient's Record and on the Seclusion Record.

PATIENT CARE ASSURANCE

WPIC policy requires a written report and thorough investigation of every incident involving patients inside and outside the hospital, and every incident involving staff members and visitors within the hospital. An "incident" is defined as "any happening which is not consistent with the routine operation of the hospital or the care of the patient." In addition to patient violence, other types of incidents that require a report and investigation include injuries sustained while the patient is being subdued, self-inflicted injury, improper medication, accidental injury, falls, recreational injury, elopement, improper commitment, attempted suicide, assault, fires, property destruction, and missing or lost personal property.

WPIC has established a Patient Care Assurance and Risk Management (PCARM) Committee to review all incidents related to patient care and to present findings and recommendations to improve the effectiveness and efficiency of patient care services. PCARM members include all members of the WPIC Executive and Management Committees and selected chiefs of services, head nurses, and program directors. WPIC's experience has shown that reviews of mandatory incident reports by the PCARM are essential to ensuring quality control in the management of patient violence and other aspects of patient care (Huber and Wolford 1981). Careful review of all incidents, including "near misses," alerts the PCARM to changes that may be needed in WPIC policies and procedures, clinical programs, training programs, staffing patterns, and resource allocations.

REFERENCES

DiBella, L.A.W. Educating staff to manage threatening paranoid patients. American Journal of Psychiatry, 136(3):333–335, 1979.

Gertz, B. Training for prevention of assaultive behavior in a psychiatric setting. Hospital and Community Psychiatry 31(9):628–630, 1980.

Hackett, T.P. How to handle the violent patient—And save your skin, too. Behavior Today 12(35):3–4, 1981.

Huber, G.A.; Roth, L.H.; Appelbaum, P.S.; and Ore, T.M. Hospitalization, arrest or discharge: Important legal and clinical issues in the emergency evaluation of persons believed dangerous to others. Law and Contemporary Problems, 45(3):99–123, 1982.

Huber, G.A., and Wolford, J.A. Investigative reporting cuts risks at psychiatric facility. Hospitals, 55(May):73–76, 1981.

Lehmann, L.S. Training in managing violent patients. Hospital and Community Psychiatry 33(1):15, 1982.

Leonard, K.E., and Taylor, S.P. Effects of racial prejudice and race of target on aggression. Aggressive Behavior 1981(7):205–214, 1981.

Levy, P., and Hartocollis, P. Nursing aides and patient violence. American Journal of Psychiatry 133(4):429–431, 1976.

Milliones, J. Construction of a black consciousness measure: Psychotherapeutic implications. Psychotherapy: Theory, Research, and Practice 17(2):175–182, 1980.

Monahan, J. The psychiatrization of criminal behavior: A reply. Hospital and Community Psychiatry 24(2):105–107, 1973.

Monahan, J.; Caldeira, C.; and Friedlander, H.D. Police and the mentally ill: A comparison of committed and arrested persons. International Journal of Law and Psychiatry 2(4):509–518, 1979.

National Crisis Prevention Institute. Nonviolent Crisis Intervention Training Program, 1984. Program available from the Institute, 401 W. Capitol Drive, Milwaukee, Wisconsin 53216.

Nigrosh, B.J. Training Workshops in Prevention and Management of Violence for Mental Health and Other Health Care Settings, 1981. A flyer published by Dr. Nigrosh, 21 Bates Street, Northampton, Massachusetts 01060.

Staff said to need training in managing violent patients. Psychiatric News, Aug. 7, 1981, 26–27.

Index

261